MARITIME WALES

MARITIME WALES

JOHN RICHARDS

TEMPUS

First published 2007

Tempus Publishing
Cirencester Road, Chalford,
Stroud, Gloucestershire, GL6 8PE
www.tempus-publishing.com

Tempus Publishing is an imprint of NPI Media Group

British Library Cataloguing in Publication Data.
A catalogue record for this book is available from the British Library.

ISBN 978 0 7524 4224 2

Typesetting and origination by NPI Media Group
Printed in Great Britain

Contents

List of Illustrations

Preface and Acknowledgements

For centuries sea-going vessels could be loaded or unloaded, at low tide, on any suitable sheltered beach, or on the banks of an accessible river. Gradually, some of these locations grew into busier and more developed shipping places – with a quay, and harbour walls to provide shelter. Later still, a floating dock might be built and perhaps even a dry dock. This book concentrates on the history of such ports and harbours in Wales: their periods of growth and decline; the kinds of cargo handled; vessels, owners and builders and the typical voyages undertaken by local mariners. Viewed as a whole, the book provides an outline of the maritime history of Wales, and there is a comprehensive bibliography so that matters of interest may be followed up in greater depth.

An explanation of certain topics may be helpful:

Ownership of Vessels

Some vessels, particularly the smaller ones, were owned outright by one person, but the traditional method of ownership was by means of shares divided into sixty-four. Thus the brig *Atalanta*, launched in 1864 at Port Dinorwic, was owned by Griffith Griffiths, master mariner, (Griffiths owned 28/64 shares), his son William Griffiths, master mariner, (8/64), Rees Jones, who had built the vessel, (16/64), Catherine Roberts, widow, (4/64), John Evans, schoolmaster, (4/64) and John Jones, painter, (4/64). The owners received their share of the profits annually, and one of them would be designated as 'managing owner'.

As the number of steamships increased, and they became bigger and more costly, a new method had to be found to finance their purchase. A system of limited liability 'single-ship companies' came to be adopted: the cost of a vessel was divided up into a large number of shares, which were advertised in a prospectus and newspaper advertisements. The manager of the ship was usually paid a percentage of the earnings.

Size of Vessels

It may be difficult today to envisage the size of vanished vessels, so an indication of this is given in the text. A vessel's measurements (length x breadth) are sometimes given and, more often, the tonnage is noted after the name – for example: *Silurian* (940). The way tonnage was calculated has changed over the centuries and figures for different periods may not be comparable. In medieval times ships came to be described by the number of tuns they could carry, a tun being a cask which could hold about 250 gallons of wine. Later, a formula based on a vessel's length, breadth and depth of hold was used to calculate the 'tons burden'. From the middle of the nineteenth century a new measurement system became standard. The figure given for a vessel in this book is, where possible, that of *Gross Registered Tons*: the volume of all the enclosed spaces of the vessel (such as bunkers, deck-houses and holds) is calculated in cubic feet, and 100 cubic feet is equal to 1 ton.

Rigs of Sailing Vessels

Sailing vessels are described by their rig. Those to be found most often in this book are:

Smack/sloop: One mast. Fore and aft sails. A small vessel, up to about 20 tons, might be called a smack. Illustration No.56 shows two sloops drawn up on the beach.

Ketch: Two masts, with the foremast longer than the mizzen mast. Fore and aft sails. See illustration No.2.

Schooner: Two or three masts (sometimes four, or even five). Fore and aft sails on each mast. A topsail schooner had square sails on the fore topmast. See illustration Nos.106 and 118.

Brig: Two masts, square sails on both.

Brigantine: Two masts. Mainmast – fore and aft sails. Foremast – square sails.

Snow: Two masts. Rigged as a brig, but with a short additional mast (carrying a small trysail) stepped behind the mainmast.

Barque: Three masts. Foremast and mainmast – square sails. Mizzenmast – fore and aft sails. There were also four-masted barques.

Barquentine: Three or four masts. Foremast – square sails. The others – fore and aft sails. See illustration No.45.

Ship-rigged: Three or four masts. Square sails on all masts.

ACKNOWLEDGEMENTS

The writer of a work such as this inevitably relies upon many earlier publications. These are listed in the bibliography.

The author is grateful for the help given by Buckley Library; Cardiff Library Service; Conwy Library Information and Culture Service; Ceredigion County Libraries Officer (Aberystwyth); Gloucestershire Record Office; Gwynedd Archives Service; Hereford Library; Manchester Central Library Local Studies Unit; County Library (Reference and Local Studies Unit) Haverfordwest and the Vale of Glamorgan Libraries. Thanks are due to the Syndics of Cambridge University Library for allowing the inclusion of three extracts from the diaries of Joseph Romilly (Classmarks Add. 6808, 6817 and 6819).

The following have given permission for the use of illustrations from their collections: Airbus, 117; Bath Central Library, 5; Bristol Industrial Museum 2, 72, 76, 80; Cardiff Library Service, 18, 54; Carmarthenshire Museums Service, 42, 45; Ceredigion Libraries, 70, 71, 73, 75; J. & M. Clarkson, 88; Director, Special Projects, Fleet Directorate, Canadian Coast Guard, Ottawa, 4; Edinburgh University Library, 3; Flintshire Record Office, 116, 119, 126, 127; Glasgow University Archive Services, 91; Glasgow University Library, Department of Special Collections, 35, 100; Gloucestershire Record Office, 121, 122; Grosvenor Museum, Chester, 120; Gwynedd Archives Service, 77, 79, 84, 86, 89, 104, 106, 122; Haverfordwest Library, 46; Sam Holland (www. samholland. co. uk), 103; Imperial War Museum, London (Negative FLM 2648), 81; Institute of Nautical Archaeology, Texas A. & M. University, 112; JoTika Ltd, 115; Kathleen & May Trust, 118; Library and Archives Canada (C-026563), 50; Liverpool Record Office, Central Libraries, 124; Llanelli Public Library, 43; J.&C. McCutcheon, 53, 57, 64, 65, 66, 67, 68, 109; National Maritime Museum, London, 55; Newport City Council Museums &

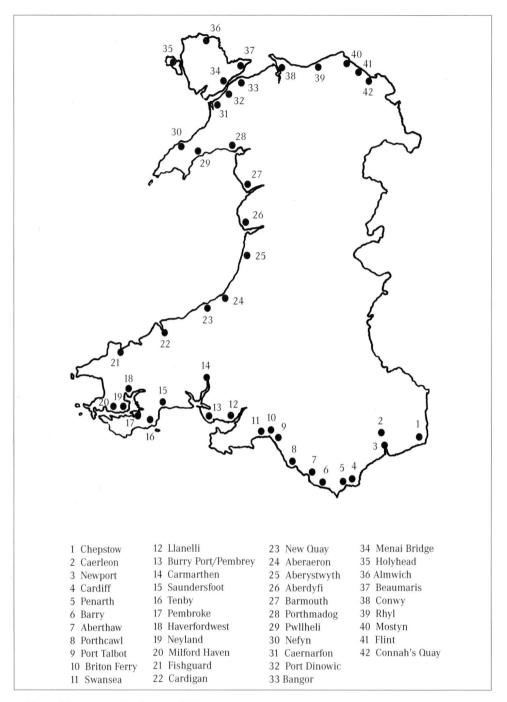

1 Chepstow	12 Llanelli	23 New Quay	34 Menai Bridge
2 Caerleon	13 Burry Port/Pembrey	24 Aberaeron	35 Holyhead
3 Newport	14 Carmarthen	25 Aberystwyth	36 Almwich
4 Cardiff	15 Saundersfoot	26 Aberdyfi	37 Beaumaris
5 Penarth	16 Tenby	27 Barmouth	38 Conwy
6 Barry	17 Pembroke	28 Porthmadog	39 Rhyl
7 Aberthaw	18 Haverfordwest	29 Pwllheli	40 Mostyn
8 Porthcawl	19 Neyland	30 Nefyn	41 Flint
9 Port Talbot	20 Milford Haven	31 Caernarfon	42 Connah's Quay
10 Briton Ferry	21 Fishguard	32 Port Dinowic	
11 Swansea	22 Cardigan	33 Bangor	

1 Map of the ports and harbours of Wales.

Heritage Services, 6; Royal Commission on the Ancient and Historical Monuments of Wales (Crown Copyright), 44, 99; The Science Museum, 113; Vale of Glamorgan Libraries, 22, 23, 28.

ONE

South Wales

CHEPSTOW AND THE WYE

In the 1070s William Fitz Osbern started to build the first masonry castle in Britain at Chepstow. Further up the river the first Cistercian abbey in Wales (and the second in Britain) was founded at Tintern in 1131 by Walter de Clare, lord of Chepstow. By the following century traffic on the Wye had increased considerably, and cargoes of foreign goods began to appear in the records: wine was taken upstream for Henry III's soldiers in 1223 and thirty-five years later Tintern Abbey provided storage, at two pence a day, for wine being carried to Monmouth. The monks of Tintern, like other Cistercians, kept large flocks of sheep and owned a vessel which took the wool to Bristol. From there Tintern wool went regularly to Flanders and by the fourteenth century it was being sold in Italy.

Chepstow became a place of trans-shipment, not only for goods carried down the Wye but also for foreign cargoes, which were loaded into smaller vessels before being taken to Bristol. There were a few locally owned boats and in May 1311 Edward II tried to commandeer one of them (properly manned and victualled) for use against the Scots. Chepstow's representatives replied that, unfortunately, they could not comply as only four vesssels were owned there – three had been wrecked and the other was away on a voyage to fetch wine from Gascony.

In the early 1550s Thomas Phaer was commissioned to report on the 'shipping places' of the Welsh coast (for details of Phaer's work see Robinson, 1972). Dr Phaer described Chepstow as:

> ... a haven of three fathoms at low water; somewhat dangerous to come to, for rocks called the Shoots. It lies over against Aust in Gloucestershire. All westerly and southern winds bring (vessels) in... The earl of Worcester is lord of the port and of the town, and dwells in a fair castle.

We can learn something of Chepstow's trade at this time from records of alleged customs offences: in July 1564 Richard Newton of Taunton imported into Chepstow, in *The British Bark*, Gascon wine, iron and resin. Christopher Dowlle, tanner, of Newland (Gloucestershire) exported from Monmouth and other places, tanned leather and calf skins. Later in the same year 150 tuns of Gascon wine were brought to Chepstow, in four different ships, for the Bristol merchants Thomas Chester, Dominic Chester and William Jeyne. In January 1565 one of the bailiffs of Chepstow had 25 tuns of his wine seized. Thomas Somerset, of Rogerstone Grange, imported 7 tuns of olive oil from Seville in 1570. Two years later the customs officer, John Leek, was himself charged with various malpractices, when cargoes mentioned in the depositions included iron, leather, salt and wine. Among the vessels listed were the *Trinity* of Swansea and the *Margaret* of Chepstow.

One or two local vessels appear in the Port Books for 1580: in January the *Charitie* (70), master John Tege, brought cargo from Bordeaux: 20 tuns of wine for Thomas Penne of London; wine and prunes for William Gittins; wine and rosin for John Pinner; wine and vinegar for Thomas Mors; wine, rosin and vinegar for Richard Grane and 2 tuns of wine for Thomas Strincter. The *Elizabeth*, master Edward Herbart, returned from San Sebastian in June bringing Spanish iron and train oil.

The first brass to be produced in Britain was made at Tintern in the 1560s and before long wire-making mills had sprung up on the tributaries of the lower Wye. Industrial activity gradually increased in the Wye Valley and by the early years of the seventeenth century the Tintern Wireworks was a thriving concern, employing 4 or 500 people, importing iron ore from Cornwall and exporting its products through Chepstow to Gloucester and Bristol. Eight of every ten boats leaving Chepstow were on their way to Bristol, carrying bell metal, copper, iron and wire, as well as agricultural produce brought down the Wye.

Industry, and the port, continued to develop throughout the eighteenth century and a dry dock opened in 1759. Cargoes of wine continued to arrive, such as these two reported in the *Gloucester Journal* in July 1755: 'Arrived at Chepstow, the *Venus*, Capt. William Bloom, from Portugal with wines'. In July 1771: 'On Monday last arrived at Chepstow – *Elizabeth*, Capt. William Butson, in twelve days from Oporto, laden with wine for Mr. Fydell'. By the 1790s the port of Chepstow was handling the output of a glassworks, a bell foundry, two brickworks and half-a-dozen paper mills. At Tintern one visitor 'was disturbed by the sight of a number of smelting-houses on the banks of the Wye, and much too near the abbey: clouds of thick black smoke and an intolerable stench, issued from these buildings, disgusting to the utmost degree, and entirely destroying the landscape'. Another important activity at Chepstow was the export of bark, used in tanning, much of it going to Ireland.

Two boats carried freight to Bristol each week, but passengers usually went by the ferry at Beachley. The Bristol press carried advertisements for 'regular trader trows' plying to Chepstow and then up the Wye to Brockweir, Tintern and Monmouth. J.T. Barber visited Monmouth at the turn of the century and reported that the commerce of the town 'depends on the navigation of the Wye, in the distribution of goods between Bristol, Hereford and adjoining districts'.

William Coxe (1801) and G.W. Manby (1802) summed up the position of Chepstow. Coxe states: 'In 1792, the shipping belonging to this place amounted to 2,800 tons, and in 1799 was increased to 3,500... upwards of 1,200 vessels annually enter and clear this port, including repeated voyages'. Manby adds: 'Chepstow is now in a flourishing state and has a trade to Norway, Russia and Oporto, and its contiguity to Bristol may be one, and the chief reason of its not having a greater share of importation'.

Chepstow Steamer Services

Steamboats began running between Chepstow and Bristol in the autumn of 1822, with two vessels competing – the *Duke of Lancaster* and the *Duke of Beaufort* – 'daily until laid up for the winter'. Then the *Wye* (60) arrived on the scene, staying in service for seventeen years from 1826. Built in Bristol by William Scott, the vessel could reach Bristol in two hours and ran five times a week in summer.

Another paddle steamer, the *Usk*, undertook a more unusual task – carrying Chartists on the first stage of their journey into exile. After the Chartist Rising at Newport in 1839, sentences of death, for high treason, were passed on John Frost, William Jones and Zephaniah Williams. *The Times* of 7 February 1840 reported subsequent events: at 11.30 p.m., with no warning, the men were ordered out of the cells at Monmouth and told to get dressed. At 1.15 a.m. they were put in a prison van, which was drawn by four horses. In the van with the prisoners were six London policemen and the gaoler; a troop of lancers provided an escort – the authorities were taking no chances in such turbulent times. This cavalcade 'passed through Chepstow to the Passage, where the *Usk* steamer was waiting for them'. Taken on board at 5 a.m. the reprieved men found themselves guarded by a detachment of the nineteenth Regiment of

2 The ketch *Emperor*, built at Chepstow in 1906, at Redland Wharf, Bristol.

Foot. The *Usk* took them to Portsmouth, where the men spent a week on a prison hulk before being put on board the convict ship *Mandarin* with 200 other transportees. They arrived at Hobart on 30 June 1840, after a voyage of over four months.

Back at home a replacement *Wye* was brought into service on the Chepstow-Bristol route in 1843. Described in advertisements as 'the fast-sailing iron-steam packet *Wye...* The voyage between Bristol and Chepstow is performed in under two hours'. The vessel was sold in 1861, but continued as a Chepstow market boat until 1867. A third *Wye* was employed for eight years from 1861.

In the year 1865 there were eighteen vessels listed in *Clayton's Register* as belonging to the port. The largest was the *Queen* (122), a brig built in 1846 whose managing owner was Thomas Sargent, also owner of the schooner *Breeze* (73), of which Robert Sargent was master. The largest fleet at this time was that of Henry Gillam, who managed a sloop, a ketch, three schooners and the *Swiftsure* (72), a three-masted schooner built at Blackwall in 1821 and originally a wooden paddle steamer.

The oldest vessel on the register in 1865 was the trow *George*, owned by Thomas Williams of Llandogo, which had been launched in 1806. Of the other five trows, three were also owned by masters living at Llandogo: *Bristol Packet* built 1812, *Good Hope* built at Redbrook in 1847 and *William and Sarah* built at Llandogo in 1860. The remaining two belonged to Thomas Swift of Monmouth: *Friends* built at Brockweir in 1844 and *William* built at Gloucester in 1846.

The 1871 census noted twelve vessels at Chepstow on 2 April. Over half were trows, while the largest were the French brig *Jean Bart* (177) and the brigantine *Princess* (159). At this time Chepstow's outward cargoes were mostly coastwise, consisting mainly of corn, timber and bark. The port's trade had been seriously affected by local transport developments: the Hereford-Gloucester Canal opened in 1845, to be followed by the extension of the rail network. (Although the railway company did provide some traffic when, in November 1878, it opened a wharf; from the following year the Chepstow Steam Boat Carrying Co.'s vessel arrived twice a week from Bristol with wheat for milling, taking away flour on the return journey. The opening of the Severn rail tunnel in 1886 provided a quick and convenient route for goods and passengers, but the Wye remained a popular destination for excursions and from 1907 steamers were able to make use of a new landing stage at Chepstow.

Chepstow and the Wye: Shipbuilding

Boats were built at several places on the banks of the Wye, for example at Llandogo, Redbrook, Tintern and Monmouth. Grahame Farr (1954) lists around fourteen vessels constructed at Monmouth between 1786 and 1853 – most were barges, but there were a few larger vessels. The *Hereford Journal* of 26 January 1825 announced that: 'In Monmouth on the stocks at Mr. W. Lambert's wharf is the *Agincourt* of 500 tons, intended for the West Indian trade. On the twenty-first the keel of a 400-ton brig was laid in the same shipyard, and contracts for three other vessels are entered into by Mr. Lambert'. Sea-going vessels like these were built in the 1820s as far upriver as Hereford and the steamboat *Paul Pry* was launched by William Radford in November 1827. On 22 December readers of the *Hereford Independent* learned that: 'The Wye Steam Boat Co.'s vessel *Paul Pry* – George Pearce, master – will start on Wednesday next, the 26th inst. (weather permitting) from Hereford to Chepstow, calling at Hoarwithy, Ross and Monmouth'. The fare to Chepstow was ten shillings with 'refreshments to be had on board by application to the steward'. This Boxing Day trip to Chepstow took four hours. Late in January the *Paul Pry* towed a barge upstream from Chepstow, but a month later left the Wye for Gloucester, moving to the Menai Straits to be employed as a tender by the St George Steam Packet Co.

Around 300 vessels were completed at Chepstow in the fifty-five years from 1750. One long-lasting partnership was that of Buckle and Davies, who launched over thirty vessels from 1812 to about 1830, including a dozen sloops (usually of 40-50 tons), half-a-dozen schooners (60-80 tons) and eight snows (100-200 tons). Their three biggest were 1814 *Ocean* (360), 1818 *Bristol* (428) and 1830 *Lord Eldon* (337), all ship-rigged.

Oliver Chapman built seventeen vessels, including seven brigs, from 1838 until his death in September 1847. They ranged in size from the sloop *Whim* (17) up to the *Rajah* (655) of 1846.

Work began on Brunel's bridge – to carry the South Wales Railway over the Wye – in 1849, with the project completed by 1853. One of those who came to Chepstow to work on the bridge was Edward Finch, who had a contract to provide iron-work. He made his construction base on land near at hand and when his contract was finished he stayed on at the same place to manufacture a variety of iron products such as bridges, dock gates, steam engines and boilers. His first venture into shipbuilding was the screw steamer *Alma* (132), which he launched in 1855. Three years later Edward Finch made masts for Brunel's *Great Eastern*.

From 1879 Finch & Co. began to build barges and tugboats, their first larger steamship being the *Rougemont* (1525) of 1882 for John Cory & Sons of Cardiff. Three more sizeable vessels followed in 1883 and 1884: *Maroon* (1591), *Radyr* (1145) and *Arrow* (1837). In 1888 Edward Finch & Co. launched *The Marchioness* (80), a steel paddle steamer which turned out to be the last packet to ply regularly between Cardiff and Bristol, continuing in service up to 1913.

During the First World War the government decided to produce 'standard' cargo ships to replace, as quickly as possible, the many vessels which had been lost. The problem was that existing yards were already working flat out and there was a shortage of skilled workers. The solution was prefabrication – parts of the vessels were to be produced at factories throughout the country and then sent off to shipyards. Edward Finch's yard at Chepstow assembled some of these ships from 1916.

In the same year a new private concern, the Standard Shipbuilding Co., was formed by a syndicate including Lord Inchcape and J.H. Silley. They began to build a new yard on The Meads, with eight slipways planned, but in August 1917 the yard was requisitioned by the Admiralty and the Standard Shipbuilding Co. was, according to Lord Inchcape in a letter to *The Times*, 'unceremoniously evicted'.

3 The steamship *Fintra*, owned by Christian Salvesen of Leith. It was built as *Tutshill* in 1918 by Edward Finch & Co. of Chepstow.

The Admiralty announced in January 1918 that it planned to develop shipbuilding on the banks of the Wye, between Chepstow and Beachley. Thirty-three slipways were envisaged and according to *The Times*, 'Chepstow will have no rival as a large shipbuilding centre'. The *Chepstow Weekly Argus* was equally impressed:

> Chepstow is to be changed out of existence and by a fortunate turn of circumstances is destined to develop into a town equal in size and importance probably to any in South Wales... In years to come old residents will be able to seek the solitude of the ruins and look from the battlements on to miles of industrial activity – on to a city of ships.

Not all were enthusiastic – there was sustained opposition from private shipbuilders and from the trades unions, who objected to the employment of military personnel and prisoners of war.

Finch's yard was absorbed into the National Shipyard in August 1918 and in the following month the standard ship *War Forest* (3,103) was launched – built by Finch but acclaimed by some as the first product of the National Yard. *War Apple* and *War Trench* were launched in 1919.

The Armistice came into effect on 11 November 1918 and soon 7,000 people left the yards on demobilisation. Two months later it was announced that the shipyards were 'being completed on a reduced scale' and were up for sale. In April 1919, 4,000 prisoners of war were withdrawn from Beachley. As to vessels under construction, a reply in the House of Commons summed up the position in December 1919: no vessels were being built at Beachley, nine at Chepstow.

In February 1920 the National Shipbuilding Yard at Chepstow was bought by the Monmouthshire Shipbuilding Co., which consisted of Lord Glanely, John Cory, T.E. Morel, T.H. Mordey, W. Leon, W.R. Smith, Sir W.S. Seager, the Fairfield Shipbuilding & Engineering Co. and the Anglo-Saxon Petroleum Co. Two monts later 3,000 people watched as the first ship launched since the takeover went down the slipway. *War Glory*, which *The Times* of 3 April described as 'not only the largest vessel so far launched on the River Wye, but has the distinction of being the largest ship ever launched in Great Britain with full steam up, completely equipped, ready for her trials'. The company went on to complete eight more standard ships, the last in August 1921.

4 The Canadian Coast Guard vessel *Mink* was built at Chepstow in 1944 as a tank landing-craft. It was acquired by the Canadian Coast Guard in 1958, and employed in Arctic waters until 1975.

In 1925 the yard was acquired by the Fairfield Shipbuilding & Engineering Co., but no vessels were built there until the Second World War, when prefabricated landing-craft were assembled.

THE SEVERN CROSSINGS

The Old Passage ferry across the Severn, between Beachley and Aust, could be dangerous. In September 1839 the superintendent of the ferry wrote to *The Times* about:

> ... a distressing occurence... The new *Despatch* sailing boat was making her sixth passage, under command of her captain (a steady, experienced sailor, who has been at the ferry for twenty-five years) with ten persons on board, including the crew, when a heavy squall capsized her, and I lament to say that all perished... including a servant lad belonging to one of the proprietors of the ferry, who was crossing in charge of his master's phaeton and pony.

There were many other accidents at the Old Passage, including that in April 1855 when another sailing vessel capsized, drowning seven people.

The first steam boats employed were the *Worcester* and the *Beaufort*. The *Worcester* (41), built at Bristol in 1827, was in service for ten years. *Beaufort* (53) was a wooden paddle vessel built at Chepstow in 1832 by Richard Watkins. It was scrapped in 1860.

The New Passage, from the Monmouthshire coast near Portskewett and Sudbrook across to the Gloucestershire side near Redwick, had been in operation for centuries before the Swedish traveller R.R. Angerstein, on his way from Bristol to South Wales, made the crossing in 1754. When he arrived at the shore he found a number of people who had been waiting for two days, hoping that the weather would improve. Eventually the ferryman decided to go, so 'twenty horses and an even greater number of passengers' were crammed on board. On the way the horses became agitated, the boat started to take in water and people became hysterical. Nearly a

5 J.C. Ibbetson's 'View on the Severn from the New Passage House in Gloucestershire, with the Ferry Boat Preparing to Depart at Low Water' from *A Picturesque Guide to Bath*, 1793.

century later the crossing continued to be uncomfortable and dangerous: on 16 March 1844 the *Monmouthshire Merlin* reported a 'dreadful calamity at the New Passage'. The passage boat *Dispatch*, 'whilst beating across from the Bristol to the Monmouthshire side of the Severn', sank with five people on board, including boatman Paul Davis, who was to have been married that day. Another who died was James Whitchurch, the 'superintendent of the boat', who left a wife and child. His father and brother had drowned when the Old Passage boat foundered in September 1839.

The first steam vessel at the New Passage was the *Saint Pierre* (30), launched at Newport in 1825, and the first steam vessel to be built there. From 1863 it was possible to arrive at the ferry by rail. On each side of the Severn, trains ran out on to piers – the one at Portskewett was over 700ft long – from which passengers could transfer to the ferry boat.

Both Old and New Passages became redundant when the Severn Tunnel was completed in 1886 but forty years later, in 1926, a diesel-engined boat to carry pedestrians and cyclists was introduced at the Old Passage. A vehicle ferry was in use from 1931: the wooden motor vessel *Princess Ida*, built in Chepstow by Hurd and Henderson, could accomodate eight vehicles and around fifty passengers. The *Severn Queen* of 1931 and *Severn King* of 1935 each had a turntable built into the deck, to make it easier to manouevre cars. The service ended with the opening of the Severn Bridge on 8 September 1966.

SUDBROOK

The shipyard at Sudbrook was started by Thomas Andrew Walker, one of the most prominent of Victorian civil engineering contractors. During his early career he had built railways in England, Canada, Russia, Egypt and the Sudan, but from around 1865 Thomas Walker was engaged on railway projects in London, at times in partnership with his brother Charles – as T.A. & C. Walker – but later on his own.

At the end of 1879 he was called in to advise on the construction of the Severn Tunnel, at the same time as he was involved in work on railways in Kent, the Prince of Wales Dock at Swansea, the Penarth Dock extension, the new Barry Dock and Railway and a reservoir at Lisvane in Cardiff. Thomas Walker sailed for South America in 1885 to finalize details of a contract for the harbour of Buenos Aires. The Severn Tunnel opened in 1886 and work started at Buenos Aires in the year following. This was also the year in which Walker won the massive contract to build the Manchester Ship Canal. Two years later he died at his home 'Mount Ballan' near Caerwent. His contract for the Buenos Aires Federal Harbour was continued by C.H. Walker & Co.

As well as taking over the Buenos Aires operation, C.H. Walker & Co. acquired the village and shipyard at Sudbrook. The village had been built for people employed on the Severn Tunnel, and Thomas Walker set up his shipbuilding yard there when the tunnel was finished and work at Buenos Aires was beginning.

The yard produced tugboats and other vessels, many of which were then employed on the company's dock contracts at Buenos Aires and Rio de Janiero: 'In connection with these works Messrs. C.H. Walker... have a fleet of more than sixty steam dredgers, barges, tugs, and other craft, most of which have been constructed at the firm's shipbuilding yards and repair shops' (*The Times* 28 December 1909). From 1889 to 1922 the Sudbrook yard completed over a hundred vessels, with the last – *Frensham* (739) – also the largest.

Early in 1944 Sudbrook village and shipyard were sold by auction at the King's Head, Newport. For £23,000 the buyer acquired 118 houses, schools, a post office, and the 'company's offices and the dismantled shipyard'.

CALDICOT

The remains of Bronze Age boats were found at Caldicot and at Goldcliff. The one at Caldicot was constructed in about 1700 BC and was made of planks sewn together with thread and caulked with moss. A smaller and later boat (about 1000 BC) came from Goldcliff. Both were propelled and steered by paddles. Goldcliff was one of many landing places on the Bristol Channel, and Thomas Phaer reported that by the sixteenth century it was, like Magor, 'another pill for small vessels... where is also much lading of things to convey to the ships at Bristol'. Small boats were built locally and perhaps a dozen larger craft were produced at Caldicot in the two decades from 1785: about half were sloops, but there were at least three full-rigged ships: *Rossetti* (193) built in 1790; *Caldicot Castle* (265) built in 1794 and *Sisters* (314) completed in 1801.

MAGOR

The vestigial remains of two early vessels have been excavated at Magor. The Barland's Farm boat, discovered in November 1993, was built in around AD 300 and was made of oak planks fastened to a wooden frame with iron nails. It was about 37ft long and 10ft wide. With a mast and sail, it was operated by a crew of three, and was large enough to transport about fifty sheep.

The Magor Pill boat remnants – dating from around the middle of the thirteenth century – were found in 1994. The craft was about 45ft long and 10ft wide and clinker-built, fastened with clench nails. There was a square-rigged sail, and it had a cargo of iron ore on board.

Thomas Phaer described Magor in the middle years of the sixteenth century as 'a pill or creek belonging to Chepstow where is great lading of small boats with butter, cheese and other kinds of victuals to ships, and is in the ruling of the earl of Worcester'.

CAERLEON

The legionary fortress at Caerleon, established in about AD 75, was garrisoned until the last years of the 3rd century. Five miles inland on the tidal Usk, Caerleon was well chosen

6 A model of the third-century Barland's farm boat.

by the Romans for ease of supply and communication and it soon became necessary for them to build a substantial quay. The trade of early medieval Caerleon was dominated by wool, as the Cistercian monks of Llantarnam were heavily involved in this trade and sent considerable quantities across Caerleon quay. The usual destination was Bristol, and from there to Flanders.

By the sixteenth century some Caerleon vessels can be identified in the records: in March 1539, for example, ten 'mariners of Caerleon' went with the *Trinity* of Caerleon to join Henry VIII's fleet assembling at Portsmouth. During the 1560s voyages by Caerleon boats were generally to Bristol. In April 1566 the *George* (18) carried a cargo of brass and pewter goods from Bristol to Caerleon on behalf of Henry Gibson, a Bristol pewterer. In the following June the *Jesus* (18) arrived with eighty stones of wool, sent by 'William Pottell of the city of Bristol, clothyer'. In September of the same year the *Trinity* (10) returned from Bristol with coal, iron and 'cottens de Manchester'. Twenty years later, some longer voyages are recorded, such as that of the *Griffin* (35) which went to Lisbon in March 1580, bringing back a cargo of salt for the merchant David Saunders of Caerleon. At the end of the sixteenth century the pattern remained much the same, with a handful of boats taking butter, cheese, oatmeal, wheat and wool to Bristol and returning with whatever cargoes they could find. In 1599 and 1600 much of the produce carried to Bristol, in such vessels as the *Joseph*, the *Dolphin* and the *Margaret*, was destined for the army in Ireland commanded by the Earl of Essex.

At the mid-point of the seventeenth century the customs official John Byrd described Caerleon as: 'a port on the river Usk between which place and Bristol is very great trade for most things in general', and 'where is far more trade than Newport'. He reported that eighty-three 'dutiable' cargoes entered Caerleon in 1654, and sixty-four were cleared outwards. A typical Caerleon vessel was the *Gift*, which went to Bristol twenty-eight times in 1656; this, and other craft, brought back tobacco, salt and wine. Longer voyages were undertaken by the *Endeavour*, which went to Britanny for salt.

Browne's *Bristol Directory* of 1785 listed the *Caerleon* as the boat running 'to and fro' from Bristol. In 1791 another directory informed readers that a regular trading vessel for Bristol 'sails every Tuesday and returns every Friday'. A significant development for Caerleon's trade came in 1795, when Nicholas Blannin's tramroad reached the river. Horses hauled drams of coal down to the wharf, as well as building materials for the new Monmouthshire Canal. Products of the Caerleon Forge and the Ponthir Tinplate Works were carried away by vessels such as the *Iron and Tin Trader*.

The decline of Caerleon as a shipping place began with the opening of the Monmouthshire Canal at the end of the eighteenth century. Competition from railways exacerbated the trend, and the use of bigger ships meant that they could no longer go up the Usk to Caerleon.

NEWPORT

Between the years 1327 and 1386 a stone castle was built alongside the river, as a focal point for the lordship of Gwynllwg. The site chosen was to prove its worth during the Glyn Dŵr rising, when the garrison of the castle received supplies by ship from Bristol: cargoes of ale and wine, oats and wheat, and more than a thousand 'fishes called hakes'. The castle's defences were strengthened with timber and other building materials, which also came by sea. Further works were set in train in the 1420s, and again building supplies were brought by sea: stone from Dundry was laboriously hauled overland to Bristol and from there loaded on to vessels for Newport. Boatloads of stone came from Penarth and thousands of slates from Cornwall. By the early fifteenth century there was a dock or watergate at the castle, which could 'receive into the castle a good vessel'.

The names of a few Newport ships appear in the fifteenth century records: in the 1440s the *Swan*; in the 1460s the *Trinity* and in the 1480s the *Christopher*, both of which traded to Ireland. The remarkable remains of a fifteenth-century ship, discovered at Newport in 2002, show that the vessel was about 82ft long and 26ft wide at the maximum, made of oak and with a keel of beech. Found with the remains were Portuguese coins and pottery, barrel staves, textiles and stone cannon balls, as well as remnants of the sails and rigging. The ship was built in about 1465.

In the middle of the sixteenth century Newport was described by Thomas Phaer: 'There is a haven good within of three fathoms, but all sands (to seaward)... All westerly and southerly winds bring in'. Vessels belonging to the town at around this time included the *James*, owned by Sir William Herbert of St Julians, the *Trinity* (24) which carried skins fom Cork to Bristol, and the *Michael* (14) which sailed regularly between Newport and Bristol. In August 1566 the *Mary Rose* (20) brought brass and pewter goods on behalf of John Northall of Bristol, a pewterer. In the following month the same merchant engaged the *Mary Rose* to take a similar cargo from Bristol to Aberthaw. Four years later the *Mary Rose* was to be found on a voyage from Waterford to Bristol, carrying skins and hides.

Thomas Churchyard, writing of Newport vessels in 1587, confirmed that 'many sail to Bristol' carrying cargoes such as butter, cheese and leather often for trans-shipment to ships going to France. Some Newport ships made longer voyages: the *Steven* went to Bordeaux, La Rochelle and Lisbon for salt and wine; the *Dragon* undertook voyages to Lisbon with lead and cloth from Bristol. A report on vessels at this time lists those belonging to Newport as: *Green Dragon* (100), *White Eagle* (100), *Griffand* (40), *Lyon* (40), *Black Lyon* (34), *Steven* (30), *Samuel* (30) and *Mary Rose* (20). There were, in addition, half-a-dozen craft of under 20 tons.

Sales of Welsh iron were increasing in the early years of the seventeenth century. In 1602 the *Jonas* (20) made several trips carrying Richard Hanbury's iron to Bridgwater, and the *Speedwell* (30) went to Beaumaris with 6 tons of iron and six pairs of millstones. But the usual voyage was still to Bristol – for example in December 1635 the *Mary Rose* took Welsh butter to be put on board the *Charles* of Bristol, bound for Lisbon, and in July 1636 butter was carried to Bristol by the *Jonas* – the *David* was to take it on to La Rochelle.

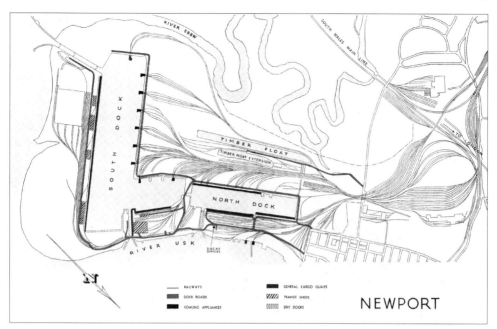

7 Newport Docks in the late 1940s.

There was an increasing trade in tobacco. In 1650 John Byrd noted that French tobacco was brought ashore at Newport from the *North Starre* of Dort, which had earlier discharged salt at Penarth and there was also a parcel of tobacco 'in a small barque of Bideford'.

Newport's maritime prospects were transformed by the Monmouthshire Canal, which opened in 1799. Several ironworks built tramroads to the new waterway, making it easier for their products to be sent to Newport. One provision of the Canal Act was of great significance for the coal trade: coal shipped through Newport paid no duty if it was being sent to Bridgwater or to any port above the Holms.

The effects on shipping at Newport were dramatic and with this expansion of trade new loading places became necessary. The *Monmouthshire Merlin* wrote on 13 January 1830 that: 'The Monmouthshire Canal with its double line of communication from Newport to Crumlin on the one side and from Newport to Pontypool on the other – its numerous wharfs, railways, and other conveniences – is perhaps one of the finest public works in Britain'. Six months later the *Merlin* reported that 'a steam engine recently began hauling coal trains from Thomas Prothero's colliery to the wharf at Pillgwelly'.

Steam power was already being applied at sea. The first steamboat service between Newport and Bristol had begun in the early 1820s, providing an alternative to the market boats which provided 'a tedious and uncertain passage'. The first two steam vessels (both built at Liverpool, and owned by the War Office Steam Packet Co.) were the wooden paddlers *Cambria* (48), which inaugurated the service in May 1822, and *St David* (48) which came on the scene five months later. Competition arrived in June 1823 in the form of the *Lady Rodney* (58), also Liverpool-built, owned by three Newport men (William Jones, Thomas Protheroe and William Williams) and one from Bristol (John Jones). The journey to Bristol took, usually, about four-and-a-half hours.

Other vessels to ply this route over the years included the *Usk* (129); built by James Lunell & Co. at Bristol in 1838, the vessel was 98ft long and was rigged as a sloop. It ran between Newport and Bristol during 1838 and 1854, before being moved to the Cardiff-Bristol service. The *Usk* was sometimes diverted from its day-to-day work: in September 1838 it took

8 A crowded excursion steamer at Newport landing stage. The transporter bridge is in the distance.

excursionists as far as the Holms to see Brunel's *Great Western* setting off for New York and in February 1840 the steamer conveyed the Chartist deportees to Portsmouth. In October 1842, at the opening of Newport Town Dock, the *Usk* towed in the schooner *Henry*.

An advertisement in the *Monmouthshire Merlin* of 9 November 1844 announced:

Steam communication between Bristol and Newport. The new steam packet company's iron-built schooners propelled by screw. The Avon and Severn Co. is run by Ebenezer Rogers at Newport. Sailings most days of the week. On certain days, mainly Saturdays and Mondays, there is a 'to and fro' service.

The after-cabin two shillings; fore-cabin one shilling. Vehicular shipping and landing charges: 4-wheel eighteen shillings; 2-wheel ten shillings. Phaeton or gig and horse, fifteen shillings. Horses, each, five shillings; rider six shillings.

The trade of Newport went on increasing during the 1830s. In one week (ending 28 October 1838) vessels arrived at Newport from Bristol, Gloucester, Ireland, London, Swansea and Quebec; they carried cheese, livestock, oats, metal and timber. In addition, ten shipments of Cornish iron ore were discharged. As for exports, that week's cargoes included bar iron, pig iron, and hoop iron, which thirty-four vessels took to Holland, Ireland and Scotland as well as to various ports in England.

On 17 October 1835 it was reported in the local newspaper that the barque *Recovery* (329) went from: 'Newport to America in Record Time'. Owned by Robert Latch, 'a regular trader to Canada', the vessel brought back a cargo of timber for Batchelor & Co., after a voyage of twenty-eight days. 'She has now completed two voyages to America in six months and seven days.'

On 4 November 1839 came the march of thousands of Chartists on Newport. Twenty of the demonstrators were killed and eight sentenced to death. Five of the capital sentences were commuted to terms of imprisonment, and three to transportation.

Three years later came a different kind of march when a new dock was opened. A procession, a mile-and-a-half long, set off from the Caerleon Road at 8 a.m. on 10 October

1842. *The Times* reported that, as well as the mayor and corporation in carriages, there were: 'Freemasons, the Druids, and Odd Fellows, in full regalia, the various clubs with banners, etc., the dock committee, and trades, with bands of music.' A detachment of the 73rd Regiment of Foot was deployed at the dock:

> At precisely twenty minutes after 10 o'clock, the tide outside having risen to the necessary height, the gates were opened, and the *Usk* steamer, which was profusely decorated with the colours of all nations, entered the lock, towing in the *Henry* schooner, on board which were the dock committee. The steamer *Hercules* followed, towing in a very fine ship, the *Great Britain* – a local barque – next came the *Tiger* steam tug, towing another fine ship, the *Rothschild*, and followed by the Channel mission-ship *Eirene*. At this moment the deafening cheers of the assembled multitude, the waving of handkerchiefs by the ladies in the grand stand, the roaring of the cannon, and the music of the various bands, who were all playing the national air 'Rule Britannia' together.

This new dock was soon outgrown – on one day, ten years later, there were 144 vessels crammed into the port. An extension to the Town Dock opened on 2 March 1858 when the barque *Great Britain* was towed in by the tugboat *Neptune*. Crowds cheered, bands played and the *Star of Gwent* reported: 'One of the crew of the *Great Britain* climbed to the top of the foremast, laid himself out on the fore-royal truck and imitated the motions of a swimmer'. After the opening of the dock extension exports of coal and iron continued to increase, as did imports of timber.

There were, inevitably, many local shipping casualties. In 1861, Newport lost *Alert*, *Bellona*, *Doctor Bunting*, *Favourite*, *General Havelock*, *Raglan* and *Young Gipsy*. They were lost in the Bristol Channel, the Mediterranean, off Cornwall and the Isles of Scilly, near Rhyl and in the St Lawrence. Other casualties in the 1860s and 1870s included: *Caerau*, *Crawshay Bailey*, *Eleanor*, *Herbert Graham*, *Minnie Graham*, *Lavinia*, *Susannah*, *Usk* and *Victory*. Several of them met their end off the coast of South America. The most bizarre incident occurred at Newport's Town Dock, when two ships – the *Constancia* of Bilbao (with 850 tons of iron ore) and the *Primus* of Whitby – became wedged together in the dock entrance. No vessel could get in or out for a fortnight.

The *National Gazetteer* described Newport in 1868: 'There are six or seven shipbuilding yards in full work, several very large timber yards in different parts of the town; also breweries, iron foundries, large anchor and chain-cable manufactories; a shot manufactory, iron factories and sail lofts, which last are principally erected on the side of the canal'. Exports included: 'pig-iron, castings, bar and bolt iron, rolled iron for armour plates, tin plates, wire, and coals'. Newport also imported provisions and 'very large quantities of timber from Canada and Nova Scotia'.

The Alexandra Dock was officially opened on 13 April 1875. Crowds flocked to the event and to see another procession, led by Newport Mounted Police, with seven bands taking part. Three years later a graving dock opened, and then a timber float. By now Newport was the fourth largest coal-exporting port of the United Kingdom.

Newport Shipbuilding

Several boat and shipbuilders were active on the banks of the Usk in the 1820s, including Matthew and David Johns, David Tudor and David Williams. In August 1825 Pride and Williams completed the first steamboat built at Newport, the *Saint Pierre* (30), which was to be employed on the Severn Passages.

John Young launched a schooner in the summer of 1834:

> The vessel is considered by competent judges to be one of the most perfect pieces of workmanship that ever was launched in the bosom of the three channels. She has been purchased by Messrs. Crisps of London and is intended for the Smyrna trade. Although

launching is becoming so common in Newport, the shores on each side of the river were thronged with spectators'. (*Monmouthshire Merlin* 9 August 1834)

In April 1837 when Young launched the barque *Amelia* (intended for 'the Liverpool-West Indies trade) there were two other vessels on the stocks. The *Queen Victoria* (150), for Waterford owners, came down the slipway in December 1837. The *Merlin* wrote, on 6 January 1838, that: 'We understand that this vessel was completed in the remarkably short period of nine weeks'. It was the fifth launch at this yard in the last eleven months.

William Perkins launched a ship of 600 tons burden in August 1834, for Bristol owners, followed by: *James Hunt* (166) in 1836; *John Panter* (254) in 1837 and *Florist* (433) in 1838.

During the period of 1843-45, Willmett and Hall built: *Anjer* (466), *Siloam* (297), *Silurian* (300) and *Sion* (360).

William Willmett constructed three barques in 1850-51: *John Henry* (556), *William Frederick* (578) and *Isca* (587).

In 1866 Newport builders completed ten vessels, including the *Crawshay Bailey* (682), which was probably the largest locally built sailing vessel. Launched by the Newport Dry Dock & Iron Shipbuilding Co., the ship was lost in 1869 on a voyage from Batavia to San Francisco. In 1867 there were eleven launchings at Newport.

Other builders at Newport included Benjamin Batchelor, Thomas H. Cook, J. Johns, the Usk Shipbuilding Co. and Mordey and Carney, who launched two screw vessels in 1884: *Camel* (182) and *Delabole* (241).

In 1865 only one steamer was listed in *Clayton's Register* as being owned at Newport: the *Thomas Powell* (272), an iron-screw vessel built at Bristol in 1856 for the coalowner Thomas Powell. There were 106 sailing vessels, of which brigs made up 36 per cent, schooners 20 per cent, barques 15 per cent, sloops 9.6 per cent and brigantines 8.5 per cent. The largest vessels were the ship-rigged *Alfred* (1,153), built in 1863 and *Norwood* (1,233), built in 1853. Of the vessels listed in *Clayton's Register*, seven brigs and one barque can be identified as having been built at Prince Edward Island in the year 1863: *Courier* (209), *Frank* (213), *Matchless* (298), *Mattie* (260), the barque *Onward* (257), *Progress* (299), *Saladin* (199) and *Surprise* (228).

Thomas Powell & Son managed a barque, three brigs and a schooner. Henry Burton operated smaller vessels: three sloops, two smacks and a barge. The Burtons were firmly established as owners by this date. Henry's father and grandfather – both named Richard Burton – bought the sloop *Bristol Packet* in 1825. Other vessels followed and in 1851 Henry's sons Edgar, Henry and William became partners. The Burtons acquired several wharves, and by the mid-1870s they were trading with the sailing vessels *Bristol Packet*, *Burton*, *Edgar*, *Emily Maria*, *Forerunner*, *Prince of Wales* and the screw steamers *Enid* (60), *Ethel* (58), *Isca* (52), *Lincolnshire* (54), *Moderator* (55) and *St David*. Twenty years later the firm operated only three sailing vessels, but had seven small steamers – *St David* had been replaced by the *City of York* (31) and there was now a *Moderator No.4*. The company was sold in 1898.

Twenty years after *Clayton's Register* the Newport fleet was of about the same number, but its composition had changed. There were sixty-eight sailing vessels registered at Newport in 1885, but there were now thirty-six steam vessels, compared with only one in 1865.

Two vessels are listed as being owned by T. Jones: *Bergamo* (778), built in 1884 and *Camargo* (608), built in 1880. The brothers Richard and Thomas Jones were engaged in the coal, iron and timber trades and entered steamship ownership in 1880 with *Camargo*, built at Sunderland. The company eventually developed into Richard W. Jones & Co., owning *Salerno*, *Alassio*, *Bergamo*, *Durango*, *Ricardo* (their first steel ship, bought in 1889) and *Elorrio*. The firm usually owned two or three ships at a time, carrying coal outwards (generally from Newport to Spain or Italy) with a return cargo of iron ore from Spain to the Mersey.

Nearly 800 vessels arrived at Newport during 1888 and the number of seamen signing on reached about 16,000. A new dock basin was opened in 1892 and in 1895 Mordey, Carney & Co. took over the facilities of the Eastern Dry Dock Co. (Newport and Sharpness), the

9 The Alexandra Docks, Newport.

Central Engineering & Ship-repairing Co. (Cardiff) and the Windsor Slipways, Dry Docks and Engineering Co. (Cardiff). Tredegar Pier and the South Dock were brought into use and in 1898 the docks company acquired the Pontypridd, Caerphilly and Newport Railway. *Kelly's Directory* for 1901 noted that: 'There are numerous foundries, steam engine and boiler works, anchor, chain, chain cable, nail factories, and shipbuilding establishments as well as dry docks for the repair of shipping.'

The port was run by the Alexandra (Newport & South Wales) Docks & Railway Co. In the final year of the nineteenth century 1,700 ships left carrying coal for foreign destinations, 1,500 departed for Ireland, and there were over 4,000 clearances of coastal vessels. Seventy-nine vessels belonged to the port.

The main imports were iron ore and timber and the principal export was coal. In 1904 the docks company could boast that, 'the Alexandra Co. can, and indeed have, put 11,000 tons of coal in a steamer in thirty-six hours', and in that year coal and coke exports totalled 4,400,032 tons.

Many smaller vessels loaded at the river bank, often coal for France, discharging pitwood on their return. To facilitate these operations a new wharf was built, as well as two coaling jetties. The Cork Steam Packet Co. ran a steamer, once a week, between Newport and Cork.

The transporter bridge opened in September 1906. The gondola, electrically operated, could carry eight vehicles and a hundred people across the Usk.

An extension of the South Dock was being built – it would open in 1914, when the large sea lock began operating. Thirty-nine people died when part of the construction work collapsed in 1909.

Newport Shipowners in the Twentieth Century

Richard W. Jones & Co.

In 1906 their two remaining vessels were put into single-ship companies: the Alassio Steamship Co. and the Elorrio Steamship Co. Subsequent vessels carried names such as *Uskside, Uskmouth, Uskhaven* and *Uskbridge*. By 1929 the Jones fleet consisted of six ships, generally carrying coal

from South Wales and the north-east of England and bringing back esparto grass (used in making paper) from North Africa to the Firth of Forth. In the early 1930s pit props were brought to Newport from the Baltic and northern Russia by the three remaining vessels. The company continued in business until 1968.

Stephens, Mawson & Co.
They were set up at Newport by a Newcastle-upon-Tyne firm as 'Stephens, Mawson & Goss' in 1878. By 1915, when the company was sold, there were six ships.

B. Pardoe-Thomas
Started the Ottoman Line with *Saracen* (3,272). He had sold off his vessels by 1920 but, in 1928, he founded the White Cross Line, operating seven ships until selling out again in 1934.

Mordey, Jones & Co.
Thomas Henry Mordey and Edmund Jones began in 1884 with two steamships taking coal to Spain, bringing back iron ore. Later vessels went to European ports and to the Black Sea. The firm survived until the death of E.W. Jones. His son continued with E.W. Jones & Son, and then (from 1924) Mordey, Son & Co., trading to Canada, Europe, the Mediterranean and the White Sea. From 1899 there was a regular service from the Bristol Channel to Antwerp.

Orders and Handford
In 1890 bought *Rosario* (1,225) and *Reggio* (1,218). The fleet of seven was bought by J. Cory & Sons in 1916.

Monkswood Shipping Co.
Started in 1928 by G.B. Bailey, with *Monkswood* (4,212), built in 1910.

B. & S. Shipping
Formed in 1933 by G.B. Bailey and R.G.M. Street. They managed the *Monkswood* and the *St Quentin* (3,528), built in 1915. By the late 1930s there were nine steamships, and a liner service was operated to South America. The business was sold in 1961.

Opposite: 10 The Newport transporter bridge opened in 1906. The gondola could carry eight vehicles and a hundred people across the Usk.

Right: 11 Coal hoists at the South Dock, Newport.

The First World War

At the start of the war in August 1914, the Hamburg-Amerika liner *Belgia* (8,132) was detained in the Bristol Channel and brought to Newport. The ship had been bought, only two years previously, from the Brocklebank Line of Liverpool. Now, renamed *Huntrick*, it was returned to British service. During the war the dry docks received about 2,000 vessels for maintenance and repair and ships came to the docks to have wireless cabins and gun mountings installed. A local tragedy occurred in February 1918 when the hospital ship *Glenart Castle* (6,576) left Newport for Brest to collect patients. The vessel was torpedoed in the Bristol Channel. Of the 186 on board only thirty-one survived.

After the war inter-racial trouble flared up on 6 June 1919. Police broke up fights and houses where foreign seamen were living had windows broken. Furniture was taken out of two houses on George Street and burned. Chinese laundries were attacked. Next night the police had more men on duty and although the mob smashed doors and windows they were driven off. Nothing more happened at Newport, but serious disturbances broke out at Cardiff. In 1922 the docks, in common with others, were taken over by the Great Western Railway. In 1932 the Town Dock was filled in.

The Second World War

Newport was bombed several times in 1940/41. In raids at the end of May 1941 twenty-three people were killed; in early July 1941 thirty-five died. Many Newport-owned vessels were sunk by enemy action, including those of Richard W. Jones & Co.: *Uskbridge* (2,715), *Uskmouth* (2,483), *Uskport* (2,462) and *Uskside* (2,706). In 1944 Newport Docks, like the other ports of South Wales, were busy with the traffic of men and supplies for the invasion of France.

After the war the British Transport Commission took over the management of the docks. At this time the North and South Docks were in operation, as were the river wharves for smaller vessels. There were also five graving docks. Exports had fallen considerably: in the last full year before the war (1938) total exports were 3,230,373 tons (95 per cent of which were coal or coke); in 1947 total exports were only 924,687 tons.

During the 1950s there was a brief resurgence of shipbuilding when the Atlantic Shipbuilding Co. constructed vessels for the Great Lakes – *Baie Comeau* in 1954, *Manicouagan* in 1955 and, in 1956, *Lachinedoc* – and for customers in the USA and Cuba. In the same decade large ore carriers brought in iron ore for the Ebbw Vale steelworks. The Spencer Steelworks at Llanwern

12 A cargo liner loading at Newport.

began production in September 1961 and three years later imports of iron ore reached nearly 2.5 million tons a year; exports of iron and steel amounted to over half a million tons.

Two dry docks shut in the 1950s and coal exports ended in 1964. The Newport Shipbuilding & Engineering Co. ceased operations in 1971, but ship-breaking continued including, in October 1955, the well-known local paddle steamer *Ravenswood* and in 1958 the ocean liner *Reina del Pacifico* (17,800).

Associated British Ports became responsible for the docks in 1981. Cargoes handled today include dry bulks, forest products (from the Far East, South America, Scandinavia, Russia and the Baltic), general cargoes, coal and coke, motor vehicles and iron and steel.

CARDIFF

The first Roman fort at Cardiff was put up in about AD 55-60. A more substantial building, parts of which can still be seen, was built towards the end of the THIRrd century. The site is on a sheltered estuary, so that the garrison could be supplied and reinforced from the sea. The Normans constructed their fortifications within the Roman remains in the eleventh century and later rebuilt the church at Llandaff bringing in stone from Dorset, Somerset and Wiltshire. From this time, trade began to develop with the harbours of the Severn Sea and particularly with Bristol.

By the sixteenth century 'in all this coast of Cardiff and Glamorganshire is great lading of butter and cheese and other provisions – partly unto other shires of Wales, and partly to Devon and Cornwall and other places'. Cardiff was, reported Thomas Phaer, 'a proper town, walled, where there is a dry haven, and beyond this is a road in the Severn called Penarth'. Rice Merrick recorded that 'the River Taff runneth near the town walls in the west part of

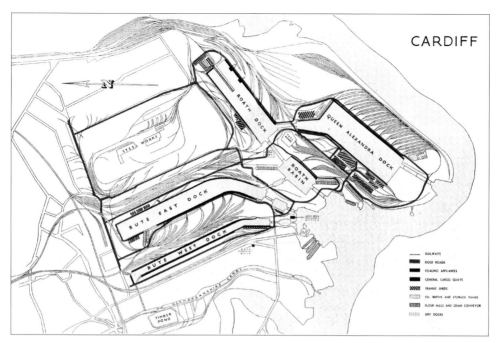

13 Cardiff Docks in the late 1940s.

the town, and washeth the wall, but somewhat too hard, for part of it is easily overturned and the sea floweth to the walls where, at the west angle, is a fair quay, to which both ships and boats resort'.

There were now several small Cardiff vessels trading to Bristol, Bridgwater and Gloucester carrying wool, grain, hides, iron, cheese and butter. Some larger vessels voyaged to the Biscay ports, returning with wine, fruit, raisins, pitch and salt.

Piracy was rife and some of the loot was sold openly at Cardiff, with the collusion of the authorities. In 1614 Sir Thomas Button was appointed 'Admiral of the King's Ships upon the Coast of Ireland', given a small flotilla and told to police a large sea area, including the Bristol Channel. Thomas (a member of the Button family of Worleton and Cottrell, near Cardiff) had commanded a pinnace at the siege of Kinsale in 1601 for which he was rewarded with a pension of 6s 8d a day and took part in several privateering voyages before being appointed to command an expedition to discover the North-West Passage. The two vessels – *Resolution* and *Discovery* – sailed from the Thames in April 1612 and the men went on to become the first Europeans to visit the western shores of Hudson's Bay. Button named their landfall 'New Wales'. After taking refuge for the winter, they were forced to abandon the *Resolution* and pack both crews into the *Discovery*. At last convinced that there was no exit to a North-West Passage from Hudson's Bay, they set sail for home in July 1613.

On his return Sir Thomas Button was given his admiral's post and began operations against pirates, taking time away from this in 1620 to go as rear-admiral with the fleet sent against the North African pirate bases. Sir Thomas was made a member of the King's Council of War in 1624, but lost his admiral's office ten years later. A friend wrote that, 'Sir Thomas died of a burning fever, quickly, much discontented that he lost his employment in the Irish Sea'.

An important part of the trade of Cardiff in Sir Thomas Button's time consisted of large quantities of butter sent to Bristol. Other items included hides, skins, wool, knitted stockings, flannel and also ringo roots (sea holly), which were sent to the apothecaries of Bristol to be made into medicines and sweets. Bristol's thriving glass industry demanded boatloads of kelp.

14 The entrance to the first Bute Dock.

In a typical week during the 1650s about half-a-dozen incoming cargoes would be declared to customs at Cardiff, with a similar number of outgoing vessels. Freight was handled at one of the main shipping places – Rumney Bridge, Leckwith Bridge and at the Bank and old quay on the River Taff.

Cardiff's growth as a port followed the development of the iron industry, particularly that at Merthyr Tydfil, and by the early 1780s there were – as well as the public quays – 'three private wharfs for shipping and landing goods, chiefly iron', on the river. The iron was at first carried to Cardiff by horses and mules, until a road was built from Merthyr to Cardiff, but this soon became worn and rutted by the heavy traffic of horse-drawn carts. The ironmasters needed better means of transport, and on 9 June 1790 an Act of Parliament authorised the construction of a canal from Merthyr to the Bank, on the river just below Cardiff. On 10 February 1794 canal boats arrived at Cardiff 'laden with the produce of the iron works'.

Two years later the canal was extended, providing a mile-long basin at Cardiff where cargoes could be transferred to sea-going vessels and a lock which allowed vessels to pass between sea and canal. The canal boats brought down iron from Merthyr but they also transported other cargoes, such as the output of the Ynysangharad chain works of Brown Lenox, which made cables for warships and transatlantic liners, including Brunel's *Great Eastern* and Cunard's *Aquitania* and *Mauretania*.

The tax concessions for coal carried on the Monmouthshire Canal were abolished in 1831, leading to a big increase in coal shipped through Cardiff. The nature of the trade was changing, as exemplified by George Insole who, rather than simply selling his coal at the quayside, sought long-term contracts, supplying local steamboat companies and shipping large quantities to the Thames, and to French ports. At the same time as coal exports were increasing, so were imports of iron ore through Cardiff. It was brought from the Forest of Dean and south-west England, but most came from Cumberland and Barrow-in-Furness.

With all this extra traffic, the conditions at the sea lock became chaotic and there were long delays. Many vessels were too large to get in and had to load cargo from lighters. This situation led to the Bute Ship Canal Bill of 1830 which enabled the Marquess of Bute (after

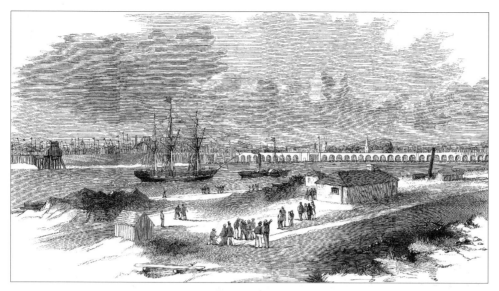

15 The official opening of the final section of the East Bute Dock, 14 September 1859. The tug *United States* is towing in the barque *Masaniello*.

an amending Act of 1834) to build his first dock, which later became known as the West Bute Dock. A feeder canal was built through the town and a new channel was dredged to allow vessels to come up to the dock, which was officially opened on 9 October 1839 when the small paddle steamer *Lady Charlotte* towed in the *Celerity*, a local schooner with the civic party on board.

By the late 1840s the foundations of Cardiff's future as a coal port had been laid: a large dock had been built by the Marquess of Bute; the Taff Vale Railway had opened, stimulating mining in the port's hinterland; the demand for coal to fuel steam boilers was growing; and the experiments of Henry de la Bèche and Lyon Playfair had established the superiority of Welsh coal for steamships.

In 1839 there were 723 steamships registered in Britain. By 1890 there were 7,400. Coal began to be stockpiled at convenient places on steamer routes and coaling stations were established all over the world. Prominent in this field was the Cardiff firm of Cory Brothers, which had over a hundred depots or agencies. The demand for coal was such that the Bute Dock was overwhelmed – vessels were queuing for a berth, and larger vessels could not get in. It was decided to build another dock, the East Bute Dock, the first part of which was opened on 20 July 1855, with the rest completed by September 1859.

There were further developments: new coal staithes on the east bank of the river; a new low-water pier for passenger steamers; the Roath Basin (July 1874) and Roath Dock (August 1887).

The Bristol Channel was a crowded place. The *Cardiff Times* of 26 February 1859 reported: 'A Magnificent Spectacle. The immense fleet of ships, numbering nearly 800 sail, which has been accumulating for weeks past, took their departure from Penarth Roads on the favourable change of wind which took place in the beginning of the week'. The *Bristol Channel Pilot* warned in the same year that: 'The space between Flat Holm and Lavernock Point is much frequented, not only by numerous coasters and other vessels proceeding to Cardiff, but by the Bristol and Newport traders and the steam packets, who creep up the north shore against the ebb'.

SHIPPING COAL, CARDIFF DOCKS, WITH THE TEN TON SHUTE.

16 An early coal-tipping appliance at Cardiff.

Clayton's Register of 1865 lists sixty-eight sailing vessels registered at Cardiff. Apart from small coastal traders there were nineteen schooners, fifteen brigs, fifteen barques, seven brigantines and five ship-rigged. Eighty per cent of owners operated a single vessel. A number of Cardiff vessels were employed in the timber trade and vessels were bought from builders across the Atlantic, for example:

Argentus (503)
A barque, 128ft long, launched at Tatamagouche, Nova Scotia in 1857. Owned by Thomas Plain, the vessel was lost in May 1865 on a voyage from Cardiff to Quebec.

Charlotte Harrison (530)
A barque, 120ft by 29ft, built in Quebec at the yard of Pierre Labbé in 1841. From around 1844 sailed from Liverpool and the Clyde to ports such as Demerara, New Orleans and New York. Registered at Cardiff from July 1859. Lost off Cape Breton Island on 17 June 1874.

Huron (428)
Built in 1841 by William Cummings at St Patrick, Charlotte County, New Brunswick. A barque managed by Thomas Plain and George Davies, who owned thirty-two shares between them. Sixteen shares each were held by William Coward, 'robe maker', and Richard Verity, 'ship's chandler'.

Monnequash (522)
A barque built at St John's, New Brunswick in 1856, owned by Richard Verity and Thomas Plain. Between 1864 and 1866 the vessel sailed to Alexandria, Cape Verde, St Vincent, Quebec and Trieste. Wrecked off Prince Edward Island in October 1867.

Steamships
There were only three steam vessels belonging to Cardiff in 1865: *Swift* (23) built in 1841, managing owner J.H. Insole; *Taff* (25) built in 1841 and owned by James Ware, and the *Velindra*

(73) 1860, of the Cardiff Steam Navigation Co. Ten years later there were fifty-two iron steamships owned at Cardiff and shipowners had begun to realise the advantages of bigger vessels for carrying coal and bringing back cargoes of iron ore or pitwood. One of the earliest larger steamers belonging to Cardiff was the *Llandaff* (280) built at Wallsend in 1865. Screw-driven, the vessel was clinker-built with an iron frame, and rigged as a three-masted schooner, 152ft by 24ft. Registered at Cardiff on 12 July 1865, when the owners, all from Cardiff, were: Alexander Dalziel, William George Noble, Charles Ellah Stalleybrass, Henry Vellacott and John Heron Wilson. By March 1869 the shareholders were: John Henry Vellacott (13/64), Henry Vellacott (12/64), Alexander Dalziel, merchant (10/64), Charles Ellah Stalleybrass, merchant (10/64), John Pybus Ingledew, solicitor (10/64) and John Fry (9/64).

Fairwater (384), a screw-driven steamer, was also built at Wallsend. It was registered at Cardiff on 29 January 1866 by the owners Henry Vellacott (12/64), John Heron Wilson (11/64), Charles E. Stalleybrass (11/64), J.P. Ingledew (10/64), Benjamin Jenkins (10/64) and Alexander Dalziel (10/64).

Charles Stalleybrass later acquired *Galatz* (571), *Hero* (373), *Lisvane* (420), *Lavernock* (444), and *Llanishen* (676).

In February 1872 the *Western Mail* advertised:

The South Wales Atlantic Steamship Co.'s new, first-class, full-powered Clyde-built steamships *Glamorgan* (2,500 tons, 500hp), *Pembroke* (2,500 tons, 500hp), *Carmarthen* (3,000 tons, 600 hp) or other first-class steamers, will sail regularly between Cardiff and New York, commencing about the end of April.

The venture was not successful, and finished within four years.

John Cory bought his first steamships in 1874; by 1885 John Cory & Sons owned seventeen vessels, all acquired as single-ship companies, and by 1889 owned 'Cory's Buildings', a five-storey office block.

Philip and Thomas Morel, from Jersey, settled at Cardiff around 1860. They were ship brokers, and developed interests in the iron-ore trade, sending their vessels to ports such as Arcachon, Bayonne, Bilbao, Brest and Cartagena. The Morels' first steamship – *Colstrup* (506) – was bought in 1876. The fleet grew to twenty-eight vessels, employed on what had become the typical Cardiff trading voyage, carrying coal outwards and bringing back grain and iron ore to British and northern European ports.

Evan Thomas of Aberporth and Henry Radcliffe of Merthyr went into business together in 1881 with a new steamship, the *Gwenllian Thomas* (1,146) – the ship's dimensions were 223ft by 30ft and it was advertised as: 'most suitable for the Bilbao iron ore trade and the grain trade from the Danube, Nicolaieff and the Azoff, where she can come from her loading berth to the sea with a full cargo without the enormous expense of lighterage'. The *Gwenllian Thomas* remained with the company until 1905. By 1890 Thomas and Radcliffe were managing sixteen single-ship companies.

Other early steamship operators at Cardiff included J. & M. Gunn, Gueret & Co., Hacquiol Brothers, Turnbull Brothers, Anning Brothers and W. & C.T. Jones. By the early 1880s over 200 steamships were owned at Cardiff.

A steam-packet route from Cardiff to Bristol was opened in 1834 with the wooden paddle vessel *Nautilus*, built in Bristol three years earlier. The *Lady Charlotte* (Cardiff & Bristol Steam Navigation Co.) was introduced in July 1835 and in September made the run from Cardiff to Bristol in only two-and-a-half hours. This daily service was well used, and in the first ten months of 1837 the two paddlers carried 12,264 passengers.

As well as services to Bristol, steamer routes developed to Cork, Portishead, Burnham-on-Sea, Ilfracombe and Weston-super-Mare. P. & A. Campbell went on to establish a monopoly in the Bristol Channel excursion trade.

The development of steam-powered vessels brought danger with it, and boiler explosions were not uncommon. On 1 November 1866 the Cardiff tugboat *Black Eagle No.2* was towing

the Norwegian barque *Aucutor* down the Avon when the boiler exploded, killing all on board and damaging nearby houses. Twenty years later six men died at the Bute Docks when the boiler of the tug *Rifleman* exploded.

For many years three redundant sailing vessels were positioned at the Bute Docks. At the beginning of the 1860s HMS *Havannah* was established as an Industrial Training Ship, to train poor and homeless boys to become merchant seamen. HMS *Thisbe* was in the West Dock from 1863 to 1892 on loan to the Missions to Seamen. The *Hamadryad* arrived in 1866, to be fitted out as a seamen's hospital, financed by a levy of two shillings per 1,000 registered tons on vessels entering the port.

Shipbuilders at Cardiff included Richard Tredwen, William Davies (at the canal wharf), Thomas Jenkin, R.H. Mitchell, Joseph Davies, William Jones, Batchelor Brothers, Charles Hill, Norman Scott Russell, Maudsley's, J. & M. Gunn, Elliott & Jeffrey and Parfitt & Jenkins. Most of them repaired vessels and built small craft – some, occasionally, launched a larger one.

Batchelor Brothers built vessels on the Taff, near St Mary Street. The *Cardiff and Merthyr Guardian* reported the launching of a boat on the evening of Saturday 10 March 1849, which was probably the last launch from that yard, as the brothers moved to a new site near the entrance to Bute Dock where they built vessels until the early 1870s.

Norman Scott Russell's yard built the iron paddle steamer *Mallorca* in 1864. The vessel was 232ft by 26ft, capable of 12 knots, and was built for service on the Barcelona to Palma route, where it continued for twenty-five years. The *Cardiff Times* described it as, 'the first iron ocean-going steamship ever built at Cardiff'. In one of the many speeches after the launch, Norman's father, John Scott Russell (who had built the *Great Eastern* and HMS *Warrior* in his yard at Millwall), described how his son, 'having seen a great deal of shipbuilding on the Thames and in foreign countries', had come to set up as a shipbuilder in Cardiff, which had: 'growth like that of an American city rather than any town in England'.

Parfitt & Jenkins made boilers and steam engines, building thirteen shunting locomotives for the Bute Docks between 1869 and 1881. They built a range of vessels, including *Bee* (31) in 1870, a tender for the Portishead Railway Co.; the steamer *Druid* (129) in 1871, which ran between Cardiff and Bristol; 1872 saw the launch of *John Boyle* (633) and, finally, the 1877 launch of *Cory Brothers* (31).

Cardiff: 1880-1918

The principal shipbuilders in 1880 were Chapman and Williams (iron) who were based between the East and West Dock Basins; Croft and Dale, situated in the West Dock; Davies and Plain, residing on the west side of East Bute Dock; Down and Grant, whose yard was between the East and West Dock basins; J. & M. Gunn, who worked from the Mount Stuart

Opposite: 17 The approach to Cardiff Docks in 1872.

Right: 18 Batchelor Brothers' shipyard at Cardiff in 1859.

Graving Dock, Stuart Street; Charles Hill & Sons (iron and wood), who were based at East and West Bute Graving Docks; Thomas Hodge of East Wharf; Parfitt & Jenkins (iron) at Tubal Cain Works and Roath Dock; William E. Pile in East Moors and William Rees, who resided between the East and West Dock basins.

In 1882 Morel Brothers, with local partners, went into business as the Bute Shipbuilding, Engineering & Dry Docks Co., taking over existing facilities. The company built steamships such as *Collivaud* (950) for Morel in 1887 – the maiden voyage being to Alexandria. In 1889, *Cardiff Castle's* (1,266), launch was reported in the *Western Mail*: 'The largest ship ever built at Cardiff was successfully launched on Saturday morning from the Bute Shipbuilding, Engineering & Dry Docks Co.'s works on the east bank of the River Taff'. The newspaper stated that it was the eighth ship to be launched from the yard and her maiden voyage was to Brazil. The vessel was renamed *Blaenavon* in 1892 and was lost after hitting a mine in 1915.

Turnbull's *Register* of 1885 lists sixty-three sailing vessels owned at Cardiff, ranging in size from *David* (12), owned by E.C. Edwards of Grangetown, up to two ships of V. Trayes & Co. – *Canute* (1,215) built in 1869 and *Glenhaven* (1,235) of 1866. The largest local sailing fleet was that of W. Brooks: *Forest Princess* (171) of 1868; *Forest Queen* (132) of 1858; *Mary Elizabeth* (177) built in 1862; *Nelson Hewertson* (240) of 1877; *Rachel Harrison* (88) of 1856 and *William Jones* (17), built in 1877. There were now 231 steamships belonging to Cardiff, with forty of them over 1,000 tons, the largest being *Rhodora* (1,763) built in 1881 and owned by F. Edwards. Seventeen of the Cardiff vessels were constructed of iron and one of steel, *Rhiwderin* (737) owned by John Cory Jnr. Many of the vessels were owned in single-ship companies.

On 1 January 1887 Cardiff Docks were transferred to a new body, the Bute Docks Co., and ten years later the Pier Head Building was built as the company's offices, just as the enterprise changed its name again, to the Cardiff Railway Co. Roath Dock was opened in 1887 and the Queen Alexandra Dock in 1907.

By the 1890s Cardiff had become famous as the largest port in the world, measured by tonnage handled. Coal accounted for 97 per cent of its exports, with 70 per cent carried by steamship. Just over half of the coal went to Europe, and one-third to South America. The boom was at its peak in 1913, when about a third of the world's coal exports went out from South Wales.

Cardiff became an important 'signing-on' port: in 1894, at Barry, Cardiff and Penarth, over 63,000 men signed on for voyages and nearly 45,000 were discharged. Although many seamen made their home locally, others, usually with very little money, came to look for a ship. Cardiff became known as a 'hard-up port' and its seamen's boarding-houses were 'hard-up houses'. J. Havelock Wilson, the seamen's union leader, called Cardiff: 'the most undesirable port in the United Kingdom, the dumping ground of Europe'.

Dozens of new steamship enterprises were started in the two decades before the First World War including:

Neale & West operated a fishing fleet at Cardiff for nearly seventy years. John Thomas Duncan and Jacques Valette formed a single-ship company in 1889 to buy the nine-year-old *Benefactor* (1,034) and by 1914 the company owned five steamers. W.J. Tatem set up a single-ship company with the new *Lady Lewis* (2,950), named after the wife of the manager of the Bute Docks. New ships followed at yearly intervals, the first eleven being built by Richardson, Duck & Co. at Stockton-on-Tees.

Owen & Watkin Williams

They became shipowners in 1895 with the *Hesperides* (2,404), which was lost two years later on passage from Santiago de Cuba to Baltimore, with a cargo of iron ore. Another vessel was bought in 1898, three in 1900 and four in 1901. Owen & Watkin Williams set up the 'Golden Cross Line' to provide a liner service to the Mediterranean ports. (A liner service kept to a fixed-sailing schedule between specified ports. Most of the other vessels at Cardiff were tramp ships, which picked up cargoes wherever they could find them.)

Edward Nicholl

Nicholl took up shipowning at the age of forty-one, and in 1904 bought the first turret ship to be owned at Cardiff – he was to buy six in all. A turret ship was built with a raised deck above the main hull. This elevated part was, usually, about half as wide as the ship's beam. By the outbreak of the First World War, Edward Nichol was managing eleven vessels.

W.H. Seager & Co.

This company was formed in 1904 to manage *Tempus* (2,981), which was employed on voyages to the River Plate, the Mediterranean and the Black Sea. By the eve of the First World War three more had been added: *Salvus* (2,259), *Campus* (3,695) and *Amicus* (3,695).

William Reardon Smith

A master mariner, Smith retired from the sea at the age of forty-four. Five years later he and his son bought the *City of Cardiff* (3,089). This, and subsequent vessels, were registered at Bideford.

The *Terra Nova* sailed from Cardiff on 15 June 1910, seen off by large crowds on shore and by the paddle steamers *Devonia* and *Ravenswood*, both crammed with well-wishers. Captain Scott had decided that the vessel should depart from Cardiff because of the high level of local support, particularly from the *Western Mail* and some of the docksmen. The *Terra Nova* entered the pack ice on 9 December 1910. Scott, Bowers, Evans (from Swansea), Oates and Wilson were to die on the way back from the South Pole.

The first successful strike of the National Amalgamated Sailors' and Firemen's Union came in 1911. The main grievances at Cardiff were low pay and the recruitment of foreign seamen. There was a good deal of violence, and cavalry reinforcements were sent to Maindy Barracks; there was a detachment from the Lancashire Fusiliers, as well as a contingent from the Metropolitan Police (who drew increasing hostility from the crowds, and responded with baton charges). Mobs attacked Chinese laundries and boarding houses and the steamer *Foric* was besieged when word got around that some Chinese men had been signed on. Knives and hammers were used, but the police managed to calm things down.

The local paddle steamers were requisitioned as minesweepers during the First World War, as were Neale & West's trawlers, ten of which were sunk. The United States entered the war in April 1917, resulting in the transformation of the Angel Hotel into the USS *Chatinouka* and US Marines guarding Cardiff Docks.

Nearly 15,000 British merchant seamen died in the war and over 200 Cardiff vessels were lost, about 70 per cent of the pre-war fleet.

The Inter-War Years

During 1919 racial violence flared up at some British ports, including Cardiff. A report to the Home Office stated that the riots began on the evening of Wednesday, 11 June:

> When some white women accompanied by men of colour were passing through one of the main streets of Cardiff on their return from a picnic. Some uncomplimentary references having been made by people in the street, the coloured men left the carriages to attack the people there, and an affray took place.

A man was killed, and later that night Arab boarding houses were attacked. The police formed a cordon across Bute Street and used their truncheons against the mob. Over the next three days there was sporadic violence, with thousands of people on the streets, attacking Arab restaurants and houses. When it all died down it was found that two more men had been killed, and a good deal of property had been damaged; the effects on race relations were incalculable. Twenty-eight men were brought to court (eighteen of them white) and received penalties ranging from fines to imprisonment with hard labour.

There was a brief post-war boom in shipping: the number of Cardiff shipowning firms doubled in 1919, and their fleet expanded to around 300 ships. The crash came a year later, when freight rates dropped and stayed low (apart from a brief recovery in 1926/27) until the Second World War. There was an overall drop in the demand for coal and between 1920 and 1937 over 240 collieries closed in South Wales. It was inevitable that vessels would be taken out of service and many shipping firms were wound up.

Measured by 'tonnage handled' Cardiff was still thriving as the third largest British port, with nearly seven miles of quays at four main docks. The north side of Queen Alexandra Dock handled food imports from Australia, Canada, New Zealand, Spain and the Middle East; the south side dealt with coal exports. Iron ore for the Dowlais Works was discharged at Roath Dock, from which steel products were exported. There was a cattle lair and an auction ring, Spillers & Bakers flour mills, and the fish quay and ice factory of Neale & West.

During the late 1920s the Great Western Railway made attempts to develop a passenger liner trade at Cardiff, but it was a coal port, with few facilities for passengers. In 1929 the *Montrose* (Canadian Pacific Steamships) called to pick up passengers, producing the local newspaper headline: 'Cardiff a second Liverpool'. There were half-a-dozen calls by liners over the next year, but nothing more.

By the start of the Second World War there were about 170 vessels based at Cardiff. Half of them were owned by five companies: the Hain Steamship Co. and Sir William Reardon Smith & Sons owned twenty-four each, with others on order. Evan Thomas and Radcliffe had fifteen, W.J. Tatem and Constants (South Wales) operated eleven each.

German air raids on Cardiff between June 1940 and May 1943 killed 350 people and seriously injured 500, but the docks were relatively unscathed. From 1942, American military supplies began to pour through and British and American servicemen were drafted in as dock labour. The ship-repairing facilities were kept busy throughout the war.

The first loss of a Cardiff vessel came five days after war was declared. Tatem's *Winkleigh* – on an independent voyage from Vancouver to Manchester with grain and timber – was torpedoed in the North Atlantic. All thirty-seven men on board were rescued and taken to New York.

Over a hundred Cardiff-owned ships were destroyed during the war, about 60 per cent of the pre-war fleet. Britain lost 1,600 merchant ships and over 30,000 merchant seamen.

In 1948 the Bute Docks were taken into public ownership. The two original docks were by now used only by smaller vessels, and there had been a disastrous fall in trade: in 1938 coal, coke and patent-fuel exports totalled 5,229,095 tons. In 1947 only 736,174 tons were exported. Shipping companies which closed down in the 1950s included Claymore, Chellew, Care, Morel, Lovering and the Neale & West fishing fleet. Bute West Dock closed in January 1964 after 125 years and Cardiff's role as a coal-exporting port ended, officially, on 25 August

19   Queen Alexandra Dock: the general cargo quay.

1964. More Cardiff companies ceased trading in the 1960s, including Frederick Jones, W.H. Seager, B. & S. Shipping and John Cory & Sons. Bute East Dock closed in January 1970 and by September of the same year the West Dock had been filled in. Nearly all the remaining shipping companies went to the wall in the 1980s.

Associated British Ports took control of the docks in 1981. On 3 April 1987, Cardiff Bay Development Corporation came into being, set up by the government as part of an initiative to bring life back to run-down areas of cities. At the millennium the Queen Alexandra and Roath Docks were still there, as was the Roath Basin. About ten ships a week visited, but 80 per cent of the cargoes handled were now inbound.

PENARTH

Penarth Roads have always provided a secure anchorage for vessels waiting to enter the Taff/Ely estuary. Thomas Phaer mentions, 'a road in Severn called Penarth, very good for ships at 3 fathom low water'. An indication of some Penarth trade at this time may be seen from a list of those charged in the 1550s and 1560s with evasion of customs duties. Robert Vesey of Gloucestershire, for example, exported tanned leather, calfskins and barrels of butter from Penarth. The owners of the goods all came from Cardiff. The *Mary* of Walberswick in Suffolk was found to be carrying thirty-nine barrels of butter from Penarth. The butter was owned by the 'alien merchants' Lewis de Pace and Henry Gonsalves of London. But John Byrd, writing in the later seventeenth century, stated that: 'Penarth is no place to load or unload goods, except in small cock boats, and that there are adjacent and near to Penarth: Ely, Sully and Barry, places where vessels usually come in and out.'

Penarth began to develop in the 1860s. The Taff Vale Railway (TVR) was experiencing difficulties at Cardiff, with coal shipments being delayed in the congested docks and railways. The TVR decided to develop its own facilities, free from the control of the Marquess of Bute: the Ely Tidal Harbour, with twelve coal tips on the north bank of the River Ely, opened on 4 July 1859 and Penarth Dock followed six years later, on 10 June 1865. The first vessel to enter was the *William Cory*, described as 'the largest collier afloat'. The dock was extended in 1884

20 Reardon Smith's *Leeds City*, built at Sunderland in 1955.

and a year later 2.5 million tons of coal were being exported. The 1881 census recorded that there were twenty-four vessels at Penarth on 3 April, about half of which were Severn trows and other small sailing craft. There were six steamships.

A certain amount of boat and shipbuilding went on at Penarth. George Down, for example, built *The Young Marquess*, and from 1882 to 1890 the Penarth Shipbuilding & Ship Repair Co. built small iron-screw vessels. On 7 May 1898, 'amid the acclamation of more than a thousand spectators', they launched the small single-screw iron steamer *Eirene* (67) for the Missions to Seamen.

From the 1850s there was a steam-ferry service between Penarth and Cardiff Pierhead, and a chain ferry worked by a windlass operated between Ferry Road and Penarth Dock. In May 1900 the Ferry Road-Penarth Dock pedestrian tunnel under the River Ely came into use, staying open for sixty-three years. The opening ceremony of Penarth Pier was on 13 April 1895, when trippers for Weston-super-Mare were embarked by the paddle steamers *Bonnie Doone* and *Waverley*.

Penarth Dock closed in 1936, except for access to the ship-repairing facilities, but re-opened when war came in 1939, later becoming one of several bases for American naval units preparing landing craft for the Normandy beaches. In 1943 the *Alberte Le Borgne* was berthed in the dock, and used to train military personnel in dock operations before the invasion. At the end of the war the dock closed again, except for ship repairs and laying up, and was shut completely in 1963.

BARRY

Thomas Phaer reported that Barry in the mid-sixteenth century had: 'a good road at four fathoms low water and a dry haven to come into with southerly or westerly winds. It lies against Minehead and Bridgwater in Somersetshire'. In April 1561 Maurice Mathew 'gent' of Barry, William Bawden and Jevan Jones were charged with the illegal export of 150 barrels of butter from Barry to Minehead. The vessel was the *Saviour* of Minehead, owned by Bawden and Mathew. The defendants said that, 'the ship was to carry goods belonging to diverse merchants of Taunton to Lisbon'. Maurice Mathew and William Bawden were charged with committing similar offences on at least six other occasions. In December 1569 the owners of

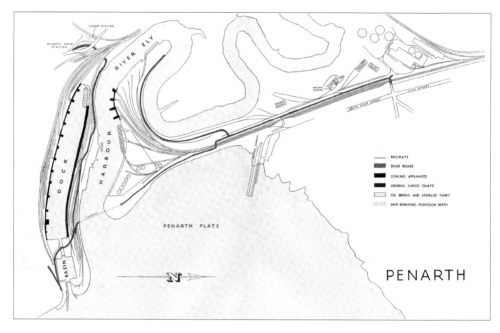

PENARTH

Above: 21 Penarth Dock and Ely Tidal Harbour in the late 1940s.

Left: 22 Building Penarth Dock, c.1860.

Below: 23 The chain ferry operated from June 1895 between Ferry Road and Penarth Dock, which can be seen across the river.

Opposite above: 24 Penarth Pier opened on 13 April 1895, when trippers for Weston-super-Mare boarded the paddle steamers *Bonnie Doone* and *Waverley*.

Opposite middle: 25 Penarth Dock.

Opposite below: 26 The paddle steamer *Glen Usk* was a regular caller at Penarth, embarking passengers for Minehead and Weston. Built at Troon, the steamer was in service with P. & A. Campbell from 1914 to 1960, apart from during the war years.

the *Julian* of Barry (David Stacey of Cosmeston, John Dyer of Cogan, John Smith Snr, John Smith Jnr, John Nichol and John Taylor of St Andrews) were alleged to have exported twelve barrels of butter and 13 tons of lead. Their vessel was seized by the customs officer.

The Barry boat which appears most consistently in the Port Books is the *Primrose* (30). From 1587 to 1595 the vessel sailed under six different masters, mainly to La Rochelle, taking out coal and 'Bridgwater cottons'. Return cargoes included honey, pitch, salt, raisins and wine.

Until the late nineteenth century Barry continued as a modest shipping place (with only a few scattered dwellings) similar to others along this coast, such as Sully, Aberthaw, Ogmore and Newton, but the settlement was to be transformed by the decision to build a dock. Congestion at Cardiff's Bute Docks had become intolerable by the 1870s, leading David Davies and other colliery owners to look for another outlet to the sea. Various alternatives were considered until, eventually, Barry was chosen. The Bill was fiercely opposed in Parliament by the Bute interests, but approval came in 1884 with the Barry Dock & Railway Act, which authorised a new dock, linked by rail with the Great Western and Taff Vale Railways.

Barry Dock opened on 18 July 1889, the first vessel to enter being the steamship *Arno* of Sunderland, 'steered by one of the directors of the Barry Co., Mr T.R. Thompson, the next vessel being the yacht of Mr. James Ware, another of the directors. These were followed by a long line of pilot boats, tugs and steamers all gay with bunting,' recorded *The Times* on 19 July 1889. The first wagon of coal was tipped into the steamer *Ravenshoe*. *The Times* told its readers that:

> The construction of the dock has already caused about 10,000 people to settle in the neighbourhood, and within the last three years no less than ten chapels have been built here.
>   The dock proper is 3,100ft in length, and the *maximum* width is 1,100ft, divided at the western end by a mole with two arms, one 1,500ft long and about 500ft wide, the other 1,200ft long and 300ft wide... At the north-east corner of the dock is a timber dock. On the north side of the dock there will be eleven fixed coal tips; there will also be four fixed coal tips on the north side of the mole, one at the end of the mole, and one at the west end of the dock. These seventeen tips are capable of tipping 4,000,000 tons of coal per annum.

The dock proved to be successful: in 1890 imports and exports from Barry Dock totalled 3,265,296 tons. In 1895 the total was 5,266,548 tons. In January 1898 a second Barry Dock opened. By 1900 total annual imports and exports at Barry were 7,486,996 tons and by 1913 were 11,736,179 tons (surpassing Cardiff). The main import cargoes consisted of pit props.

The Barry Railway Steam Vessels Act of 1904 permitted the company to operate steamers between Barry and anywhere on the coast between Ilfracombe and Weston-super-Mare (both inclusive). Excursions could be run to other places, provided that the trips started and finished at Barry. The Barry Railway hoped that it could avoid these restrictions by putting their vessels into a holding company – the Barry and Bristol Steam Shipping Co., the 'Red Funnel Line' – and began a service from Cardiff to Weston. Litigation followed, and in 1908 the Barry Railway proprietors were forced to abide by the provisions of the Act. Their steamers at this time were the *Barry*, *Devonia*, *Gwalia* and *Westonia*, which had all been sold by 1910.

A visitor to Barry Docks in the 1930s would have seen innumerable railway lines; the sidings could handle, at any one time, 6,000 loaded coal wagons and 3,000 empty. There were coal hoists all round No.1 Dock and along one side of No.2 Dock. On the south side of No.2 Dock were a cold store, transit sheds and a large flour mill, which received grain by conveyor directly from the ship. In 1934 coal and coke exports amounted to over five million tons, with nearly 2,000 vessels clearing outwards.

During the Second World War Barry Docks became a huge military supply base, especially for oil products, handling a total of 20,000 vessels. From the summer of 1940 to the summer of 1941 there were seven air raids; little damage was done, but one person was killed and eighteen injured.

After the war the management of the docks was transferred to the British Transport Commission. There had been a disastrous decrease in coal and coke exports: in 1938 the total

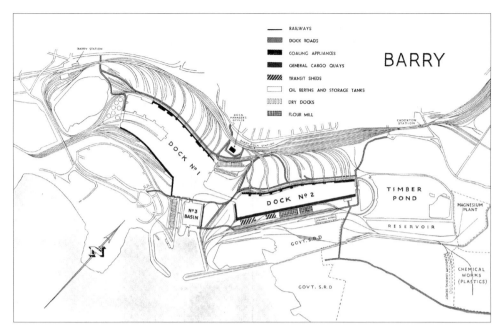

Above: 27 Barry Docks in the late 1940s.

Right: 28 The breakwaters at the entrance channel to Barry No.1 Dock.

29 Barry No.2 Dock, *c.*1900.

was 5,578,100 tons, but in 1946 this had dropped by 70 per cent. The export of coal ceased in 1976. A welcome addition to the port's trade came in the 1960s and 1970s, when the Geest Line imported bananas through Barry.

Associated British Ports was given control in 1981 and the main trade of Barry Docks developed to support the local chemical industry, handling containers, dry and liquid bulks and timber products.

ABERTHAW

In the sixteenth century the most frequent destination for Aberthaw boats (often carrying butter or wool) was Minehead, which in favourable weather could be reached in two hours. During the seventeenth and eighteenth centuries Aberthaw became the most significant shipping place between Cardiff and Neath. Most of the vessels were small, but there were a few large ships – such as the *Long Thomas* (200) and *Great Thomas* (100) – sailing as far as the West Indies. A big vessel, fully loaded, had to discharge some of its cargo at Minehead before continuing with the remainder to Aberthaw; smaller boats would then fetch the cargo left at Minehead. Imports at Aberthaw included items such as brandy, cloth, iron, oil, pottery, salt, soap and wine.

Vessels belonging to Aberthaw in the 1660s included the *Blessing* (masters Arthur Sweet and William Sweet), *Marie* (masters John Spencer and David Martin) and *Speedwell* (Thomas Spencer and Christopher Spencer). Nearly all their voyages were to Minehead, with only an occasional one to Bristol. In the year 1668/69 *Speedwell* made fifteen recorded trips to Minehead, *Marie* did nineteen and *Blessing* twenty-six.

In the nineteenth century agricultural produce was carried to the growing towns of Cardiff, Neath and Swansea and by the 1850s a vessel went to Bristol every fortnight. There was a considerable trade in Aberthaw limestone to all parts of the British Isles.

Nash Point, near Aberthaw, was a notorious hazard for shipping and many vessels met their end there. One of the worst wrecks was that of the paddle steamer *Frolic*. Built at Greenock and originally used on the Glasgow to Belfast run, the vessel had only recently become employed on the Haverfordwest-Tenby-Carmarthen-Bristol route. The *Frolic*, on the way to Bristol, was wrecked on Nash Sands in the early hours of 17 March 1831. All on board perished and bodies were washed up along the coast for months afterwards. *The Times* published a letter from Haverfordwest (dated 21 March):

> It is generally believed that between seventy and eighty have perished... From Tenby: General M'Cleod and four servants; Major Boyd, his wife, and three servants; two children, and seven others unknown. From Milford: Eighteen sailors going to join South Sea whalers; three servants from Castle Hall; one servant from Beulstone; one servant from Picton Castle; three runaway apprentices of J. Matthias's; a son of Mr. Griffiths – the currier – of Prendergast; a Colonel in the army... and his servant; a Mr. George, of Pater; Mr. Anderson, of the dockyard, his only son and eldest daughter;... and the entire crew of fifteen or seventeen. One of the Captain's children was buried on Saturday; he has left eight alive, and Mrs Jenkins large in the family way. The steward has left his wife in the same way, and four small children'.

The tragedy led to the construction of a pair of lighthouses at Nash Point.

PORTHCAWL

The small vessels of Newton Nottage made regular voyages to Minehead with butter, sheep, pigs, wool and stockings, as well as some coal and lead. In 1672 the Newton vessels included

30 The *Gwalia* and *Westonia* at Cardiff. They were owned by the Barry Railway Co. (Red Funnel Line) from 1905. *Gwalia*, nearest the camera, was sunk in June 1940 during the evacuation from Dunkirk.

31 Coal hoists at Barry No.2 Dock.

Ann, Five Brothers and *Speedwell*. A decade later these craft, and others, were still serving the Newton to Minehead route, sometimes venturing as far as Bristol.

During the early nineteenth century there were thoughts, but little action, about a tramroad to carry coal from the Llynfi Valley to the sea. Eventually a committee of landowners and industrialists was set up, which turned down a proposed route to the harbour at Newton in favour of one to Pwll Cawl Bay. The Duffryn, Llynfi & Porthcawl Railway Act of 1825 provided for building a tramroad or railway and constructing a loading jetty. The first, horse-drawn, wagons rumbled along the tramroad in 1828, each journey taking six hours to the new tidal dock.

Another Act of Parliament in June 1840 authorised extending the quay wall and providing better facilities for loading coal. In 1845 Porthcawl Dock was finally linked to the railway system, providing easy access from the Llynfi and Ogmore valleys. A pilotage guide of 1859 reported that: 'This little port carries on a trade in coal and iron, though it cannot contain more than eighteen or twenty vessels of 50 or 150 tons. It has now become much frequented by coasters and vessels in the coal trade'.

On 22 July 1867 a new dock opened, with a gated entrance and a longer breakwater. It had a wharf of 2,300ft and four high-level coal-tipping appliances. Much of the impetus for this new work had come from John Brogden & Sons, seeking a convenient outlet for their coal and iron. Trade grew, carried in small coastal vessels, 70 per cent of them under 100 tons and only about one in five driven by steam. Half of the vessels arrived in ballast, and nine of every ten departing carried coal, most of it from Brogden collieries.

With many fluctuations, coal shipments reached their peak in 1892 when over 800 vessels entered the dock, about half of them steamers. Most vessels still arrived in ballast, but if a vessel did bring in cargo it was probably either iron ore or pitwood. Dependence on a single commodity, coal, would cause problems for the port, as would the fact that larger ships could not enter. By the end of the nineteenth century bigger and better-equipped docks had opened, particularly at Port Talbot, which was well placed to handle coal from the Garw, Llynfi and Ogwr valleys. Porthcawl's import and export trades were lost, and the dock officially closed in 1906, although a few boats brought in building materials from Bridgwater and Sharpness in the years before the First World War.

The *Samtampa* – a Liberty Ship built at Portland, Maine – was lost on 23 April 1947. The vessel developed engine trouble during a gale and was driven on to Sker Rocks, near Porthcawl, where she quickly broke up. Attempts to get a line aboard were unsuccessful. The Mumbles lifeboat was launched, but returned an hour later, having failed to make contact with the *Samtampa*. The crew took the lifeboat out again, in the dark. It was later found on rocks near the *Samtampa*. The eight lifeboatmen died, as did the thirty-nine men on the *Samtampa*.

PORT TALBOT

The Cistercian abbey at Margam was founded by Robert, Lord of Glamorgan, in 1147. From the beginning the monks owned boats and in 1188 they sent a vessel to Bristol to bring back food for 'a very large crowd of beggars' who were starving at the gates. The usual reason for the abbey's boats going to Bristol was to take wool, returning with goods such as salt, iron and corn.

The abbey was dissolved in 1536, when the property was acquired by Sir Rice Mansel. His grandson Robert decided on a seafaring career, helped along the way by his relative Lord Thomas Howard. In 1591 Howard led a flotilla against the Spanish treasure fleet, with Robert Mansel of Margam in command of one of the vessels, but the Spanish fleet proved to be too strong for their would-be plunderers. Five years later Howard was vice-admiral of the force sent to Cadiz; Mansel was placed in command of a ship after the death of its captain, and later knighted by the Earl of Essex.

In June 1597 Howard took part, again as vice-admiral, in the 'Islands Voyage' to the Azores. Sir Robert went with him and afterwards put in considerable sea service until the year 1604,

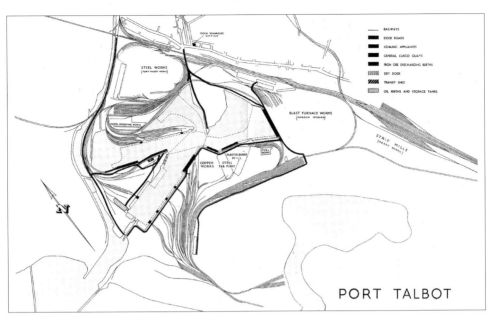

RAILWAYS
DOCK ROADS
COALING APPLIANCES
GENERAL CARGO QUAYS
IRON ORE DISCHARGING BERTHS
DRY DOCK
TRANSIT SHED
OIL BERTHS AND STORAGE TANKS

STEEL WORKS
(PORT TALBOT WORKS)

DOCK MANAGER'S
OFFICE

BLAST FURNACE WORKS
(MARGAM WORKS)

STRIP MILLS
(ABBEY WORKS)

PLASTER BOARD
MILL

FUEL
WORKS

COPPER
WORKS

STEEL
FAB. PLANT

N

PORT TALBOT

32 Port Talbot Docks in the late 1940s.

when he managed to secure the appointment of Treasurer of the Navy (with the aid of the Surveyor of the Navy – fellow Welshman Sir John Trevor – and another relative, the Lord Admiral Charles Howard, now Earl of Nottingham).

As Treasurer, Mansel was able to amass a fortune. In due course he sold the Treasurer's post, becoming 'Vice-Admiral of England' in 1618. Two years later he commanded a fleet sent against the pirate headquarters at Algiers, but after this his duties were land-based and minimal. He died in 1652.

In the latter half of the eighteenth century the Margam Estates were inherited by Thomas Mansel Talbot and it was his son, Christopher Rice Mansel Talbot, who initiated the development of Port Talbot.

Up until the nineteenth century Aberafan harbour was used only by small craft. In 1834 C.R.M. Talbot and local businessmen obtained an Act of Parliament enabling them to form the Aberavon Harbour Co., which dredged a new channel and built a dock. A weekly steamer service ran to Bristol from 1847 to 1851, taking four to five hours in the *Talbot* (160), an iron-screw steamboat, built at Neath Abbey Ironworks.

A pilots' guide of 1859 reported that:

The harbour, distant ¾ of a mile from the sea, is a floating dock, upwards of a mile in length, with a depth of 16 to 20ft water at all tides; it is entered by a lock 44ft wide and 140ft long. In the river is a very good level hard, for vessels to ground upon and a shipwrights' shop adjoining. The Port Talbot pilots will generally be found stationed at the Mumbles. A steam-tug, for the purpose of towing vessels in or out, is also stationed in this harbour.

Locally owned vessels listed in *Clayton's Register* of 1865 were: *David Jenkins* (104), schooner, built in 1864; *Peri* (134), brigantine, built in 1855; *Sarah* (62), schooner, built in 1844. All three were owned by David Jenkins. There were also: *Fairy* (72), schooner, built in 1857, owner John Jones, master mariner; *Gem* (48), dory, built in 1856, owned by W. Jenkins; *John Daniel* (92), schooner, built in 1830, owned by J. Mansfield, shipbuilder; *Leader* (107), schooner, built in 1858, owned by Nicholas Bate, master mariner; *Rival* (78), built in 1846, owned by John

Port Talbot Docks.

33　Port Talbot Docks in the first decade of the twentieth century.

Harris; *Secret* (100), schooner, built in 1863, owned by Joseph Foley, master mariner; *Xerxes* (79), schooner, built in 1839, owned by C.R.M. Talbot, Margam.

The death of C.R.M. Talbot was followed by the formation of the Port Talbot Railway & Dock Co. in 1894. In the 1860s the entrance lock and breakwater had both been lengthened, but now new docks were built. The company owned over thirty miles of railways, and ships were loaded by a conveyor-belt system, the first in a South Wales port. These modern facilities and quick turnround took trade away from Swansea and the port of Porthcawl went under completely.

There were now two docks at Port Talbot: the Old Dock (fifty-five acres of water) was entered via a channel from the New Dock (thirty-five acres). There were eight hydraulic coal tips and, for general cargo, a dozen cranes. The entrance was sheltered by two long breakwaters. A double-graving dock was constructed, which could accomodate two vessels at once. The Crown Preserved Coal Co.'s works made patent fuel, which could be loaded at the company's wharf.

By the 1920s, when the Great Western Railway took over, a considerable trade in iron ore had developed, with imports for Baldwin's steelworks going directly from vessel to works. In 1938 exports of coal and coke amounted to 1.5 million tons, but by 1946 the figure had dropped to 262,017 tons. The principal import was iron ore. In 1952 the Abbey Works was completed next to the Margam and Port Talbot steelworks and in the 1960s a deep-water terminal was developed for iron-ore carriers.

The Port Talbot Docks, run by Associated British Ports, can now accomodate – in the Inner Docks – vessels up to 8,000 dwt and 426ft long; in the Tidal Harbour vessels up to 180,000 dwt and 950ft in length. Each year thirteen million tonnes of imported coal and iron ore are handled, mostly for Corus UK.

BRITON FERRY

The Briton Ferry Estate was part of the lands of Margam Abbey. After its dissolution the estate was first owned by the Mansel and then by the Villiers and Vernon families.

34 The electric conveyors for shipping coal at Port Talbot.

35 Briton Ferry, from William Daniell's *A Voyage around Great Britain*, 1814.

36 The opening of Briton Ferry Dock in 1861.

Industrial enterprises developed on the estate during the nineteenth century: an iron works was founded in the 1840s, and by the end of the century Briton Ferry had become established as an important centre of steel-making.

The 1851 Briton Ferry Dock & Railway Act provided authority for building a harbour. The intention was to carry coal from the Afan and Llynfi valleys and most of the capital came from railway concerns: the Vale of Neath Railway, the South Wales Railway and the Swansea Valley Railway. Land was bought from the Earl of Jersey and the South Wales Mineral Railway was opened. A railway line was laid (Glyncorrwg-Cymmer-Tonmawr-Briton Ferry) which was operated for thirty years from 1855 by the Glyncorrwg Coal Co. Brunel's Dock – 1,600ft long and 400ft wide, and with an entrance basin – came into use in 1861. Twelve years later it was taken over by the Great Western Railway. The dock shipped considerable quantities of coal, mostly coastwise, until it closed in 1959.

NEATH

Thomas Phaer reported that at Neath, in the middle years of the sixteenth century, there was 'a pill within a bay for small boats where is a mine and trade of coals'. A century later coal was still being exported – there were about fifty recorded cargoes of coal in a year, most of it going to North Devon – and there were imports of 'Rochelle wine', salt and pitch.

By the seventeenth century a copper-smelting industry had been established at Neath, relying on regular shipments of Cornish ore, unloaded at wharves on the river and loading coal for the return voyage.

The lower part of the River Neath was a convenient place to build vessels, with sheltered sites and supplies of timber close at hand, particularly on the Margam Estate which, during the eighteenth century, supplied timber not only to local builders, but also to the Admiralty. Early nineteenth-century shipbuilders included Allen & Lully, Grainger & Evans, Walters & Llewellyn and William Thomas.

Neath Abbey Ironworks

The works made iron rails and other equipment for the Stockton & Darlington Railway, the first public passenger steam railway, which opened in 1825. The ironworks also built and installed marine engines. For example, in 1822 engines were provided for the paddle steamer *Glamorgan* (59), the hull of which had been built at Rotherhithe.

Vessels built at Neath Abbey Ironworks included: *Pioneer*, an iron 'steam towing vessel' and *Prince of Wales* (182), an iron paddle steamer, 120ft by 17ft, which ran between Swansea and Bristol. Both were built in 1842. In 1845 *Henry Southan* (Neath Abbey's first iron-screw steamer, 103ft by 17ft) was built; *Neath Abbey* (98), iron screw, 97ft by 16ft was built in 1846. The year 1847 saw the production of *Talbot* (160), iron screw, 134ft by 17ft. In 1848 *La Serena*, an iron barque, was launched for Henry Bath and Robert Eaton of Swansea. Intended for the South American ore trade, it was the first iron vessel to go round Cape Horn, and was to break the record for the return voyage to the west coast of South America, arriving home after five months and nine days. 1850 saw the launch of *Princess Royal* (149), iron screw, 114ft by 17ft. 1853 saw *Lapwing* (20), iron screw, 65ft by 9ft, launched for G. Francillon of Gloucester; *Ellen Bates* (1,098), an iron full-rigged ship for Edward Bates of Liverpool – the largest vessel built by Neath Abbey – also made her maiden voyage in that year. *Flying Scud*, an iron ship designed by J.D. Lewis and named by Sarah Ann Jones, daughter of the works manager, first set sail in 1876. It was owned by Captain Rosser of Swansea.

In the early eighteenth century Humphrey Mackworth built the first floating dock in South Wales at Neath, and in the following years the river was straightened and embankments made. Although the river was navigable for three miles or so inland, the approach was difficult, with an awkward bar to negotiate. During the 1840s efforts were made to improve the channels leading to the coal wharves by dumping slag from the copper works into the river. This was not successful and Acts of Parliament were obtained in 1843, 1874 and 1878 to allow improvements to be made by the Neath Harbour Commissioners.

The screw steamer *Neath Abbey* (98), newly built at Neath Abbey Ironworks, inaugurated a twice-weekly service between Neath and Bristol in August 1846. The owners, from Neath, were Jonathan Rees (ironmonger), Evan Evans (brewer) and Paul French (druggist). The *Neath Abbey* was re-registered in 1886 by the Neath and Bristol Steamship Co. and from the early 1890s was employed on the Swansea-Bristol route by the Swansea & Bristol Shipping Co. The vessel was wrecked at Nash Point on 19 June 1894. Three of those on board were saved by the Porthcawl rocket apparatus crew, but four were drowned.

In 1863 imports at Neath totalled 86,371 tons, of which copper ore made up nearly 50 per cent. Exports were 208,829 tons and nearly all coal. Ten years later imports were 102,268 tons (40 per cent copper ore, 26 per cent bar and pig iron and 13 per cent copper ore). Exports totalled 284,045 tons, of which 96 per cent was coal. Various schemes for improving the shipping facilities were suggested from time to time, including the building of a floating dock, but nothing came of these, and the problems of navigation and the increasing size of vessels led to the inevitable decline of Neath as a port.

SWANSEA

Swansea has always been associated with ships and the sea, but it was from the fourteenth century that trade began to develop, with increasing numbers of vessels arriving to load coal. Shipping places needed to be improved and by the sixteenth century quays had been built along the river, where cargoes of wine and salt could be discharged and coal loaded. Most of the traffic was coastal.

The volume of trade increased considerably in the eighteenth century, with the establishment of works for smelting copper, lead and zinc as well as for making iron and tinplate. Coal was exported and copper and lead ore were imported, usually across the river banks. In the 1730s the first river dock was constructed, and forty years later an Act of Parliament authorised work

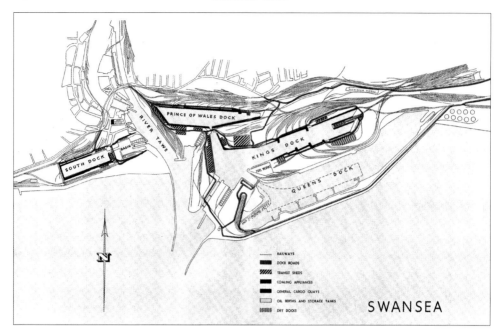

37 Swansea Docks in the late 1940s.

to improve access to the harbour. Even so, larger vessels often had to anchor outside the bar, and barges were employed to trans-ship cargoes.

Pilots were necessary to make sure that vessels arrived and left safely, a cost item which appears in the accounts of the *Betsy* (40), which arrived at Swansea from Bridgwater in April 1776 with a cargo of bricks, cloth and elm planks. The master's accounts for the return journey, with a cargo of twenty-five chaldrons of coal, survive in the Somerset Record Office: the total cost was estimated to be £32 and 2s. Almost a quarter of the cost was taken up by duties of one kind or another, including payments for 'logs and bondsmen' and 'putting in the logs and land officer', town dues and harbour dues. The duty payable on the coal amounted to over £6. Another quarter of the cost went on labour: a man to shift the coal, help and 'ales' during the discharging of cargo (six to seven days), hire of horse and messenger (to inform the consignee of the cargo's arrival), four men for twelve days (total £1 and 16s), two men at £2 and 10s, one boy at 15s. The master's wages were £1 and 15s. Pilotage ('help into Bridgwater') cost 9s. 'Help out of Swansea' was charged at 8s and 6d.

An Act of Parliament in 1791, and subsequent legislation, led to the building of breakwaters and the deepening of the water over the bar. Exports of coal and imports of copper ore were growing, and ore came to be sold by weekly auction, the 'Swansea Ticketings'. A potential buyer wrote on a 'ticket' the price he was willing to pay for a quantity of ore and the ore went to the highest bidder. Similar ticketings, attended by agents from South Wales, took place in Cornwall.

In 1827 the first vessel with foreign copper ore arrived. Up to that time ore had been brought from Cornwall, Anglesey, Ceredigion, Ireland and north-west England, but later Swansea crews made regular voyages to Cuba. The brig *Emulous*, for example, returned from Cuba in March 1832 with a cargo of 'copper ore, fustic and elephant tusks'. In the 1830s and 1840s vessels such as *Armata, Castor, Cobrero, Cubana* and *Charles Clarke* made the voyage. In September 1839 the *Sarepha* made the Cuba trip in a record two months and twenty-six days, but the dangers inherent in such enterprises may be seen from reports in *The Cambrian* during the first three months of 1845: the *Lady Pirie* arrived at Swansea with copper ore from Cuba but five people had died during the voyage; the barque *Lady Scott* (owned by J.C. Richardson, at that time Mayor of Swansea) was wrecked on the way back from Cuba and the *Cobrero*, another regular Cuba trader, was wrecked on Crooked Island, Bahamas. Swansea vessels were also to undertake, regularly, the even more difficult and dangerous voyage around Cape Horn to the west coast of South America.

The first cargo of copper ore direct from Australia arrived at Swansea on 27 June 1846, in the brig *Amelia* of Kirkcaldy, and regular shipments of ore began to arrive from South Australia, providing an opportunity to carry migrants in the opposite direction; *The Cambrian* of 21 April 1848 advertised: 'Emigration to Australia. For Adelaide, Direct from Swansea, The fine fast-sailing barque *Jenny Jones*'. The vessel 'has superior accomodation for Cabin and Steerage Passengers. Terms moderate.'

Just over five years later, on 12 August 1853, *The Cambrian* announced the arrival of 'the ship *Shackamaxon* from Adelaide, with 800 tons of copper ore for Leach, Richardson & Co. She also brought twenty-three packages of gold bullion, containing 94,106 ounces, produce of Victoria, for the South Australia Banking Co.; 170 bales of wool, seven bales of sheep-skins; likewise some specimens, the produce of South Australia'. In addition there were about forty passengers, including 'the Lord Bishop of Adelaide'. On a previous voyage the *Shackamaxon*, an American ship, had left Liverpool on 4 October 1852 with 696 migrants. Scarlet fever broke out on board and sixty-five died, most of them children. The vessel arrived at Port Adelaide on 19 January 1853, when a Court of Enquiry was convened to examine the conduct of the ship's doctor.

Local sea routes were becoming busier: in 1830 steam packets went twice a week to Bristol, and once a week to Ilfracombe. Boats trading to London included *Brothers*, *Eliza*, *Henry*, *Sarah*, *Paul* and *Jane*. Bristol traders were: *Eleanor*, *Rose*, *Phoenix*, *Swansea Trader* and *Swansea Packet*. Trading regularly to Gloucester were: *Abeona*, *Halcyon* and *Sarah*. Goods could be carried, by river and canal, to 'Worcester, Stourport, Birmingham and all parts of the North'.

Shipping facilities at Swansea were improved by an Act of Parliament in 1836, which authorised a 'New Cut' (840 yards by 55-70 yards wide) to bypass a bend of the river. The original course of the river was made into a floating harbour, a project finished in 1842, with lock gates added ten years later. This became known as the North Dock. The river itself was still used intensively and there were many wharves, generally owned by coal or copper companies. By now, 90 per cent of the world's copper was being smelted in the area of Llanelli, Neath and Swansea, with a continuous flow of shipping bringing ore in and taking copper products out.

The South Dock opened in September 1859, but within a decade the two docks were becoming congested. *The Cambrian* gave a list of problems in 1872: not enough coal tips; the limited capacity of the railway sidings and too few wagons and the dock area was too small. The Swansea Harbour Act of 1874 authorised a new dock, the first to be built on the east side of the river. Originally known as the East Dock, it was renamed 'Prince of Wales Dock' at the official opening in 1881 although it was not, in fact, completed until the following year.

By the early 1880s there were three docks – North, South and Prince of Wales – whose facilities attracted steamship operators to Swansea and encouraged the development of the overseas trade in tinplate. During the 1890s extensions and improvements were made to all three existing docks, and another new dock, the King's Dock, with seventy acres of deep water, was opened in 1909.

Swansea Shipbuilding

Swansea grew into an active centre of boat and shipbuilding. Builders included: Henry Mansel who built the *Revenge* in 1667 and, later, the *Friend's Adventure*. In 1765 Henry Squire obtained a lease from the corporation of 'banks or yards for building of ships situated on the Strand'. William Jones built a dry dock in 1766. Members of the Llewelling family built vessels from around 1808 to 1830.

In July 1810 a notice in *The Cambrian* referred to 'Meager & Richards, carpenters'. A year later they are described as 'shipbuilders', and members of the Meager family were to continue

38 The North Dock at Swansea in the 1880s. The floating timber has been unloaded over the side of a ship.

in this business until at least the 1870s. Typical vessels launched were: *Hussey*, a sloop, in February 1821; November 1834 saw *Pascoe*, a schooner for Pascoe and Grenfell, hit the water for the first time; in August 1844, *Henry*, a schooner 'for the copper trade' was launched; March 1857 saw the launch of *Mary Jane*, a schooner for Captain Prust. In August 1874 the steamship *India*, a 'Portuguese troopship', was in Meager's Graving Dock; it was described as 'the largest ship seen in this port'.

The Swansea Iron Shipbuilding Co. was not a long-lived enterprise. In 1849 they launched the steamer *Fire Fly*, which was delivered to Chile after a passage of sixty-four days, and the *Augusta*, an iron steamer for Schneider & Co. of Loughor.

The Richardsons built vessels for the Cuba and Chile trades, including three barques: in 1851 *Owen Glyndwr* (373); in 1857 *Duke of Beaufort* (412) and in 1861 *Marquess of Worcester* (419).

From the mid-1820s local shipbuilders were faced with severe competition from cheaper vessels built on the east coast of Canada, especially at Prince Edward Island. The vessels could be sailed to Swansea with a cargo of timber or oats and then sold or, of course, retained for future voyages, a practice common to several Wesh ports.

Sales of some of these vessels were advertised in *The Cambrian*, including:

August 1853 For Sale: the schooner *Echo*, just arrived from Prince Edward Island. Apply Mr. W.H. Tucker.

August 1854 Arrived – *Perseverance*, schooner. Lying at Swansea to be sold.

December 1868 For Sale: the brigantines *Aladdin* and *Jenny Lind*, expected from Prince Edward Island. Also the brig *Edith*. Apply to W.H. Tucker, Jnr.

August 1869 For Sale: the schooner *Trot*, lying in Beaufort Dock; just arrived from Prince Edward Island.

39 Swansea's South Dock in the early years of the twentieth century.

40 Building the Prince of Wales Dock, Swansea.

September 1876 For Sale: 16/64 shares in the brigantine *Emily*, built at Prince Edward Island, now at Bristol.

Swansea Shipowners

The Bristol & Glamorgan Steam Packet Co. ran steamboat services between Swansea and Bristol from April 1823 until 1843. The first vessel on the route was the paddle steamer *Glamorgan* (59), built in 1822 at Rotherhithe and fitted with engines at Neath Abbey Ironworks. On 4 August 1834 the Revd Joseph Romilly travelled from Bristol to Swansea in the *Glamorgan*:

> Started by *Glamorgan* steamer at 1.30 p.m. An invalid lady was so frightened at having to go down the ladder into the packet that she cried bitterly and screamed; it was with the greatest difficulty that another lady, her companion, and two gentlemen (who seemed relations) prevailed upon her to go aboard. These two men sailed about two miles with us to talk to her, but she continued sobbing all the way. We were now only four cabin passengers, the two ladies, a gentleman-like invalid youth and myself; the women didn't eat so the captain had but two companions at dinner... Arrived off Swansea with magnificent moonlight at 10.30 p.m.; anchored for want of water. At 11 p.m. came a pilot boat and took me and the young man ashore.

Joseph Tregelles Price

Based at Neath Abbey Ironworks and operated the Swansea to Bristol route from 1843 to 1858 with the vessels *Lord Beresford*, *Princess Royal* and *Prince of Wales*, a vessel which did the run in under six hours in 1858.

James Wathen Pockett

Ran services from 1858 to 1880, as did his son William Pockett, from 1880 to 1890. When J.W. Pockett took over the Bristol route from J.T. Price in 1858 he also acquired the *Lord Beresford* and the *Prince of Wales*. Other steamers employed by the Pocketts were the *Henry Southan* and the *Velindra*, which was bought from the Cardiff Steam Navigation Co. in 1868. This vessel was a big improvement on the previous steamers, and ran to Bristol in under four hours.

William Jenkins

By the middle of the nineteenth century the principal Swansea owner was William Jenkins, most of whose vessels were built at Bideford, including the barques *Agnes Blake* and *Alicia*, which sailed to Cuba and Valparaiso. In 1845 another barque, *Catherine Jenkins*, sailed from Newport to the West Indies with coal, in 1846 from Swansea to Valparaiso, in 1848 to Coquimbo and in 1849 to Valparaiso. It was announced in 1852 that the vessel was to be sold by auction. Later issues of *The Cambrian* reported: 'June 1854, arrived at Swansea from Coquimbo with copper ore for Mr. Lambert; March 1855 from Coquimbo with copper for C. Lambert and H. Bath; August 1855 from Cuba, copper ore for Mr. James Petrie. February 1856 wrecked on Oxwich Point.'

William Jenkins's *Emperor of China* was at London in May 1847; in 1849 it returned from Port Adelaide; in May of that year it left Swansea with patent fuel for Trincomalee. By April 1850 the vessel was back at London from Calcutta.

The *Rajah of Sarawak*, built for William Jenkins by George Cox of Bideford, was delivered to Swansea in March 1850 and within a month left for Calcutta. The *Rajah* was at Melbourne early in 1856, and later in the voyage the crew had to repel an attack by Chinese pirates.

Principal Shipowners in 1865

There were 118 Swansea vessels on *Clayton's Register* of 1865 of which five were steamers: *Augusta* (125) built in 1849, was owned by Henry Vivian; *Havre* (177) built in 1864, owned by

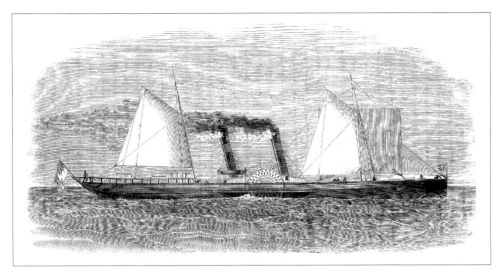

41 *Velindra* was built at Millwall for the Cardiff Steam Navigation Co. and acquired by J.W. Pockett of Swansea in 1868. The vessel could reach Bristol in about four hours, and was also employed on summer excursions to Ilfracombe and Padstow.

Henry Bath; *Morfa* (299) built in 1862, Arthur Vivian. The *Prince of Wales* (80) built in 1842 and *Henry Southan* (96) built in 1849 were both owned by J.W. Pockett.

Of the 113 sailing vessels, nearly half were schooners and one-third were barques. The largest vessel was the *Marshal Pellissier* (743), a barque, built in 1856 and owned by John C. Richardson. The oldest was the schooner *Speedwell* (69) of 1803, owned by W. Rees, master mariner.

Henry J. Bath operated twelve vessels: nine barques, two ship-rigged and a schooner. The names of several of them showed the influence of the 'Last of the Mohicans': *Deerslayer* (347), *Delaware* (377), *Hawkeye* (504), *Mohican* (357), *Pathfinder* (313) and *Uncas* (433).

J.C. Richardson managed eight barques. Henry J. Madge had five vessels and James Stuck four: *Eliza* (137), schooner, of 1857; *Emilia* (215), barque, built in 1832; *Ford Mill* (223), brig, built in 1838; *Victoria* (62), schooner, of 1830.

Principal Shipowners in 1885

There were 181 sailing vessels belonging to Swansea listed in Turnbull's 1885 *Register* including thirty-one steamers, of which William Philip Ching owned three: *Cruiser* (5), of 1881; *Pioneer* (16), built in 1878 and *Royal Albert* (37) of 1851. The largest steamship on the register was the *Gwenllian Thomas* (732), built in 1882, whose managing owner was E. Thomas of Porthcawl.

The Swansea Merchant Ship Owners' Co. was set up to take over the sailing vessels of Henry Bath & Sons. The company operated *Delta* (437) built in 1865; *Epsilon* (521) of 1865; *Gamma* (556) also of 1865; *Gloria* (735) built in 1868; *Hawkeye* (504) of 1864; *Henry Bath* (490) built in 1863; *Iota* (551) launched in 1866; *Kappa* (491) also built in 1866; *Pampero* (588) of 1864; *Theta* (518) built in 1865; *Uncas* (433) of 1861 and *Zeta* (640) built in 1877. Hit by a decrease in the number of copper cargoes, the business ceased trading in 1895.

J.C. Richardson managed ten and G.S. Richardson nine vessels.

Letricheux and David had two steamers built: the 1883 *Abermaed* (1,111) and, in 1884, *Abertawe* (1,336); they traded to France, Greece, Italy and Spain.

In the last year preceding the First World War Swansea exported about 4.5 million tons of coal. Such shipments were badly hit in the post-war period, although by the 1920s greater quantities of tinplate were being exported. Oil was brought from Llandarcy by pipeline, and a jetty had been built so that oil-burning vessels could refuel without entering the docks.

Queen's Dock opened in 1920, with the south side being used by the ships of the British Tanker Co., carrying oil from the Persian Gulf. Swansea grew into the largest oil port in the United Kingdom, with oil pumped directly from the ship into large tanks, and from there to the refineries at Llandarcy, four miles away.

Swansea was also a considerable fishing port. The Castle Steam Trawling Co. had been operating out of Milford Haven since the 1880s, but moved its fifteen steam trawlers to Swansea's South Dock in 1903. By 1914 the company had nineteen vessels, but the whole fleet was requisitioned for minesweeping in the First World War, when six were lost. After the war the company was acquired by the Consolidated Steam Fishing & Ice Co., which already owned over a hundred vessels. During the 1920s the firm based two-dozen trawlers (all registered at Grimsby) at Swansea, where they were often joined by vessels from other ports. The area of their operations now extended to the seas off Portugal, Spain and North Africa.

Swansea steamship owners on the eve of the Second World War included:

Ambrose, Davies and Matthews
In the Brynmor Steamship Co.: *Aelybryn* (4,986) built in 1938; *Brynmor* (4,771), of 1936; *Dan-y-Bryn* (5117) and *Ger-y-Bryn* were being built at Burntisland.

In the Cook Steamship Co: *Cefn-y-Bryn* (5,164), also under construction at Burntisland.

Stockwood, Rees & Co.
Dillwyn Steamship Co.: *Josewyn* (1,926), of 1919; *Ronwyn* (1,894), built in 1918.

Swansea and its docks were a primary target for German bombers. The first raid was on 27 June 1940, with the worst period being that of the Blitz of February 1941 which left 230 people dead and over 400 injured. Altogether there were forty-four raids, which killed 387 people and injured 841.

After the war the British Transport Commission took over a run-down port with diminished trade. In 1938 exports had totalled 4.4 million tons (of which 85 per cent were coal or coke). In 1946 they added up to 1.6 million tons. The trawlers disappeared from Swansea in the years after the Second World War.

In the opening years of the twenty-first century Swansea had a container terminal at the east end of the King's Dock, and a ferryport terminal on the east bank of the river for the ferries to Cork. There were two dry docks and seventeen quayside cranes. Queen's Dock handled liquid-bulk cargoes for local chemical plants, and there were fuel jetties and storage tanks. Timber arrived regularly from the Baltic and the Far East.

TWO

West Wales

LLANELLI

By the end of the seventeenth century regular cargoes of coal were being loaded at Llanelli, and several shipping places had developed. The more permanent ones were to be: the Carmarthenshire Dock, built by Alexander Raby between 1797 and 1799 as a small tidal dock; Pemberton's Dock, originally a quay to load coal brought along the Wern Canal. It was built in 1794 and made into a tidal dock in 1803. Acquired by the Llanelli Copperworks Co. in 1807, by the early twentieth century it was badly silted and later filled in. The Copperworks, or Nevill's Dock, was built in 1805 as a tidal dock – but within two decades it had been converted into a floating dock and became the town's main shipping place, remaining in use during the first half of the twentieth century. It was closed in 1951 and later filled in.

The New Dock, opened in 1834 by the Llanelli Railway & Dock Co., was taken over by the Great Western Railway in 1889. Commercial traffic came to an end in the 1930s, and the dock was filled in after the Second World War.

The North Dock was opened in December 1903 and used until the 1970s, but the shifting sands made it increasingly difficult for the larger vessels to approach.

The area developed into a major centre for the manufacture of tinplate and by the 1830s there were over thirty works at Llanelli, with about three-quarters of their production being exported to the United States. In the early years of the nineteenth century, copper ores were transported to Llanelli from Cornwall, Ireland and North Wales, but from the 1830s Cuban ore began to be imported through Llanelli Docks. Cargoes were brought in by vessels owned elsewhere, but in 1841 local ironmonger David Hughes bought the new brigantine *Elizabeth Hughes* (183) for the copper trade, and by 1846 the Llanelli Copperworks was managing its own fleet of a dozen vessels. Ore arrived from South Africa, North America and Newfoundland, as well as from Cuba, and by 1870 over half of the lead ore imported into Britain came to Llanelli. There were more coal shipments and by the 1850s they amounted to around 400,000 tons.

The volume of trade through Llanelli Docks was affected by two developments: tinplate exports dropped from 1891, when the McKinley Tariff was imposed by the United States government; coal production from the Amman Valley began to be sent out by rail through Swansea, rather than through Llanelli. There was some increase in trade in the years following the First World War, but it slumped again in the 1930s.

When the British Transport Commission took over at Llanelli in 1948 they inherited the North Dock, 1,000ft long by 400ft wide, with cranes, coal-loading machinery and a large transit shed, and the Carmarthenshire Dock, 350ft long and suitable for vessels laid up or being repaired.

Nevill's Dock was owned by the Nevill's Dock & Railway Co. and was 680ft by 110ft with three tidal berths. The Great Western Wharf was tidal, and handled the traffic of Richard Thomas & Baldwin's steelworks.

From the 1960s to the 1980s sand was loaded at the Carmarthenshire Dock and some use continued to be made of the North Dock: during the first half of the 1970s shallow-draught vessels brought in cargoes of grain.

Llanelli Shipowners

Sir Thomas Stepney
Sir Thomas, who had coal-mining interests, took delivery of the brigantine *Elizabeth* (100) in 1747; it had been built for him at a cost of £610. He had a quarter share of the sloop *Hazard* (29), built at Llanelli, and was part-owner of other vessels, including the *Prince Charles* (95), which cost £840 to build.

Alexander Raby
He had acquired vessels in the early nineteenth century to carry iron ore from Lancashire for his iron works, and to ship coal from his collieries.

Ralph Stephen Pemberton
He owned a handful of small vessels, mostly carrying coal, from around 1814.

R.J. Nevill
His vessels carried copper ore from Anglesey, Cornwall and Ireland, and took copper products to warehouses at Bristol, Liverpool and London. From the 1820s Nevill ran regular advertised services to Bristol and Liverpool, where his cargoes were often trans-shipped to larger vessels. One such vessel owned at Llanelli was the barque *Suir* (431), acquired by John Biddulph and George Jones Webb in 1840, and employed in carrying coal to North America and bringing back timber. In 1843 the vessel passed to R.J. Nevill and Charles Nevill Broom.

George Jones Webb
Webb operated eighteen vessels between 1837 and 1846.

Simon Samuel
Samuel had shares in around three-dozen local vessels, including the snow *Wee Tottie*, built in the north-east of England in 1845. On one voyage the *Wee Tottie* took a cargo of iron rails from Cardiff to Cuba, and then went direct from there to St Petersburg where a cargo was loaded for Dublin. Other voyages took the snow to the Bay of Biscay, Brazil, South Africa and Australia, before it was wrecked in 1864.

The list of vessels owned at Llanelli in 1865 included only one steamer, *Leopard* (42), built in 1861 and belonging to the Llanelli Steam Navigation Co. There were fifty-three sailing vessels, of which half were schooners and one-third brigantines. The largest was the barque *Glanmor* (520) of 1855, managed by Simon Samuel, sail maker of Llanelli. He was also managing owner of two brigs and a schooner.

C.W. Nevill, Copper Works, Llanelli
Managed ten vessels at this time, nearly all schooners.

Townsend Kirkwood
Kirkwood, of Bideford, owned: *Brothers* (132), a brigantine, built in 1859; *Why Not* (97), a schooner, built in 1859; and *Yeo* (43), a smack, built in 1862.

Steamboat Services
There had been small steam vessels at Llanelli from around 1829, when steam tugs began to be used. A larger steam vessel, *Hercules*, was built at Gravesend for the Llanelli Railway

& Dock Co., and employed from 1837 to take freight and passengers to and from Bristol. The Llanelli Steam Navigation Co. was formed in 1862, buying the newly built *Leopard* for a service between Llanelli and Bristol. When the vessel was sold to Swansea owners in 1867 it was replaced by the *Cambria* (134), a new screw steamer built by W.H. Nevill, which remained in service until 1887 when the company was wound up.

A vessel for a service to Liverpool was launched in 1867. The *Llanelly* (304) was a screw steamer built by W.H. Nevill and managed by C.W. Nevill. Built to carry cargo and twenty passengers, the *Llanelly* was owned on the sixty-fourth system by shareholders in Lancashire and Somerset, as well as those from Llanelli. The vessel sank off the Bishop Rock in 1873, with no loss of life.

A second *Llanelly* (374) was built at Preston, but this time it was placed into a new joint-stock company, the Llanelli & Liverpool Steam Navigation Co. The new steamer arrived at Llanelli in September 1875. Another vessel, the *Burry* (327), came into service four years later, to voyage between Llanelli and the Lancashire and Cumberland ports. The South Wales & Liverpool Steam Navigation Co. was set up in 1886. Based at Liverpool, the company took over the *Llanelly* and the *Burry*.

Llanelli Shipbuilding
Craig *et al.* (2002) provide a list of eighty-five vessels built at Llanelli between 1815 and 1889. Among the builders were:

Edward Jobling
Built a slipway in 1845. From it he launched *May Welch* (137), a brigantine, in 1846; in 1848 *Elizabeth* (80), a schooner; in 1850 *Pandora* (224), a brig, was launched; 1851 saw *Cambria* (40), a smack, being introduced. The brig *Pandora* was the largest vessel built up to that time at Llanelli. In December 1850 the vessel left London to become part of a whaling expedition, voyaging to the Pacific and up to Alaska. On the way home the *Pandora* called at the St Lawrence, loaded timber, and arrived at Gravesend in December 1853, after an absence of three years. The brig later traded to South Africa.

James Bevans
Built twenty vessels, nine of which were schooners, between 1846 and 1868. His biggest vessels were the snow *Gem of the Sea* (190) built in 1855, and the brigs *Hetty Ellen* (189) in 1860 and *Coquette* (299) of 1868. James Bevans also constructed the paddle steamer *Samson* (111), launched in 1861. The *Gem of the Sea* was owned initially by the builder, with his son as master, but was later acquired by master mariner Henry Rees. Voyages were made to the Mediterranean, the Black Sea and the Caribbean, until the vessel was lost off the French coast in 1885.

W.H. Nevill
Nevill took over Edward Jobling's yard and extended it. Twenty-seven vessels, all made of iron, were built between 1863 and 1874. There were eight brigs, six schooners, five barques, three barquentines, two brigantines and at least three steam vessels. The largest vessels were the barques: 1864's *Oliver Cromwell* (415); 1866's *Towy* (324), *Blonde* (329) and *Brunette* (333), and in 1869, *Hinda* (476).

The life of one of Nevill's vessels, *Concord*, has been traced by R.S. Craig (1989-90). *Concord* (278), a brig, was ordered on 19 August 1864 at a cost of £4,500. To finance the purchase the company issued 950 £5 shares. Launch day was 2 November 1864, with fitting out completed by 14 December. The *Concord* was 125.6ft long by 23.9ft wide by 14.3ft deep.

The usual crew was master, mate, boatswain, cook/steward, four able seamen, one ordinary seaman and an apprentice. The masters were: 1865-68 Stephen Cloke; 1868-74 Thomas Cloke; 1874-80 John Rees and 1880-81 W.H. Gurnett.

42 The Llanelli-built *Naiad*, painted by Reuben Chappell (1870-1940). The schooner was launched in 1867 by W.H. Nevill.

Returning from Malta on her maiden voyage, the brig collided with another vessel in the Straits of Gibraltar, and had to make for Malaga for repairs.

On all her voyages the *Concord*'s outward cargo was coal. Eighteen voyages were made to Cagliari with the return cargo of lead ore. Five voyages to the Mediterranean for sulphur. Five followed to Spain to pick up ore. Three voyages to Madeira with a cargo of coal, then to South Carolina (ballast) and home carrying phosphate rock. Two trips were taken to Puerto Caballo, Venezuela, returning with copper ore. Two voyages to Cuba for sugar. Single voyages with coal to Egypt and returning with wheat; South America for wheat via West Africa, then back to Marseilles. In 1881, having left the River Plate, *Concord* disappeared. All nine men on board were lost.

Samuel Brothers

Built four vessels at Llanelli: *S.T.* (325) an iron barquentine, launched in 1880; in 1882 *Owain Tudor* (227) an iron steam vessel was launched; *Fawn* (330), a steel steamship, was built in 1884; 1889 saw *Gogo* (132), a dredger. They obtained three damaged screw steamers and rebuilt them: in 1883 *Gazelle* (588), originally built in 1869; in 1885 *Springbock* (823), originally built in 1863 and in 1889 *Lady Bertha*, originally built in 1877. Samuel Brothers placed the vessels into three single-ship companies in 1890, and worked the ships on the short sea routes, including those to France and Spain, with occasional trips to the Mediterranean.

Twentieth Century Llanelli Shipowners

Aaron Stone and W.M. Coombs

They had acquired their first steamship in the 1890s, *Electra* (517), which was bought from Enoch Lewis of Aberdyfi. Their second vessel, *Galtee* (565), was bought in 1903. Other steamships to come into the fleet were *Jason* (798) and *Charlaw* (890), which was lost after becoming stranded near the entrance to Mostyn Harbour in August 1905. The *Lizzie*, another purchase from Enoch Lewis, was acquired in 1906.

43   Grain boats in the North Dock at Llanelli, 1972.

When the Stone and Coombs partnership broke up, Coombs retained *Electra*, *Galtee* and *Jason*. Stone kept *Lizzie*, the most modern vessel, which was fitted with triple-expansion engines.

Stone and Rolfe

In 1909 Aaron Stone formed the Lizzie Steamship Co. and bought the *Mary Hough*, which was renamed *Gwladmena*. He took on a new business partner, Joseph Rolfe. In 1917 Stone and Rolfe formed the Channel Transport Co. with Thomas Donking of Middlesbrough, acquiring the steamer *Solway Prince* (317), which was sunk by a U-boat in June 1917. Their vessel *Allie* (1127) was sunk by a submarine off the French coast in the same year. In 1919 Stone and Rolfe became major shareholders in Walford Lines, based in London. The first motor ship owned at Llanelli, the *Lottie R.*, was ordered by Stone and Rolfe in 1937.

During the Spanish Civil War, Stone and Rolfe's *Glynwen* was damaged and *Isidora* sunk. The *Isidora* had been damaged during an air attack at Valencia on 25 April 1938, and was sunk in Castellon harbour in June, after being bombed and machine-gunned. The crew were ashore at the time.

Coombs's Afon Steamship Co. took over *Afon Dulais* (987), *Afon Gwili* (874) and *Afon Towy* (684) in 1920. Both the Coombs fleet and that of Stone and Rolfe stopped trading in the 1950s. The port of Llanelli closed officially in 1951, but a few vessels used the North Dock in the 1970s.

BURRY PORT

The creek at Burry was typical of many around Wales: a shipping place used by small vessels to load and unload coastal cargoes. In 1566 the *Jesus* (8) is recorded as trading to Laugharne and Barnstaple, carrying coal on the outward journey and coming back with a mixed cargo. It had a crew of three and belonged to Owen ap Jenkyn. In November 1586 William Johnes, merchant of Llandeilo, imported from Bristol a cargo of iron, cheese, soap and raisins. From time to time horses arrived from Ireland; on 17 August 1599 eight horses and two colts from Wexford were the cargo.

Sea-borne trade at Burry was transformed when a new harbour was opened in 1836. It was given the name of 'Burry Port' and was at its busiest in the second half of the nineteenth century, when Burry Port and Pembrey became the main shipping places for coal from the Gwendraeth Valley. Hobbs (1859) wrote that Burry Port:

> ... is advantageously situated about half a mile to the eastward of Pembrey Harbour; it possesses great depth of water, is well sheltered, and there is an excellent roadstead within a short distance southward. Also here is a wet dock, which will admit large vessels, the entrance at the dock gates being 45ft. The exports are similar to the adjoining harbour of Pembrey.

The Burry Port & Gwendraith Valley Railway opened in 1865, and a new West Dock at Burry port, to cope with the increased coal trade from the Gwendraith collieries, came into use in 1888.

The Burry Port Steamship Co.
They ran the *Udea* (147) from 1873 to 1880, carrying cargoes for the Burry Port Lead Works until it closed in 1877. The *Udea* was bought by C.W. Nevill of Llanelli.

Francis J. Evans
In the early years of the twentieth century Francis Evans and his father Thomas Gwynne Evans ran a few small sailing craft. In 1913 Francis Evans acquired *Lizzie Ellen* and, in the following year, ventured into steam with the management of *Helen* (216), built in 1900 and owned by T. Randall Evans. The *Helen* was sold in June 1916.

Evan Jones
Jones had financial interests in collieries, metal works and shipping. He ran his shipping investments in conjunction with Francis J. Evans and the brokers Randell and Smith. He bought *Edith* (710) in 1917, and became part-owner of *Brynawel* (410), *Glynarthen* (825), *Pembrey* (549) and *Pemsco* (370). The Norwegian-owned steamer *Smaragd* (487) had been built at Chepstow in 1889. After becoming stranded at Burry Port the vessel was salvaged, and then repaired at Appledore. In 1916 it was placed into the Smaragd Steamship Co., in which half the shares were held by Evan Jones and a quarter each by Francis J. Evans and Arthur Morgan, the harbourmaster. Morgan had saved the vessel by having it hauled off the sandbank using hawsers connected to a railway engine.

By the 1920s there was little commercial shipping at Burry Port.

PEMBREY

Early in the eighteenth century coal was being worked on Lord Ashburnham's estate at Pembrey. M.D. Matthews (2004) has analysed the estate accounts for the years 1714-1721, finding that during this period there were 553 coal-shipping transactions, of which only about 5 per cent were local sales. The origins of vessels loading the coal were: Devon 38 per cent, mostly from the Taw/Torridge estuary, Cornwall 26 per cent and Ireland 8 per cent. Only a few of the vessels belonged to Welsh harbours; two from Aberystwyth and one each from Carmarthen, Llanelli, Oystermouth and Mostyn. Pembrey collieries owned a sloop called *Wern Collier No.3*, sold in 1798, and another named *Anne*; two sloops − *Eleanor and Catherine* and *Hero* − were bought in July 1810. In three months in 1815 the *Hero*'s travels were: Carmarthen-Cork (bark); Cork-Cardiff (pigs); Cardiff-Cork (coal); Pembrey-Somerset and South Devon (coal); Kidwelly-Bristol (tinplate); Bristol-Kidwelly (timber).

44 The East Dock at Burry Port, 1995.

The first public harbour opened in 1819, from which cargoes of 'Pembrey culm' were despatched to the harbours of West and mid-Wales for well over a century. Culm was anthracite dust which, when mixed with clay, was used as a fuel. Some Pembrey vessels ventured on much longer voyages. One was the brig *Eliza* (185), which had been built at Prince Edward Island in 1842. By 1845 the owners were John Thomas, farmer of Pembrey, with 44/64 shares and David Thomas, shopkeeper of Pembrey, 20/64. The master was the twenty-one-year-old John Thomas, son of David. The mate was another John Thomas. Ports visited by the *Eliza* included Ancona, Kronstadt, Liverpool, Malta, Messina, Naples, St Petersburg and Venice. After a voyage of nearly seven months, the vessel arrived at San Francisco at the time of the Gold Rush. The crew deserted and the *Eliza* became one of the hundreds of ships stuck in San Francisco harbour. The brig was sold by the authorities in April 1854.

In the 1840s Pembrey harbour was: 'capable of holding eighty sail of the largest class of coasting vessels in perfect security in the roughest weather, and with all winds'. But the harbour approaches silted badly and the port eventually became redundant.

KIDWELLY

There was some sea-borne trade at Kidwelly in the thirteenth century. Evidence for this survives from the time of Henry III, who gave the shipmaster Robert of Kidwelly a permit to sail to Gascony with a cargo of hides and wool, returning with wine. Kidwelly was already suffering from silting in the early sixteenth century, to the advantage of other shipping places. John Leland reported that trade at Carmarthen: 'has increased since Kidwelly haven decayed'.

In March 1566 a cargo arrived at Kidwelly from Bristol for local merchant Roger Collins: 2 tons of iron, white soap, black soap, twenty fardels of linen, brass and pewter, six coffers of drywares, four seams of wood ashes and 5,000 laths. In the following December a vessel arrived with more goods for Roger Collins, this time from Ilfracombe: 1.5 tons of iron, seven pieces raisins, four fardels of linen, six stones of cheese and 1.5 hundredweights of sugar. Twenty years later the trade with North Devon was thriving, and there was also commerce with Ireland and France.

Between 1766 and 1768 Thomas Kymer built a canal, three miles long, to bring coal from the pits of the lower Gwendraeth Valley. Some attempts were made to improve the shipping places, but the silting up of the Gwendraeth estuary was always a problem. M.D. Matthews (2004) has examined the accounts of Thomas Kymer's collieries at Kidwelly: in 1769 half of the sales went to Devonshire and one third of the vessels loading coal came from that county. A total of 144 vessels came for Kymer's coal, and he owned around a dozen barges which moved small cargoes around the local shipping places and as far as Carmarthen, Laugharne and Llanelli.

Vessels built at Kidwelly in the four decades after 1785 included seven sloops, a smack, a brig, a brigantine, three snows, a schooner, and three unspecified craft. The brigantine was the *Albion* (71), built in 1787 and registered at Beaumaris, the shareholders being Benjamin Wyatt, agent for the Penrhyn Quarries, William Williams, the sub-agent, John Cooper (architect, Beaumaris) and, later, William Jackson, the innkeeper of the Bangor Ferry Inn. The vessel was in regular use carrying slate from Port Penrhyn to London for Samuel Wyatt. The schooner built at Kidwelly was the *George and Jane* (42), launched in 1823 and later owned at Carmarthen.

Pigot's Directory of 1844 listed fourteen pubs in Kidwelly, including the 'Pelican Inn and Excise Office'. The *Union*, under Captain Jones, sailed to Bristol once a fortnight, and *Pigot's Directory* informed its readers that coal was exported to Cornwall, Devon and Ireland. The publication boasted that: 'The quay is convenient and the harbour safe, and vessels of considerable burden can come close up to the wharf'. No mention was made of the silting.

Thirty years later *Worrall's Directory* wrote that: 'The Gwendraeth Valley Mineral Railway connects the port with extensive anthracite collieries in the Pontyberem district,' but, in spite of developments such as this, navigation problems at Kidwelly caused trade to move to Burry Port. By the first decade of the twentieth century very little coal was shipped from Kidwelly as most of it was taken to Swansea, and Kidwelly harbour closed in the 1930s.

CARMARTHEN

The Normans arrived in Carmarthen by ship and materials for their castle also came by sea. In 1230 and 1254 large quantities of stone were shipped from Chepstow for work on the fortifications and in the 1280s a ship brought crossbows, quarrels and armour, for Dryslwyn Castle, to Carmarthen. There is also a record of the transport of 300 pounds of silver from London to Dryslwyn via Bristol, and around the year 1298 stores were sent from Bristol for Carmarthen Castle.

Commercial activity began to develop; eighteen casks of wine, which fetched forty shillings each, were unloaded from vessels at Carmarthen in 1305/06. Most medieval foreign trade at Carmarthen was for salt from La Rochelle and wine from Bordeaux.

In 1326 Carmarthen became a staple for leather, hides, lead, tin and wool. The Ordinance and Statute of the Staple (by Edward III in 1353) decreed 'That the staples of wool, leather, wool-fells and lead grown or produced within our kingdom shall be perpetually held in the following places,' and there followed the names of ten towns in England, four in Ireland and Carmarthen in Wales.

The silting of the river caused continuing problems for Carmarthen, situated as it was ten miles from the sea, and vessels often had their cargoes brought upriver by lighters. John Leland observed in the 1530s that, 'beyond Llanstephan before the haven mouth lieth a bar, so that ships lightly come not in without a pilot'. In order to control river traffic the Mayor of Carmarthen was made, in 1547, 'Admiral of the River Towy from the bridge of Carmarthen to the bar of the river'. At around this time Thomas Phaer viewed Carmarthen as:

An ancient town well-traded and peopled, where is an old castle of the King's in the keeping of my Lord of Pembroke... and here is the great passage of leather, tallow and hides by reason of the merchants. All this country is very bare of corn and be not able to live of their own provision, for most part of their tillage is oats, and are served of wheat and malt out of the Forest of Dean and other parts.

There were over 300 households at Carmarthen in 1566, when local vessels included *Nyghtingall* (50), owned by Richard Lewis Hopkin and David Ieuan, which traded to France, as well as to Bristol. The other boats went only as far as to Bristol. They were: *Angell* (28), owned by 'Gr. Pontin, Moris Hancok and Moris Thomas'; *Mathew* (18), owned by Richard Lewis Hopkin; *Nycholas* (8), owned by Richard Lewis Hopkin and William David; *Mary David* (8), owned by Richard Lewis and Nicholas Roche and *Trynytie Burley* (8), owned by William Burley and John Phillyp.

Overseas trade in the second half of the sixteenth century was still concentrated on Bordeaux and La Rochelle, but there were now more voyages to Ireland, the Channel Islands and the Iberian Peninsula taking cargoes of butter, cheese, cloth, hides, skins and coal. It was not all plain sailing: in 1592 merchants of Carmarthen complained to the Court of Admiralty that four vessels of the town had been looted by pirates 'in their passage from Bristol to Carmarthen laden with silks, velvets, wine, oil and divers other merchandises, amounting to the value of ten thousand pounds'.

During the eighteenth century large quantities of butter were still being shipped out of Carmarthen, but the town's official records from November 1757 show that not all was well with the trade: 'Whereas the exportation of butter out of this County Borough for many years past hath been very great... many complaints have been made about the malpractices of farmers.' For example, filling their casks with 'bad and unwholesome produce' and putting stones in the bottom of the casks. In future, every cask would be examined and weighed by officials appointed by the mayor. In the same month the *Postillion*, carrying a cargo of butter from Carmarthen to London, was lost with all hands.

Matthews (1999) has analysed the records of vessels arriving coastwise from Carmarthen at Bristol in 1789/90. Seventeen different Carmarthen vessels visited Bristol on seventy separate occasions during the period from 5 October 1789 to 27 September 1790. They were, on average, 32 tons, the smallest being the *St David* (15) and the largest *Emlyn* (54). *The Universal British Directory* of 1794 lists nineteen vessels as belonging to the port of Carmarthen, with ten of them making regular voyages to London (taking six to ten weeks), and nine to Bristol. Of these nineteen vessels, ten had been built at Carmarthen.

The quay was extended up to the bridge in 1804, and a dry dock constructed. Two years after this *The Cambrian* reported that:

A fine ready-rigged brig was, on Monday evening last, 5 May 1806, launched at Carmarthen. She is called the *Priscilla*, in honour of Mrs Rees, the lady of Mr John Rees, merchant, and principal owner. The men had scarcely time to strike off one bridle when she darted into the water carrying away the other bridle in most majestic style. The evening being favourable, there was an immense assemblage of persons present at the ceremony. On the following night the owners entertained a select party of eighty friends with a cold supper, consisting of every delicacy in season, and the glass circulated freely until a late hour.

The vessel appeared in *The Cambrian*'s pages on three more occasions: on 27 December 1817, advertised for auction at Carmarthen, part share in the brig *Priscilla*; on 4 July 1818, announcing she would be loading at London for Milford Haven and Carmarthen and on 19 September 1818, announcing that the brig *Priscilla* was for sale.

Eighteen months later the *Priscilla* was making a voyage to Nova Scotia, taking migrants, and aiming to bring back a cargo of timber. After disembarking the passengers, Captain Phillips and four men set off upriver to collect a raft of timber. When it was finally stowed, *Priscilla's* homeward cargo was listed as: 3,668ft of pine; 1,360ft of birch; 39ft of ash, 270 log staves; 375 billet staves, plus cordwood.

The ship sailed on 11 June 1820 and was soon in trouble; the vessel began to leak, the weather was deteriorating and the crew had to fight the rising water by constant pumping. On 18 July the thankful mariners were able to beach the vessel at Pilglas in the Towy. Five days later a pilot helped to move the battered brig some of the way upstream towards Carmarthen. He then left and was expected to return for the next tide but, as the log notes, 'he got drunk and forgot to come on board'. Unloading the cargo took six days, and an overhaul of the vessel began.

On the next voyage, once more to Nova Scotia, vessel and crew again suffered in a gale and heavy seas, forcing them to turn back. The brig sank in Swansea Harbour. (For a detailed account of these voyages see James, 1983.)

The *George and Jane* (42), a schooner, had been built at Kidwelly in 1822/23. Something of the work of such a vessel may be appreciated from the following account of the schooner's voyages in 1836 (Craig 1985):

Departed:	Cargo Discharged:
2 January, Carmarthen to Emsworth 416 qtrs oats	25 January
6 February, Falmouth to Swansea 60 tons copper ore	18 February
27 February, Carmarthen to Southampton 371 qtrs oats	13 April
30 April, Carmarthen to Cardiff 60 tons coal	3 May
6 May, Carmarthen to London 400 qtrs oats	1 June
24 June, London to Tenby 48 packages of furniture	10 July
23 July, St Clears to Glasgow timber	31 August
3 September, Glasgow to Newry general cargo	8 September
12 September, Newry to Gloucester 400 qtrs corn	2 October
12 October, Gloucester to Carmarthen 36 tons salt	21 October
8 November, St Clears to Waterford 27 tons oak bark	4 January

A larger vessel than *George and Jane* was the *Queen of the Isles*, built at Pembroke in 1834 and registered at Bristol. Owners from Carmarthen included Thomas Lewis, grocer; Griffith Harries, merchant; Job Jones, merchant; John Lewis, merchant; Charles Jones, furrier and Amy Howell, grocer. Voyages were made to St Helena, Pernambuco, the Caribbean and then regular trips to the Mediterranean. The vessel was lost in 1846. In that year the total number of sailing vessels belonging to Carmarthen was eighteen. There were no steam vessels.

There was a steamboat service between Carmarthen and Bristol, on and off, from 1830 to 1870. The first vessel to be employed was the wooden paddler *Frolic* (108), which began a weekly voyage of Bristol-Carmarthen-Tenby-Haverfordwest in October 1830. The vessel was wrecked off Nash Point during the night of 16 March 1831.

The *County of Pembroke* ran once a week for about four months in 1834, but the service then seems to have been in abeyance until 1842, when the *Phoenix* appeared. One of the vessels employed later was the *Juno* (298), built at Bristol in 1853 for the Bristol General Steam Navigation Co. It was sold in May 1863 as a blockade-runner for the Confederate States of America. In September of the same year, the *Juno*, with a cargo of cotton and tobacco, was captured off Wilmington by the USS *Connecticut*.

There are records of over seventy vessels built at Carmarthen in the last quarter of the eighteenth century and the first quarter of the nineteenth. Among the biggest were the snows: *Carmarthen* (225), built in 1805; *Hero* (174), built in 1814 and *Albion* (168), of 1812. The last vessel to be launched at Carmarthen was the wooden steamboat *Lilly*, in 1865.

The quay was still in use by small vessels in the late nineteenth century, and even in the 1930s a handful of vessels called annually, usually to discharge flour from Bristol.

45 A barquentine at Carmarthen in around 1900.

ST CLEARS

The *Thurloe Boat* was owned by Edmund Thurloe and John Laugharne in the seventeenth century, and John Bevan, 'gentleman', had *Bevan's Boat*. By 1700 the quay at St Clears could be described as 'always busy either with exports of corn and general produce from an extensive area of country or with imports of coal, limestone and the simple groceries and draperies then in demand'. The largest vessel to be built at St Clears was the schooner *Sophia Wells* (131) of 1839, the main shareholder being Charles Cooke Wells, 'gent. of Tenby'. A voyage was made to Quebec in 1841, but the rest of the time was spent going to and from the Mediterranean, fetching grain from the Black Sea, wine from Marsala and raisins from Smyrna. Deviating from this routine, the *Sophia Wells* was wrecked in 1846 whilst on passage from Kronstadt to Belfast.

LAUGHARNE

Thomas Phaer thought that, 'Laugharne and Llanstephan be two poor towns' and in the 1560s there was only one vessel, the *Michael* (18) – owned by David Allen and John Palmer – trading to Bristol with a crew of five. Goods sent from Laugharne at this period included butter, cheese, cloth and skins. In return came mixed cargoes, such as that for John Palmer 'clothier of Laugharne' who received from Bristol on one boat: 'oil, one barrel of honey, 3 tons of brass, 2 cwt. cheese, four packs linen, eight chests, four cupboards, 1 cwt. crocke brass, 100 doz. pan brass, two hampers dry wares, 2 cwt. black soap, ½ cwt. alum'. Laugharne may well have been a transit place for cargoes from Bristol to Carmarthen. In January 1567 the *Margett* of Laugharne arrived with the following cargo for Thomas Jones, shoemaker, of Carmarthen: iron, forty-dozen calf skins, leather, three packs of cloth, soap and two chests of drywares. These were probably taken on to Carmarthen by lighter.

Around the middle of the seventeenth century Henry Butler and Henry Langston owned *Assistance* and *Samuel*, engaged in coastal trade, and Henry Langston had a half share in a ferry boat.

Zachary Bevan was a well-off farmer and merchant of Laugharne. At the time of his death in 1715 he owned a large house and three farms. He was a coal shipper and a dealer in grain, salt, tobacco and malt. He was also a builder, quarried stone and produced lime. From Zachary Bevan's account books for 1689 to 1714 Matthews (2003) has built up a picture of his shipping activities. He was part-owner of several vessels, including *Ann and Sarah*, *Carolina Merchant* and *Tenby Merchant*. He had a 1/16 share in the *Susannah* and interests in the *Factor* (built in 1690) of Milford Haven, the brigantine *Hopewell* and the Neath barque *Beginning*. The records show how he hired coasting vessels to carry his cargoes: the ketch *Diligence* made seven voyages in 1692, mostly from Laugharne to ports such as Dublin, Waterford and Youghal, but there was also a trip to Liverpool and one to France. In the same year Bevan sent barley and wheat to Ireland in the *William and Alice* of Kinsale and corn from Laugharne to Dublin in the *Truelove* of Ilfracombe, which then went on to carry salt from Chester to Tenby. He hired the *Owner's Adventure* to transport butter in 1700 and the *Speedwell* of Northam took corn from Laugharne to Kinsale in the same year.

Zachary Bevan's multifarious business interests included transatlantic shipping and, particularly, the tobacco trade. In April 1689 the *Elinor and Jane* carried a consignment of his tobacco, and four years later the *Hester* brought him 2 tons of tobacco from Virginia. In August 1692 he bought a quarter share in the *Yarmouth* (110) from a widow in Bideford. Bevan also had a quarter share in the pink *Katherine* – a pink was a flat-bottomed vessel, usually square-rigged, with a narrow stern – and his accounts for February 1692 show that another part-owner, Sir Hugh Owen, was due to receive 753 bags of tobacco for 'his proportion of the last voyage in ye Katherin Pinke'.

SAUNDERSFOOT

Saundersfoot in the early nineteenth century was a hamlet of perhaps a dozen dwellings. A few coal workings sent their coal and culm down to the beach, where it was loaded into small coasters at low tide, an activity that had been going on for the last 300 years.

In the early 1830s the quantities of coal and culm exported from Saundersfoot increased and the collieries were able to use the new railway and harbour. Local coal fuelled the Stepaside Iron Works, which operated from 1849 to 1877, transporting its products along the railway to the harbour, as did the foundry of David and Parcell and the local brickworks.

Hobbs (1859) wrote that:

> Since the completion of this harbour in 1832, several additions have been made; but the most recent consist of an extension of the piers, by which the entrance has been much reduced, and the greatest security given to vessels in the harbour. New jetties and quays have been erected, and the accommodation for loading vessels considerably increased... Many vessels load here the valuable anthracite coal and culm of this district.

In one week in 1863 eight vessels sailed (with coal, culm or iron) to Ireland, Port Talbot, Cardigan, South Devon, and the south coast of England.

Coal was still being loaded in the 1930s, but production stopped just before the Second World War, leaving what was by now a big industrial village and a disused railway. Fortunately for the local economy, holidaymakers had already begun to take over.

TENBY

A harbour wall was built in the middle of the fourteenth century, as commerce with Bristol Channel ports developed. Wine was already being imported, a trade which was to be carried on for another 200 years. During the medieval period cargoes of coal, cloth and corn went to Spain, Portugal and France in return for wine, salt, raisins, pitch and Spanish iron. Coal and corn were sent to the east coast of Ireland.

By the second half of the sixteenth century the manufacture of cloth was in a prolonged depression and a later report stated that the town had decayed 'by the loss and discontinuance of the trade of clothing'. But wine continued to arrive, for example on 26 May 1550 the *Mores* of Morlaix arrived with linen cloth and Gascony wine; 10 March 1551 *Mary George* of Tenby, master Thomas Parrott, brought in Gascony wine; 11 April 1551 *Mary James* of Tenby, master David Wogan, arrived with a cargo of Gascony wine and salt.

In 1566 there were perhaps nine vessels belonging to Tenby, including the *Mary James* (40), *George* (16) owned by Richard Rede and which 'saileth with four men and useth most commonly to Ireland afishinge and upp Severne' and Nicholas Lange's *Saviour* (12), which also went 'upp Severne', as well as to North Wales. Fifty years later there were around two-dozen, the largest being the *Gift* (80) and the *Daniell* (70). In March 1599 the *Jesus* went to La Rochelle with coal and cloth, but on the return voyage the vessel was captured by Spanish pirates, looted and burned. The crew escaped from La Coruña and made their way home.

George Owen of Henllys noted in 1603 that some coal was transported from south Pembrokeshire to Ireland and France; by 1790 Tenby was handling around one third of all coal exports from Pembrokeshire, a trade which was later lost to Saundersfoot.

Tenby was served by a steamer service, sometimes sporadically, from 1822 to the 1890s. The first vessel to appear was the *St Patrick* which inaugurated the route between Bristol and Liverpool, via Dublin, with a call at Tenby. Many other steam vessels served Tenby, including the *Frolic* (which went to Bristol via Carmarthen), the *George IV* and the *Palmerston*, both of which ran Bristol-Ilfracombe-Tenby. The *Palmerston*, built at Bristol in 1823, was a wooden-paddle steamer owned by the Bristol Steam Navigation Co. The Revd Joseph Romilly boarded the *Palmerston* at Tenby on 5 August 1837 and recalled:

> We moved off in a dirty Tenby steamer of 80hp named *Palmerston*. We had not got 100 yards when we were enveloped in steam, which escaped in a most unexpected manner; there was a slight explosion, and bye and bye the engineer came to inform us that they had put on too great a pressure of steam and that something in the boiler had given way, that they must pump out all the water, repair the damage and endeavour to sail by the next tide. It was most happy for us that we escaped with so slight inconvenience from so great a danger, and we had every reason to be most thankful to God.

The Welsh name of Tenby is Dinbych-y-Pysgod, 'Tenby of the fish'. Famous from the Middle Ages, the fishing in the early days was concentrated on Carmarthen Bay, but boats later ventured further away to the coast of Ireland. The arrival of the railway in the 1860s made it easier for the catch to be sent to the industrial areas of South Wales, and by 1880 there were about twenty local sailing trawlers (each crewed by two or three), not to mention those which visited every year from Brixham. By the end of the First World War fishing from such vessels had practically finished at Tenby.

In the two decades before the war there had been, as well as the trawlers, more than seventy 'lug-rigged' boats, engaged on inshore fishing with lines and nets. As the numbers of people visiting the resort increased, so these boats began to be used for pleasure trips.

PEMBROKE

Pembroke is dominated by its castle. The first Norman defences on the site were erected by Roger de Montgomery at the end of the eleventh century and the building of the great stone fortress was begun about a hundred years later. Thomas Phaer reported that, by the 1550s:

46 The paddle steamer *Star* at Tenby, sketched by Charles Norris on 30 June 1838.

The castle of Pembroke, wherein was born the renowned Prince King Henry VII... is sore decayed, despoiled and defaced, which is a great pity for the situation is both strong and princely. Here is great transporting to Ireland of corn and money and many other things to other places without control, for men may do what they will ere they be spied by the officer, and pass when they please by reason of the haven being so large and secret.

Two small Pembroke craft were noted in 1566: *Anne* (12), owned by Henry Adams and Thomas Holland and *Mary* (16) owned by Richard Lymton, Phyllipp Scorlocke, William Ffrowyn and Owen White. Each vessel had a crew of four, traded to Ireland and North Wales, and went fishing in the Severn Sea.

Pembroke was a prosperous town by the middle of the eighteenth century with a good many vessels based there. Much of Pembroke's trade later migrated to Haverfordwest and Milford Haven, a movement accelerated by the arrival of railways.

47 Tenby harbour.

THE ROYAL DOCKYARD

The Royal Dockyard was founded in 1814 at Pater, soon to be known as Pembroke Dock. Two years later the first two vessels were launched: the frigates *Valorous* and *Ariadne*.

Eventually there were to be thirteen covered slipways for building ships, necessary because on an uncovered slip, battered by rain, a ship's timbers were likely to rot. For many years the yard was not equipped for fitting out and vessels had to be taken to Plymouth or Portsmouth. When the yard began to make steam vessels these were sent elsewhere for their machinery, but later ships had engines and guns fitted locally at Hobbs Point. In 1906 a jetty was constructed across the Carr Rocks as another place for fitting out.

In 1844 the defensible barracks was erected, and forts were built at Thorne Island and Stack Rock. During the 1850s two Martello Towers were put up at the north-east and south-west corners of the dockyard. The railway arrived at Neyland, on the other side of the river from the dockyard, in April 1856, which made it easier to bring in supplies. Eight years later the Pembroke & Tenby Railway opened. By this time over a thousand people were employed at the dockyard.

Altogether, nearly 250 vessels were launched at Pembroke Dock, including four Royal Yachts: 1843 *Victoria and Albert*; 1855 *Victoria and Albert*; 1870 *Osborne* and 1899 *Victoria and Albert*.

Some of the Warships Built at the Royal Dockyard

Date	Name	History
1823	*Hamadryad*	The frigate which became a seamen's hospital at Cardiff.
1827	*Clarence*	Eighty-four guns, launched during the visit of the Duke of Clarence (later King William IV).

1834	*Tartarus*	A paddle steamer, with four guns. The vessel was designed by Sir William Symonds, Surveyor of the Navy from June 1832.
1837	*Gorgon*	A paddle steamer with a speed up to 8.5 knots. Designed by Sir William Symonds and perhaps the first effective steam warship.
1846	*Conflict*	A small sloop and the first warship with a screw propeller.
1847	*Lion*	At the time of its launch the largest ship in the navy.
1852	*Duke of Wellington*	Laid down as a sailing vessel. The ship was lengthened by 30ft, fitted with screw propulsion and launched on 14 September 1852, the day the Duke of Wellington died. It was the largest vessel yet built for the Royal Navy.
1856	*Alert*	A wooden sloop, 160ft long. A low-power steam engine was installed at Chatham. There were seventeen guns and a crew of 175.
1861	*Pandora*	A wooden screw gunboat, barque-rigged.
1867	*Penelope*	Iron-clad, with twin screws, ten guns and a crew of 350.
1878	*Mercury*	A dispatch vessel. *Mercury* and her sister ship *Iris* were designed to be the fastest ships afloat.
1882	*Edinburgh*	A battleship 325ft long by 68ft broad, with a speed of 14 knots. There was a crew of 400.

Other large battleships built at Pembroke Dock included 1882 *Collingwood*, 1885 *Howe*, 1886 *Anson*, 1888 *Nile*, 1891 *Empress of India*, 1892 *Repulse* and 1896 *Hannibal*.

In 1874, *Alert* was refitted for Arctic exploration: the hull was strengthened, and the guns were stripped out, to be replaced by four breech-loaders. Rigged as a barque, and given a more powerful, compound engine, the *Alert* could do 7.5 knots using 6 tons a day of 'best ordinary Welsh coal'. There was now a crew of sixty-one.

Alert took part in the 1875 expedition (with *Discovery*, a steam whaler commissioned into the Royal Navy) to investigate the earth's magnetism. Commanded by Captain George Nares, the vessels sailed up the east coast of Canada. *Alert* became stuck in the ice for nine months at latitude eighty-two degrees, the first European vessel to reach so far north. Three sledge parties set off, and the one led by Commander H.A. Markham managed to attain a record northerly latitude. HMS *Alert* gave its name to the settlement on Ellesmere Island described today as the 'most northern permanently inhabited settlement in the world'.

48 Pembroke Dock during the visit of the Duke and Duchess of Edinburgh in 1882.

49 The dispatch vessel HMS *Mercury* was launched at Pembroke Dock on 17 April 1878. Designed, along with sister ship *Iris*, to be the fastest ship afloat.

50 HMS *Alert* was launched at Pembroke Dock in 1856. On an expedition to investigate the earth's magnetism she became stuck in the ice off the coast of Canada for nine months.

The *Alert* went off surveying around the Pacific in 1878, before returning to Chatham in 1880. Adolphus Greely (of the United States Army) had, in 1882, gone four miles further north in the Arctic than Markham, but had disappeared. Two expeditions went off to find Greely and his group, but with no success. The *Alert* was lent to a third expedition, which finally managed to rescue the eight survivors. In his State of the Union Address, on 8 December 1885, United States President Grover Cleveland said: 'The Arctic exploring steamer *Alert*, which was generously given by Her Majesty's Government to aid in the relief of the Greely expedition, was, after the successful attainment of that humane purpose, returned to Great Britain'.

The vessel had, in fact, been transferred in May 1885 to the Canadian government, for surveying duties in Hudson's Bay. When these were finished, the *Alert* became a tender, serving buoys and lighthouses around Nova Scotia and then in the Gulf of St Lawrence. The ship was still on loan and when finally sold to the breakers (for £814) the money went to the British government.

In October 1866, off the coast of West Africa, *Pandora* collided in the dark with the gunboat *Griffon*, which sank. Two years later, the vessel was in action with two other gunboats against 'piratical tribes' in the Congo. In 1875 *Pandora* was sold for the Arctic voyaging of Sir Allen Young. In 1878 it was bought by James Gordon Bennett, the New York newspaper owner, and renamed *Jeanette*. An expedition was to be mounted to try to reach the North Pole. The United States Navy would man the vessel, but Bennett was to meet all costs. The *Jeanette* left San Francisco on 8 July 1879, under the command of Lieutenant George Washington DeLong. There were thirty-one on board, and the dogs, sleds and two handlers were collected in Alaska. Passing through the Bering Strait, the *Jeanette* became stuck in the ice in September 1879 and for nearly two years the ship was carried helplessly in a north-westerly direction. On 13 June 1881 the Pembroke Dock vessel sank. Hauling three boats and supplies, the thirty-three men set off towards the delta of the River Lena, 700 miles away. Twenty died, including DeLong.

The launch of *Edinburgh* was in March 1882, when the Duke and Duchess of Edinburgh steamed up the Haven in the paddle dispatch vessel HMS *Lively*. (Prince Alfred, Duke of Edinburgh was the second son of Queen Victoria; his wife was the Grand Duchess Maria Alexandrovna, daughter of Tsar Alexander II who had been assassinated in the previous year.) The Lords Commissioners of the Admiralty had arrived earlier – by Great Western Railway – and boarded the Admiralty steam-yacht *Enchantress*. The town was *en fete*: the Royal Welch Fusiliers and the Castlemartin Yeomanry Cavalry were on parade, the band played the British and Russian national anthems, and the route was packed with spectators. 'The utmost enthusiasm prevailed, and the decorations were profuse. An arch in Meyrick Street bore the word "Welcome" in Russian'.

The Times reported that:

> The launching apparatus provided for the use of the Duchess was made in the Royal Dockyard, and was presented to her Royal Highness by Chief Constructor Warren. The handle of the lever is beautifully carved, and surmounted by a golden lion, on one side being a silver plate bearing an inscription, and on the other the Royal Standards of England and Russia. The box in which the handle is enclosed is handsomely carved, the lid being inlaid with a drawing of the *Edinburgh* in a frame of intricate work, with the Russian crest.

After all this, the *Edinburgh* was not ready to enter service for over five years. The warship was stationed in the Mediterranean from 1887 to 1894, and was then put into reserve, being sold for scrap in 1910.

Seven hundred people were dismissed from the dockyard in 1906, provoking a letter to *The Times* (2 June) from Thomas C. Meyrick:

> Pembroke Dock, which now contains about 12,000 people, is entirely the creation of the dockyard, and is absolutely dependent on that establishment for its existence. The town does

51 The launch of HMS *Edinburgh* by the Duchess of Edinburgh.

52 HMS *Andromeda*, launched at Pembroke Dock on 30 April 1897. This was the most powerful warship built so far at the dockyard.

not possess a single other industry of any character, nearly every inhabitant deriving his livelihood, either directly or indirectly, from the dockyard. The men employed in the yard reside mostly at Pembroke Dock and Pembroke and number about 2,500.

The cruiser *Curaçao*, launched in 1917, was the last warship, other than a handful of submarines, to be built at Pembroke. The vessel survived until October 1942, when it was rammed by the liner *Queen Mary* off the coast of Northern Ireland and over 300 men died.

During the First World War more than 4,000 people were employed at the dockyard, but layoffs began with the end of hostilities, and from then on the yard's future became increasingly uncertain. The last vessel to be launched, on 3 May 1922, was the Royal Fleet Auxiliary's oil tanker *Oleander*.

Royal Air Force Pembroke Dock was established at the dockyard in 1930, when the airmen of 210 Squadron arrived with their Supermarine Southampton flying boats. During the Second World War the Royal Air Force presence expanded greatly, more squadrons flew in and Sunderlands and Catalinas became familiar sights over and on the Haven with training flights, anti-submarine patrols and convoy protection sorties.

On 19 August 1940 German bombers set oil tanks blazing at Pemboke Dock. Firemen were sent from all over the country and five, from Cardiff, died. In 1940 and 1941 air raids continued; in one of them thirty-two people were killed and hundreds of houses damaged.

The Royal Air Force finally departed twelve years after the end of the war, but a small area remained in use as a depot by the Royal Navy until the 1990s, and the shipyard of R.S. Hayes was also located in part of the old dockyard. In 1953 Hayes converted the *Ocean Layer* (ex-*Empire Frome*) into a cable-laying vessel and in 1956 launched the trawler *Norrard Star*.

At the beginning of the twenty-first century Pembroke Port, based at the former dockyard, was run by the Milford Docks Co. There was a ferry terminal for the Irish Ferries service to Rosslare.

HAVERFORDWEST

Haverfordwest, at the tidal limit of the Western Cleddau, was an ancient shipping place, symbolised by the town's Common Seal (used from the early fourteenth century) which depicts a single-masted ship. In a Charter of 1479 the mayor was designated 'admiral of the port', entitled to 200 apples from every such cargo discharged at the port. Just over a century later, some typical cargoes recorded at Haverfordwest were: On 5 December 1585 the *Mary* (7) of Northam – master Charity Mussell, merchant John Miles of Barnstaple – loaded at Haverfordwest for Barnstaple brass, wool, frise, skins, ginger and yellow wax. On 20 January 1586 the merchant Harry Taylor of Haverfordwest sent to Devonshire on the *Cherubyn* (12) of Minehead: '180 stones of wool, forty pieces of frise, fifteen-dozen calf skins, 500 yards *lystes*'. On 27 January 1586, the merchant William Graffinge of Minsterworth, Gloucestershire aboard the *Ann* (8) of Fremington brought from Barnstaple: ninety stones of cheese, a hundredweight of beef and a side of bacon. Another cargo from Barnstaple was carried in the *Angle* (10) of Northam – merchant James Rowth of Haverfordwest – including iron, linen cloth, three hampers of 'haberdashery wares', 4 hundredweights of 'congers', alum, tallow, shoemaker's thread, frise, figs, a piece of red cloth, butter and ginger.

George Owen of Henllys, writing in 1603, refers to the 'apple men of the Forest (of Dean)' who arrive 'with barques laden with apples and pears.' Other imports included wine and salt. At this time nearly 90 per cent of vessels arriving at Haverfordwest came from the Bristol Channel.

The Clerk of the Peace made a list of vessels based on the Cleddau in 1795. There were forty, thirty-seven of which were lighters, two were sloops and one a 'boat'. Hugh Barlow, esquire, owned eight vessels that worked between Cresswell Quay and Milford Haven. John Daniel, a shipwright, operated two lighters and a sloop, the *Swallow* (Matthews 1999). S. Lewis's

53 Royal Air Force Pembroke Dock was established at the dockyard in 1930. The Sunderland flying boat was a familiar sight during the Second World War.

Topographical Dictionary of Wales (1833) described Haverfordwest as 'a seaport, borough and market town... The modern capital of Pembrokeshire'. It continues:

> From its central situation it attracts considerable trade, chiefly coastwise: the exports are principally oats and butter, with a small quantity of leather and bark; the imports are chiefly groceries, manufactured goods, and other miscellaneous articles, for the supply of shops. Coal is brought by water from Newport in Monmouthshire, and from Liverpool... The river is navigable to the bridge for barges, to a lower part of the town for larger vessels, and to a place immediately below the town for ships of 250 tons burden.

Butter, cheese, eggs, barley, oats and wheat were sent to Bristol.

The Cleddau passes through the Pembrokeshire coalfield and coal was shipped from places such as Hook, Landshipping and Creswell. Coal had been loaded at Cresswell Quay from the 1280s, when it was being transported to Aberystwyth for the men building the castle. Barges were often taken down to Lawrenny or Llangwm Pool, where their cargoes were trans-shipped. The river traffic began to diminish as trade was transferred to Neyland and Milford, although coal was to leave Hook by small steam vessels up to the 1920s.

The paddle steamer *Frolic* ran once a week to Haverfordwest-Tenby-Carmarthen-Bristol from October 1830 until the vessel was wrecked in March 1831. The *Benledi* provided a similar service in 1836, followed by the *Star* (1836-47), which was too big to go up the river and had to transfer freight for Haverfordwest into barges.

The railway arrived at Haverfordwest in 1853 and by end of the century there was little river trade.

NEYLAND (NEW MILFORD)

Mr Brunel decided that the railway terminus at Neyland would be: 'at a point where the water is sufficiently deep for the largest steamers to come up to the pier. When the line is opened to Neyland (Milford Haven) a large American and Irish traffic is anticipated' reported

The Times on 21 June 1855. The first train arrived on 15 April 1856, on the completion of the South Wales Railway line from Gloucester. The terminus was to cover twelve acres and could handle railway engines and trains, freight, mail and passenger services. To the railway company, Neyland became 'New Milford'.

A London firm, Ford and Jackson, won the contract to run a twice-weekly (later three-times-a-week) passenger and goods service to Waterford, the voyage lasting about eight or nine hours. In 1863 the South Wales Railway was incorporated into the Great Western Railway, which continued to operate a daily service from Neyland (New Milford) to Waterford. Three years later a service began to Cork, but this was later handed over to the City of Cork Steam Packet Co. The GWR ordered three new iron-paddle steamers from Simons & Co. of Renfrew: *Limerick* came into service in 1873, *Milford* and *Waterford* in 1874. They took around eight hours to get to Waterford, with each vessel licensed to carry 400 passengers in winter and 500 in summer.

When Fishguard became the Packet Station in 1906, rail and sea traffic moved there, although a steamer still went from Neyland to Waterford once a week.

Hopes were high for a liner trade from Neyland. On 1 August 1857 the *New York Herald* carried an account of 'a convention held at Old Point, Virginia, in aid of Mr. Dudley Mann's proposed Atlantic steamship ferry'. The plan was to operate four steamers between Milford Haven and Chesapeake Bay. Nothing came of this ambitious project, but just over a year later on 11 September 1858, *The Times* reported that:

> The steamship *Prince Alfred*, Captain Jarvis, 2000 tons burden... now coaling at Neyland, will sail on Monday, the thirteenth inst. for Melbourne, Sydney and New Zealand, to take up the duties of the Royal Mail intercolonial packet service between Sydney and New Zealand. The *Prince Alfred* takes a full complement of passengers and cargo.

The *Portugal* was a screw steamer, rigged as a barque and built at Blackwall by C.J. Mare. Originally called the *Calcutta*, she was acquired in 1859 by the Anglo-Luso-Brazilian Royal Mail Steam Navigation Co. In 1859 the *Portugal* sailed from Neyland to Lisbon and on to South America, but any ideas about a regular service from Neyland were soon abandoned.

If the passenger-liner trade came to nothing, there was still fishing; with an ice factory, and a covered fish market (built in 1908) sending off trainloads of fish.

Railway services came to an end in June 1964 and the Hobbs Point ferry closed in March 1975 when the Cleddau Bridge opened.

MILFORD HAVEN

The waterway of Milford Haven has always been of strategic importance, particularly in relation to Ireland. Both Henry II (in the twelfth century) and Richard II (in the fourteenth) assembled their invasion fleets in the Haven and there were, at times, fears of invasion fleets arriving. In August 1405 a French force of over 2,000 men disembarked, on their way to support Owain Glyn Dŵr and eighty years later Henry Tudor, born at Pembroke, landed at Mill Bay on his way to Bosworth and the crown.

In the middle of the sixteenth century Thomas Phaer reported on this important harbour:

> The haven of Milford, mete for all ships and all winds to come in and out at their pleasure and to lie safe at fourteen fathoms low water with pills and privy creeks an incredible number. For, as the report is, there may lie a thousand ships not to be seen one of another by reason of crooked pills and great banks, whereof the number is not easy to be reckoned, by the space of sixteen or twenty miles. And to my sight appeareth no less but the same to be true, for it is to behold a wonder. This haven of Milford lieth against Padstow in Cornwall. North and south the towns of Pembroke and Haverford West within the haven, and the country adjoining fruitful of corn

and all good provision as England. Milford is the great resort and succour of all pirates and enemies in storms, whom the country cannot resist to lie at their pleasure, for the two bulwarks which the king's majesty began stand unfinished and the iron work stolen and defaced...There is also some ordnance but to no purpose.

A survey commissioned by the commander of the 1597 Spanish Armada reported that:

Milford is the finest port in England. The harbour is approached with a north-east heading. There is an anchorage of one league at the mouth. At low water it has sixteen fathoms at the mouth and within there are eight or seven fathoms. It is a protected harbour and is six or seven leagues round about. There is room for countless ships. There is no fortress, and but one tower at the entrance. On the right side it is not strong, it usually has two pieces of artillery, which cannot prevent an entry. It is six leagues to the head of the river. There is an open village. It has water, meat and grain in abundance, There are many Catholics and the people are naturally enemies of the English and do not speak their language. (Loomie 1963)

The Spanish Armada did not come, but the Civil War brought skirmishes to the Haven in August 1643, with the arrival of the Royalist vessels *Fellowship* and *Hart*, both recently captured from Parliament's fleet. Captain Burley summoned some of the local gentry to the *Fellowship* in an attempt to recruit them to the King's cause. Now two Parliamentary vessels – *Bonaventure* and *Swallow* – sailed into the Haven, and the *Fellowship* and the *Hart* found themselves back in Parliamentary hands. In February of the following year five of Parliament's ships captured the fort being built at Pill, as well as the the Royalist vessels *Globe* and *Providence*. In 1649 a Parliamentary army under Cromwell left Milford Haven for Ireland.

William Hamilton, who had acquired his local estate by marriage, decided to increase its value by promoting a new town and in 1790 obtained:

An Act to enable Sir William Hamilton, Knight of the Most Honourable Order of the Bath, his heirs and assigns, to make and provide quays, docks, piers and other erections; to establish a market, with proper roads and avenues thereto respectively, within the Manor or Lordship of Hubberston and Pill in the County of Pembroke.

Hamilton's nephew Charles Francis Greville acted as his agent, and in 1791 invited Quakers, who had emigrated from Nantucket to Devonshire to move to Milford and undertake South Sea whaling from there. Government pensions were awarded to Timothy Folger, Samuel Starbuck and their wives, and about fifty people arrived at Milford in 1792.

A shipyard was leased to the Admiralty in 1796, and Harry and Joseph Jacob of London were contracted to build vessels for the Royal Navy. They became bankrupt in 1802, the year in which Sir William Hamilton decided to visit his property, bringing with him his wife (Emma) and Admiral Lord Horatio Nelson. Entertainments provided included a fair, a cattle show, a regatta and a commemoration of the battle of the Nile. Nelson announced that the Haven was, along with Trincomalee, the best he had seen. He boosted Sir William's new town and lauded the new vessels being built, the American whalers, the Custom House and the Irish Packet service. Sir William died in the following year and Francis Greville inherited the estate. He died nine years later and it passed to his brother Robert Fulke Greville.

Vessels Built for the Royal Navy at Milford Haven

Date	Name	History
12 April 1804	*Nautilus*	Sixth rate with eighteen guns.
6 March 1806	*Lavinia*	Fifth rate with forty guns.
1 April 1809	*Milford*	Third rate with seventy-four guns.

54 The frigate *Surprise* at Milford Dockyard in 1812. Sketched on the day before launch by Charles Norris.

1811	*Portsmouth*	A transport.
1812	*Surprise*	Fifth rate with forty-six guns.
1813	*Myrmidon*	Ship-sloop with twenty guns.
1814	*Rochfort*	Second rate with eighty guns.

Nautilus, *Lavinia* and *Milford* were begun by Harry and Joseph Jacobs, but completed by the government. The government wanted to buy the site of the shipyard, but terms could not be agreeed and so a new dockyard was established at Pater (Pembroke Dock) from 1814.

During the early part of 1806 the *Nautilus* was one of the vessels patrolling the coasts of France and Spain. In May, her crew helped to cut out a small Spanish vessel from the harbour at Cartagena. Seven men were wounded in the operation. Four months later, commanded by Edward Palmer, the *Nautilus* was to be found as part of a squadron reconnoitering the Dardanelles. Edward Palmer died when the *Nautilus* was wrecked on Anikythera, north of Crete, on 4 January 1807.

During 1808 the *Lavinia* was employed on blockading duties off the French coast. In August 1809 the *Lavinia* led the line of battle when a frigate squadron forced the channel between the batteries on the Scheldt. She was lost in 1868 after a collision with a steamship at Plymouth.

The *Milford* was the flagship of Admiral Fremantle in July 1813 when the batteries at Fiume were bombarded and then stormed. Ninety vessels were taken; about half of them were returned, thirteen became prizes and the rest were destroyed. A month later, boats from the *Milford* and the *Weazel* landed on the island of Rogoznica, off the coast of Dalmatia, and attacked the French garrison. The *Milford*, under Captain John Duff Markland, took part in the siege of the castle at Trieste, when marines and guns were landed; the French surrendered after three weeks.

By the 1820s the *Surprise* was a prison hulk at Cork, holding many Irish men, women and children who were being held until a convict ship could transport them to Australia.

55 The barque *Lyderhorn*, built at Milford Haven in 1892 by T.L. Oswald for J.R. De Wolfe & Son, Liverpool.

Some civilian building continued at Milford; there was Hogan's yard and graving dock at Hakin; Roberts Brothers were on the east side of Hubberston Pill and Watson and Winshurst at the old dockyard. George (1964) lists the numbers of vessels built as: sixteen in the 1810s; twenty-two in the 1820s; twenty-one in the 1830s; twenty in the 1840s; ten in the 1850s and twelve in the 1860s.

T.L. Oswald moved his shipbuilding yard from Southampton to Milford in 1890, launching the full-rigged ships *Speke* and *Ditton* for Leyland Brothers of Liverpool and in 1892, two four-masted steel barques: *Lyderhorn* (2,914), measuring 311ft by 42ft, for J.R. De Wolfe of Liverpool and *Windermere* (3,050), measuring 320ft by 43ft for Fisher & Sprott of London. In 1893 Oswald repaired the North German Lloyd liner *Spree*, which was towed into Milford Haven after suffering a broken propeller shaft. Three trawlers were launched before the yard closed in 1895: *Ayaconora*, *Sea Gull* and *Seamew*.

The Packets to Ireland

A daily packet service was inaugurated between Milford and Waterford in 1787. Up to 1821 the six packet boats were owned privately, and chartered to the Post Office. A steam vessel came into service in 1824, taking eight or nine hours over the voyage. A report published three years later lists the vessels in use as the *Crocodile*, *Meteor*, *Sovereign* and *Vixen*, each with a crew of fifteen.

The steamers moored off Milford, which meant that passengers had to be ferried to and fro in small boats, but in 1835 the Admiralty pier was completed across the river at Hobbs Point, and the ferries terminated there.

The Domestic Packet Service, run by the Post Office, was taken over by the Admiralty in January 1837, but the packet route closed in 1848 after it became possible to send the Irish mail by rail to Bangor, and then by coach to Holyhead.

From the 1830s people could travel from Milford Haven to Bristol by paddle steamer, the first being the *County of Pembroke* (110) which was in service from August 1831, serving Pater and Haverfordwest. A fast passage to Bristol took thirteen hours.

LAYING THE FOUNDATION-STONE OF THE HUBBERSTON DOCK AT MILFORD HAVEN.—SEE NEXT PAGE.

56 The foundation stone of a new dock at Hubberstone was laid on 11 August 1864 by Mrs Potter, wife of the chairman of the Great Western Railway. The ship in the background is in Hogan's graving dock at Hakin.

On 3 March 1854 *The Cambrian* carried the news that the Australian Direct Steam Navigation Co. was planning a service from Milford Haven to Australia, via Panama. The Panama Canal would not be opened for another sixty years, so passengers would have to disembark, cross the isthmus, and board another ship to carry them across the Pacific. The scheme's promoters had been hoping for government subsidies, and in the absence of these abandoned their plans.

On 3 May 1858 an advertisement in *The Times* read:

> Steam to New Zealand, via Milford Haven – The *Lord Ashley*, mail-screw steamer, under contract with Her Majesty's Government, will sail direct for Auckland – from London – on 10 May, calling at Milford Haven to embark passengers and cargo on 15 May positively. Passengers availing themselves of this opportunity will avoid all the dangers and accidents of the voyage down Channel.

The *Lord Ashley* (422), an iron-screw vessel, was a sister ship of the *Lord Worsley* which left London at around the same date for Wellington. The two ships were to remain in New Zealand, chartered for a government contract to carry mail, passengers and freight between Sydney and New Zealand ports. The *Lord Ashley* embarked sixty passengers at Milford – who were, according to *The Otago Times*, 'going out under the auspices of the Provincial Government of Auckland' – and departed on 26 May, with nearly a hundred passengers in all. The reporter at Milford Haven wrote that, 'the event, being the first of its description, caused considerable excitement'.

Proposals to build a dock at Hubberston Pill dated back to at least 1814, but now something was done. On 26 September 1864, *The Times* reported:

57 The *Great Eastern* at Milford.

The almost unequalled natural resources of this harbour are at last about to be turned into some practical account, and, as a first step in that direction, the foundation stone of the Hubberston Docks has been laid, and the works are already in progress. The new Milford Docks are also to be commenced without delay, and there is every probability that the Newton Noyes Ocean Pier will be carried out as well.

It would be nearly a quarter of a century before Milford Haven Docks were open to shipping.

The Great Eastern
The *Great Eastern* (18,915), 689ft long and 118ft wide and the largest vessel in the world, spent the winter of 1861/62 at Milford Haven for repairs to paddle wheels and steering gear, damaged on a transatlantic voyage.

After employment as a cable-laying ship, the *Great Eastern* came back to Milford Haven in the summer of 1875. Day trips to see the vessel came from far afield, and the Milford Dock Co.'s shareholders were informed that:

The *Great Eastern* entered the docks on the second instant and will shortly be placed upon a gridiron preparing for her, where she will remain several months for overhauling and repair. The presence of the great ship in the Dock will, no doubt, increase the public interest in the undertaking and further the objects of the Company.

The *Great Eastern* was still at Milford Haven in 1881, when it was advertised for sale. Four years later the ship was acquired by Edward de Mattos and then chartered by Lewis's, who moored it in the Mersey to publicise their department store during the 1886 Liverpool Exhibition of Navigation, Travelling, Commerce and Manufacture.

At the 1881 census, taken on 3 April, there were 179 vessels in the Haven, many of them having sought shelter from a gale. The *Great Eastern* was recorded with twenty-one people on board, including the chief engineer, his wife and four children. There were five other steamers, three of them belonging to the Great Western Railway and employed on the ferry service to Waterford. The three steamers were: *Limerick*, *Pembroke*, and *Malakhoff*, which had been built thirty years earlier at Millwall by John Scott Russell, who had also built the *Great Eastern*. The fourth steamer was another Irish ferry, the *Briton* (282), owned for the previous seventeen years by the Bristol Steam Navigation Co. The only screw steam vessel of the five was the *Drumhendry* (89) in Dale Roads.

The largest of the sailing vessels was the brig *Eothen* (215), built at Cardiff in 1849, now owned at Stornoway. Of the rest, there were sixty-nine schooners, twenty-five smacks, eleven sloops, six brigantines, four ketches and a pair of cutters.

Milford Haven Docks opened on 27 September 1888. The first vessel to enter was the steam trawler *Sibyl*, a prophetic sight because accommodating trawlers was to became the chief function of the docks. The first aim of the dock and railway companies was, however, to develop a port which would attract the transatlantic liner trade, and the directors and shareholders of the company must have been gratified by the the headline in *The Times* of 25 October 1889, 'The New Atlantic Port'. The article went on to describe the arrival of the Anchor Line steamship *City of Rome* (8,415), which arrived from New York, via Queenstown (Cobh), at 5.30 p.m. on 24 October. It anchored in Dale Roads, with passengers being brought ashore by tender:

> Temporary accomodation had been provided on the dock side for the reception of the 122 passengers and the 160 packages of luggage brought over. The Customs examination occupied a little over an hour, after which the passengers, who were all members of Barnum's company, were free to enter the special train. Having landed her passengers, etc., the *City of Rome* left for Liverpool. The Great Western Railway's special train from Milford Haven to London consisted of two powerful engines, a van, ten saloon carriages and baggage vans, the whole being illuminated with gas... The directors and officials of the Milford Docks Co. left with the train, and it was expected that the whole distance to Paddington would be covered in six hours and seven minutes.

'Barnum's company' was Barnum and Bailey's 'Greatest Show on Earth', the original 'three-ring circus', which opened a fortnight later at Olympia in London. One newspaper described it as a 'combination of circus, wild-beast show and curiosity museum'.

Ten years after the opening of the dock there was still no liner trade. A fresh attempt was made in December 1898, with what was announced as 'a new service to Canada'. The press reported that:

> A considerable number of persons travelled down from Paddington yesterday to Milford Haven, on the invitation of the chairman of the Canadian Steamship Co. and of the chairman of the Milford Docks Co. The special object of the expedition was to participate in the inauguration of a new line of steamers to Canada, bound for a new port by a new route.

The port was a small fishing settlement – Paspebiac, on the Baie des Chaleurs – whose main attractions seemed to be that it was connected to a railway, and was said not to freeze up. The new route was heard to be described as 'starting from a port which hardly anybody uses, for a port of which very few persons have heard the name'.

The ship employed for this venture was the *Gaspesia* (3,829). In the view of *The Times*:

> The company is making a modest beginning. The *Gaspesia* is not a new vessel and by no means an ocean greyhound. She is quite sound and of very substantial construction... She is nothing more than a comfortable thirteen-knot vessel of old-fashioned type built to carry cargo and to accomodate passengers.

The ship was formerly the *Galicia*, built twenty-five years before by Robert Napier & Sons of Glasgow, making a maiden voyage to Valparaiso in April 1873 for the Pacific Steam Navigation Co. *Galicia* had recently been acquired for £8,000 by the Canadian Steamship Co., and renamed *Gaspesia*.

58 The Anchor Line steamship *City of Rome* arrived at Milford from New York on 24 October 1889. Over a hundred passengers disembarked. They were all members of Barnum and Bailey's Show, and left by special train for London.

The vessel arrived at Milford Haven Docks on 6 December 1898. Llanelli tinplate and 200 tons of coal were taken on board. Seventy-five passengers had come with the *Gaspesia* from Liverpool, and three-dozen more were expected to embark at Milford Haven – the ship could accomodate over 600 – and the *Gaspesia* left on 8 December.

On the return voyage from Canada the *Gaspesia* carried 1,300 sheep and cattle, but had to take them to Liverpool because Milford Haven had no licence to import animals. The vessel left Liverpool on 8 January 1899 and, after being delayed by ice, arrived at Paspebiac on 25 January. Departing ten days later the *Gaspesia* was trapped in the ice on the same evening and was held for seventy days.

In September a Reuters' telegram reported that the *Gaspesia* was in distress during a gale off Cape Breton, but by November it could be found plying between Greenock and Genoa. The ship was later publicly referred to, by the chairman of the Milford Docks Co., as 'the unfortunate *Gaspesia*'. The whole scheme for a liner service to Canada had fizzled out.

It came to be realized that the future of Milford Docks was as a fishing port, and a fish market and ice-making plants were established, as well as a new wharf. In the first decade of the twentieth century there were sixty-five steam trawlers based at Milford Haven, and many smaller fishing vessels. From April to October a fleet of perhaps 200 herring drifters would operate from the port. In 1912 the *Pembrokeshire Herald* was able to write: 'The fish trade is Milford Haven's sole industry and everything and everybody in the town depend on it. Directly or indirectly, between 1,500 and 2,000 people are engaged in it.'

The Haven was often used as a base for naval exercises, and in the years before the First World War a fleet of large warships might be seen anchored in Dale Roads, accompanied by many smaller vessels. One such event took place in August 1886, prominently reported in *The Times*. The exercise took the form of an attack on a defended passage, the chief objective being to find out what role torpedo boats could play in such an operation, and also to practise with the 'search lights' which had been installed at Stack Rock, South Hook Fort and Angle Bay.

59 A naval exercise to test torpedo boats was held at Milford Haven in August 1886.

The torpedo boats at this time were powered by steam, and were typically about 125ft long by 13ft beam. A crew of fifteen could be carried along at 22 knots, but it was not a comfortable ride:

> The occupants of a torpedo boat are so tossed about and jolted from side to side as their craft run through or over the waves that any attempt at eating or drinking is put out of the question by reason of necessity of holding on to avoid being thrown overboard.

There were also the smaller second-class boats, which could be hoisted on board ship.

Around noon on the first day, warships of the Channel Fleet steamed into the Haven: *Minotaur* and *Agincourt* (both five-masted), together with the ironclads *Iron Duke*, *Monarch* and *Sultan*. They were accompanied by the torpedo-supply ship *Hecla*, five torpedo boats, four gunboats and some tugboats.

The defensive forces were, on land: three artillery batteries, two companies of mine-laying engineers and a battalion of infantry. On water: six picket boats, three gunboats and five first-class torpedo boats (which were older, smaller and slower than those provided for the attacking force). These torpedo boats were sent off to attack the fleet, but, 'there was in this action nothing to be seen save spray by any person not actually engaged'. The attempt on the defended passage came after dark, bringing into action searchlights, gunboats, torpedo boats, five shore batteries and infantry.

In addition to the vessels taking part, for two or three days the waterway was crowded with all kinds of craft – from barges to expensive private yachts – packed with spectators. Excursions arrived from as far away as Cardiff, and a Naval Correspondent reported in *The Times* that:

> In honour of the event the occasion was made the excuse for a general holiday in Milford Haven and surrounding towns, and all shops and places of business were kept closed

60 Milford Docks in the late 1940s.

throughout the day. The influx of excursionists was even greater than on the preceding day and from an early hour in the morning both New and Old Milford were thronged with visitors, whose numbers so continued to increase before evening that it seemed as though the whole countryside had been drawn to the Haven by the fire of the guns.

At the end of the exercise the fleet moved up to the anchorage off Milford Haven town to take in stores, near 'the unused spacious new docks'. It was noted that 'Milford Haven has already begun to subside into its normal condition of tranquil torpor'.

When the real war broke out in August 1914 the *Haverfordwest and Milford Haven Telegraph* let in be known that:

Government vessels are stationed near the harbour entrance for the purpose of challenging, and if needs be, searching all incoming craft, and searchlights are played upon them from the forts... Torpedo boats are hovering around the entrance to Milford Haven Docks and practically everything is being challenged.

Trawlers were employed as minesweepers during the war, and trawlers from the east coast and from Belgium moved to Milford Haven, where there is a plaque:

Erected by Steam Trawler Owners and people of Ostend who were resident in this town during the Great War 1914-1919 as a mark of gratitude to the British nation in general and the people of Milford Haven in particular. For the hospitality received here during the period of exile from Belgium.

Milford Haven continued as an important fishing centre in the 1920s, and by this time more herrings were being landed here than anywhere else in England and Wales. In the subsequent

61 Solva.

decade a good deal of the catch was brought into port by vessels from the east coasts of England and Scotland, although Milford Haven itself still had over a hundred trawlers.

During the Second World War, Atlantic convoys assembled in Dale Roads and from 1940 to 1943 twenty-six Dutch trawlers were engaged on minesweeping duties.

On 25 April 1943 two landing craft sank at the entrance to the Haven. Only three of the seventy-five men on board survived, and six more died in rescue attempts. For some months Milford Haven became the assembly point for thousands of soldiers, and for the equipment, supplies and vessels needed for invasion of Normandy.

After the war fishing activity dwindled away, from seventy-eight trawlers in 1953 to only twelve in 1979. During the 1960s Milford Haven became an oil port, with terminals and refineries being built by Esso (in 1960), BP (in 1961), Texaco (in 1964), Gulf (in 1968) and Amoco (in 1973).

The tankers brought an extra hazard to the Haven: in August 1973 the Liberian-registered tanker *Dona Marika* grounded, with 10,000 tons of high-octane fuel. The people of St Ishmael were evacuated and the crew of thirty-eight rescued by Dale coastguards.

The empty oil-tanker *Pointsman* was in Milford Haven Docks for routine repairs on 15 June 1984. There was an explosion at 2.30 p.m. followed, after an interval, by two more. Four people were killed and seventeen injured (ten of these were firefighters).

The large oil tanker *Sea Empress* ran aground at the entrance to the Haven in February 1996, leaking 72,000 tons of crude oil into the sea, polluting over a hundred miles of shoreline, preventing any fishing and killing, it is thought, over 20,000 seabirds.

SOLVA

George Owen described it as 'a portlet for small shipping'. Cargoes such as barley and oats were sent to Bristol. In the late eighteenth century warehouses were built, and some small vessels were based there. Activity in the harbour increased between 1859 and 1861 when a lighthouse was being built on The Smalls, twenty-one miles off the Pembrokeshire coast.

Cornish granite was brought to Solva, where it was handled at a new quay, named Trinity Quay after the Corporation of Trinity House, the builders of the lighthouse. Limestone was a regular import at Solva, where there were ten limekilns.

Steamers called from the 1860s up to the early twentieth century, providing links with Cardigan Bay and Bristol. They included the Aberayron Steam Navigation Co.'s *Prince Cadwgan* (which sank after hitting the rocks at Solva in September 1876) and the *Ianthe* and *Norseman* of the Aberayron Steam Packet Co.

PORTHGAIN

Abereiddi and Porthgain are two creeks lying between St Anne's Head and Strumble Head. In the middle of the nineteenth century Porthgain came to be the busier shipping place, exporting granite and slate.

The United Welsh Slate Co. bought two vessels in 1890: the iron *Maggie Ann* (57) had been launched in 1868. In December 1890 the vessel sank near Abereiddi on a voyage from Porthgain to Southampton with a cargo of roadstone. No lives were lost. *Edith* (89), made of wood and completed in 1878 at Berwick-upon-Tweed, was lost in April 1894 when she caught fire while carrying lime from Llanelli to Aberaeron. The *Marion* (125) was also employed by the company.

Between the years 1902 and 1904 the harbour was improved, to cope with an increased demand for roadstone.

United Stone Firms bought five new steamers in 1909: *Dean Forest, Liscannor, Mountcharles, Multistone* and *Porthgain*, as well as the older *Hopetoun* and *Volana*. Trade continued until the 1930s.

THREE

Cardigan Bay

Five hundred years ago Cardigan Bay had 'no ships, barks or vessels' other than 'certain fisher boats of the burthen of 4 or 5 tons at the most and these maintained by poor fishermen for the only use and exercise of fishing'. A report written at the end of the sixteenth century concluded that this was 'a bad coastline, and on this account every year many of those fishing for herring are lost' (Loomie 1963). In autumn the herring appeared in the Bay, precipitating three months of work for the villages along the coast.

FISHGUARD

There were two distinct shipping places: Goodwick and Lower Fishguard. By the sixteenth century, as well as catching herring, trade was developing with West Wales harbours, the Bristol Channel and Ireland, with occasional longer voyages.

The most famous event in Fishguard's history is the French invasion of 1797. The plan was to send a French fleet to the southern coast of Ireland, with the aim of landing 14,000 men to aid an Irish rising. A smaller expedition was to threaten either Chester (having come ashore on Cardigan Bay) or Bristol, after sailing up the Bristol Channel. The principal invasion of Ireland was called off because of bad weather, but the other force was ordered to carry on, sailing from Brest on 16 February 1797. There were four vessels, all newly built: the frigates *Resistance* and *Vengeance* (each with forty-two guns and a crew of 350), the corvette *Constance* (twenty-four guns) and a fourteen-gun lugger, the *Vauteur*. The soldiers, led by the American William Tate, consisted of a thousand convicts and fifty trained soldiers.

This force appeared off the Pembrokeshire coast, no more than three miles from Fishguard, on the evening of 22 February. Boatloads of men, arms and equipment were brought ashore, and the four vessels of the flotilla sailed away.

As soon as the French were seen attempts were made to assemble the defence forces. During the next day, about 600 men gathered at Fishguard: sailors from Milford Haven, militia, volunteers and yeomanry. That evening Tate offered to discuss his surrender, but was told that negotiation was out of the question. At 2 p.m. on the following day the invaders laid down their arms on Goodwick Sands, before being taken off to prison. The story of Jemima Nicholas, and the red-cloaked women mistaken by the French for soldiers, has often been invoked to explain the rapid collapse of this last invasion of Britain.

Over fifty small vessels were owned at Fishguard in the early nineteenth century, but a directory of 1833 pointed out that at Lower Fishguard the small quay was in a very bad state and as a result vessels now tended to go to Milford Haven. 'Fishguard is daily becoming more impoverished' and trade is now 'very inconsiderable'. Corn and butter were carried to Bristol and Liverpool. Shop goods were imported, as were coal, culm and limestone from Milford

LOWER FISHGUARD HARBOUR

62 Lower Fishguard harbour.

Haven. Some of the bigger vessels were general carriers, loading cargoes at Bristol, Liverpool, Milford Haven and London and taking them to Ireland. A new pier and quay were built at Lower Fishguard between 1860 and 1862.

The new harbour at Goodwick opened on 30 August 1906. Two million tons of rock had been blasted away in order to build four railway platforms and a quay, and there was now a breakwater 2,500ft long.

Fishguard was to be the new packet station, and the Irish ferries' base was moved there from Neyland. The ferry operation was operated by the Fishguard & Rosslare Railway Co. (which was owned by the Great Western Railway and the Great Southern & Western Railway) on routes to Rosslare and Waterford, the service being provided by three new triple-screw steamers, built by John Brown's on the Clyde: *St George*, *St David* and *St Patrick*. *St Andrew* followed two years later. A day and night service (except on Sundays) was operated until the outbreak of war in 1914.

Efforts were made to diversify the trade of the port, particularly by encouraging large ocean-going vessels. The first liner, the Booth Line's *Lanfranc* (6,287), called on 2 April 1908, when the passengers landed by tender and travelled on to London by train. The ship's owners, Alfred Booth & Co., had been founded in 1866 and ran liner services to northern Brazil and up the Amazon. The route just taken by the *Lanfranc* was Brazil-Lisbon-Oporto-Fishguard. Next stop, her home port of Liverpool.

Three weeks later a second Booth Line vessel arrived. The *Antony* (6,446), the Booth Line's largest ship, was met by *Sir Francis Drake*, a new tender built by Cammell Laird at Birkenhead, and a railway train took passengers to London in five hours.

Passengers and mail between London and New York, on the big transatlantic liners, went by rail through Liverpool. Perhaps a quicker and more convenient route would be to use,

63 The dining room of Booth Line's *Lanfranc*, the first ocean liner to land passengers at Fishguard, on 2 April 1908.

say, Southampton, Plymouth, Fishguard or Holyhead? On 20 June 1909 White Star liners, on their way from New York to Liverpool, began calling at Holyhead. The response by their great rivals Cunard, after pressure from the directors of the GWR, was to initiate eastbound calls at Fishguard.

On Tuesday 31 August 1909 *The Times* reported that: 'The Cunard liner *Mauretania*, which left New York on Wednesday morning last, called yesterday afternoon at Fishguard, thereby inaugurating a new and shorter route between New York and London'. Local people had flocked to the coast to watch the arrival of this famous ship, three tenders were made ready, and as the *Mauretania* dropped anchor cheering was heard from the spectators and 'an informal salute' was fired from the coastguard station. As the 240 passengers landed they were presented with sprigs of heather by girls in Welsh costume, before boarding their special train for London. The Cunard company announced that: 'at present all Cunard liners from New York will call at Fishguard.'

The *Mauretania* arrived for a second time on 20 September 1909, after a record passage from New York to Queenstown of four days, thirteen hours and forty-one minutes, at an average speed of 25.61 knots. It was pointed out that: 'The *Mauretania* now holds all the eastward and westward records for highest daily runs, fastest passages and highest average speed per hour.' On this occasion the tenders brought ashore 250 passengers, 1,154 bags of mail and 1,500 packages.

Nine days later the *Campania* anchored at 2.15 a.m., and in December the *Lusitania* arrived.

During the following year, Cunard liners calling at Fishguard landed a total of 14,300 passengers (8,300 'saloon', 4,000 'second cabin', and 2,000 'third class') and 55,825 bags of mail. An announcement was made that next season the Cunard ships from Boston would also be calling.

Above and below: 64 and 65 The *Mauretania*'s first visit to Fishguard.

Above and below: 66 and 67 The *Mauretania*'s first visit to Fishguard.

68 A poster by Odin Rosenvinge. Cunard vessels called at Fishguard from 30 August 1909 until the outbreak of the First World War.

In the years leading up to the First World War calls were made by the Cunarders *Carmania*, *Caronia* and *Lusitania* but the *Mauretania* was always the star attraction. On 22 December 1910 the *Mauretania* anchored at 10.22 p.m. after a crossing of four days, fifteen hours, fifty-seven minutes. It was only twelve days, four hours and thirty-nine minutes since the liner had left Liverpool for New York, and 'for several days past officers of the Cunard Line and the Great Western Railway have been gathering here to complete the extraordinary preparations required to give an extraordinary finish to an extraordinary voyage'. They were accompanied by a number of journalists, one of whom described the scene:

> Four special trains were drawn up in the station, and the mail train was out on the breakwater, while three tenders, with steam up, lay ready to dash out to meet the big ship at the harbour mouth... a special corps of twenty Customs officers drafted from London and other ports were in waiting.

Six hundred passengers were brought ashore, 'although some of them were disappointed to find no sleeping cars in any of the trains'.

During 1911 the *Lusitania* made a dozen appearances at Fishguard, but on three voyages did not come to the harbour; on 6 and 27 March the weather prevented it, and in September the liner went straight on to Liverpool rather than land passengers at 1 a.m. The last call of 1911 was on the morning of 22 December, when 720 people disembarked. The last Cunarder, *Carmania*, arrived from New York on 6 August 1914 – two days after the declaration of war – with a cargo of gold worth £2,500,000.

Ships of the Blue Funnel Line first visited Fishguard in 1910, when voyages were advertised, 'To Australia via Las Palmas and Cape Town. Saloon passages £40 to £50; *Aeneas* (10,000 tons) leaves Glasgow 18 November; Fishguard 19 November. *Ascanias* (10,000 tons) Glasgow 30 December; Fishguard 31 December'. *Aeneas* and *Ascanias* were both new sister ships built for Alfred Holt's Blue

69 The *Aeneas* (Blue Funnel Line) at Fishguard on 19 November 1910. Passengers boarded by tender and half-an-hour later the liner sailed for Cape Town, Adelaide, Melbourne and Sydney.

Funnel Line by Workman Clark & Co. in Belfast. Holt's had up to now been involved in carrying frozen meat and fruit from Australia, and taking passengers on this scale was a new venture. The plan was that the vessels would load freight at Glasgow and embark passengers at Fishguard.

Passengers joining the *Aeneas* left London by special train at 11.28 a.m. on 19 November 1910, arriving at Fishguard harbour at 4.30 p.m. Half an hour later the *Aeneas* sailed on her maiden voyage, scheduled to be in Cape Town by 9 December, Adelaide on 28 December, Melbourne on 1 January 1911 and Sydney on 6 January. After three weeks in port, she would set off from Sydney on the homeward trek.

There had been plans to build deep-water berths for liners at Fishguard, but they were abandoned. The bread-and-butter work of the port remained the ferry service, and in 1930 came a second *St Patrick* and in 1934 a second *St David*, together with *St Andrew*.

During the Second World War the docks were operated by the Ministry of War Transport and the ferries, except *St Patrick*, were requisitioned for war service. On 13 June 1941, on passage from Rosslare to Fishguard, the *St Patrick* was bombed and sunk off Strumble Head. The vessel went down in five minutes, and seventeen crew members, a gunner and twelve passengers died. Elizabeth May Owen, a stewardess, was awarded the George Medal for her bravery in saving passengers trapped on the lower decks.

The hospital ship *St David* was sunk on 24 January 1944 during the Allied landings at Anzio. There were 226 people on board and 130 survived.

After the war the Fishguard to Rosslare ferry started again with the *St Andrew*, and on 1 August 1948 Fishguard, like other railway ports, was taken over by the Docks & Inland Waterways Executive of the British Transport Commission. Today, the ferries and port are operated by Stena Line: a 'Superferry' takes three hours and thirty minutes from Fishguard to Rosslare, and a 'Fastcraft' one hour and twenty minutes.

NEWPORT

During the sixteenth century the Pembrokeshire town of Newport had a busy sea-borne trade, mostly with Bristol. Thomas Phaer described it as 'a barred haven to serve a small ship with a westerly or northerly wind upon a spring tide. The country bare of corn but plenty enough of cattle'. By the eighteenth century slates were a well-established export cargo, and boatbuilding was carried on up to the late nineteenth century.

A quay was built at The Parrog in 1825, although the beach continued to be used for discharging and loading cargoes. An 1830s directory describes a small harbour, the entrance partly obstructed by a sandbank, the main exports being corn, butter and quarried stone. Coal, culm and limestone were imported.

Some of the Davies family, Cardigan shipowners, lived at Newport. The Davies vessels operated from Newport during the nineteenth century included five smacks, three schooners and two snows. By 1880 *Slater's Directory* had to report that 'The trade of Newport was at one time more considerable than it is now', although 'in some seasons the salmon and herring fisheries are profitable; and the bay forms an excellent harbour of refuge from easterly and southerly winds'. Some maritime trade continued at Newport until well after the First World War.

CARDIGAN

Cardigan was to grow into a busy harbour. By the fifteenth century coal and limestone were imported coastally, and trade had developed with Ireland. Cargoes of herrings were sent to Ireland throughout the seventeenth and eighteenth centuries and in return came the casks, nets and salt necessary for the herring trade. The port developed rapidly in the last quarter of the eighteenth century, shipping Cardigan brick, Cilgerran slates and Llechryd tinplate. Some vessels went as far as North America.

Cardigan Shipowners

Patrick Brown (1784-1847)
Brown was a merchant who owned, or part-owned, a number of vessels. He was sole owner of a brig and five sloops, built between 1799 and 1830.

Thomas Edwards
In business as a ship's chandler and as a merchant, owning a riverside warehouse in Cardigan. Vessels were acquired to bring in his cargoes: the snow *Betsey* (115), built by William Jones at Cardigan in 1841, three schooners and two sloops.

The Stevens Family of Llechryd
Operated a number of vessels as part of their slate business including two smacks; *Union* (26), built at Cowes in 1813 and *Ruby* (21), built at Cardigan in 1839; the schooner *Stevens* (57), built at Cardigan in 1856 and the brigantine *Elizabeth Stevens* (197), built at Ipswich in 1871. They were part-owners of the Aberystwyth-built schooner *Alberta* (90) and the Cardigan-built ketch *James* (25).

The Davies Family
Played a large part in the commerce of Cardigan for much of the nineteenth century. They handled a variety of goods, including timber, wine and slate, and they participated in the emigration trade, with vessels leaving from Cardigan, Caernarfon and Liverpool. Much of the following account of the family's trading activities is based on Jenkins 1984.

Vessels managed by the Davies family included: *Alliance* (126), a brig, built at Bideford in 1796. *Alliance* made regular voyages to Sweden for timber, and was then employed trading to Ireland. On passage from Cork to Limerick with the *Barbadoes* on 14 August 1813, both vessels were captured and set on fire by the American brig *Argus* (twenty guns), commanded by Lieutenant William Henry Allen. The *Argus* had attacked twenty vessels in the previous three

Left: 70 Sailing vessels 'taking the ground' in Cardigan harbour during the nineteenth century.

Opposite: 71 The schooner *Ezel* being repaired at Cardigan during the nineteenth century.

weeks, and was being sought by HMS *Pelican* (eighteen guns), which saw the blazing vessels and gave chase; after an engagement of forty-five minutes, the American vessel surrendered, having had ten men killed and thirteen wounded. Lieutenant Allen died four days later at Mill Prison, Plymouth, and was buried with full naval ceremonial.

Eliza (147) a brig, built in 1800. Captured by the French, but released in 1814.

Albion (166) a snow, 72ft by 23ft, built at Milford Haven by William Roberts in 1815. In 1817 and 1818 she made voyages carrying slate and emigrants to New York and Quebec, and in the latter year carried migrants from Caernarfon to Perth Amboy, New Jersey. The voyage took forty-five days.

On 11 January 1819 the *Albion* conveyed migrants from Cardigan to St John's, New Brunswick. In that year over 7,000 immigrants landed at St John's, about 70 per cent of them from Ireland. The New Brunswick authorities were anxious to attract new residents, and laid out settlements: most of the Welsh went to Cardigan, in York County. Later in the year the *Albion* sank off Wexford, with the loss of all on board (Thomas 1986).

Active (142) a brig, built at Cardigan, sailed regularly to Canada in the 1820s, carrying emigrants and bringing timber back.

Triton (260) a snow, built in 1836 at Sunderland, was another of the Davies vessels to make frequent transatlantic voyages. She was lost in 1864.

Some of Thomas Davies's vessels were built in North America, including: *Mary Anne Newell* (251) a brig, built at Prince Edward Island which was bought in 1857; *Goliath*, built at Quebec, bought in 1863 and wrecked in the St Lawrence; *Black Swan* (297) was a barque, built in Nova Scotia and purchased in 1867, and *Anne Wilson* (415), a barque, bought in 1871, was built at Pembroke, Massachusetts.

An analysis of Davies vessels shows that of the total of thirty-seven, fourteen were brigs (tonnage 90-251) and eleven sloops (tonnage 33-59). Twelve of their vessels were built at Cardigan and others built locally came from New Quay, Llangranog, Newport, Llanddewi Aberarth, St Dogmaels, Derwenlas and Milford Haven. The rest (apart fom the North American vessels) were built in Chepstow, the north-west of England, North Devon, Sunderland and one, a brig, was built way up the River Severn at Bridgnorth in 1849.

There were eighty-five Cardigan vessels on *Clayton's Register* in 1865: fifty-one schooners, fifteen smacks, twelve brigs and seven brigantines. The oldest vessel listed was the schooner *John* (70) built in 1777 and owned by T. Davies, master mariner of Liverpool. The largest vessels were brigs: *Triton* (260), built in 1836 and owned by David Davies; *Ocean Queen* (180), of 1854 and *Princess Royal* (180), built in 1851, both of which were owned by John Thomas (shipbroker of Cardiff).

Sixteen of the vessels had managing owners living in Cardigan town: eight schooners, seven brigs and one brigantine. Five schooners and two smacks were owned at St Dogmael's.

The Cardigan Steam Navigation Co.
Their first vessel was the *Tivyside* (108), 100ft x 18ft, built on the Clyde in 1869 for Thomas Davies & Co. In 1885 the vessel was acquired by the Cardigan Steam Navigation Co., but the business was wound up in 1888, and *Tivyside* was sold to Thomas Jenkins of Carmarthen.

The Cardigan Commercial Steam Packet Co.
The shareholders were nearly all local people, mostly shopkeepers. Their first vessel, in 1877, was the *Seaflower* (150) built at Port Glasgow, which ran to Cardiff and Bristol. On passage from Cardiff to Cardigan it collided with and sank the brigantine *Charlotte*, but the sailing vessel's crew were rescued. The *Seaflower* was held to be at fault, and the company had to pay damages, which forced it into liquidation, with the steamer being acquired by William James, ironmonger.

A new company, with the same name, was registered in May 1879 and the *Seaflower* was bought back. It was sold in 1902 and for the next two years the services to the Bristol Channel were operated by the *Mayflower*, until the company ceased trading in 1904.

The Bristol & Cardigan Trading Co.
Founded in 1909 by four Cardigan business men, to re-start a steamer service to Bristol with the *Saint Tudwal* (198), built in 1895 at Wallsend for Thomas Lewis, Bangor. The vessel was sold in October 1915. Nineteenth-century imports to Cardigan included coal, culm and limestone

– there were seven limekilns on the south bank of the Teifi at Cardigan – and timber from Norway and North America. Exports included slate, oak bark and agricultural produce. The volume of traffic through the port was affected by the arrival of the railway in 1880 and by the problems of navigation caused by the bar and the silting estuary. By 1914 there was almost no trade through the harbour, but in 1926 James Davies and John Lloyd Richards bought the steamer *Teifi* (244), built in 1912 at Selby as *Aegir*. The vessel traded from Cardigan to Bristol and Liverpool with cement, coal and fertilisers, until November 1930, when it struck a wreck near Cardiff and sank; all the crew were saved.

British Isles Coasters Ltd
The company was registered in April 1936 and owned Lloyd's Wharf at Cardigan and ran regular services to Liverpool with *Drumlogh* (311). The other vessels were increasingly employed away from their home port: *Eskburn* (472), *Orchis* (483) and *Enid Mary* (582). Later acquisitions were *Suir* (58), *South Coaster* (513), *East Coaster* (469) and the diesel-engined *West Coaster*, bought new in 1938. The company's last two vessels were sold in 1946.

ABERPORTH

Samuel Lewis's *A Topographical Dictionary of Wales* (1833) noted that there were 485 inhabitants at Aberporth and that it was 'pleasantly situated on the shore of Cardigan Bay, St George's Channel, and is a small cove near the mouth of the river Howny, forming a commodious, though small port'.

Opposite: 72 *Tivyside*, launched on the Clyde in 1869 for Thomas Davies & Co. of Cardigan. In 1885 the owners were the Cardigan Steam Navigation Co. Three years later the steamer was sold to Thomas Jenkins of Carmarthen. The photograph shows the *Tivyside* in the final years of the nineteenth century after lengthening and when owned by John Bacon, of Liverpool.

Right: 73 The steamer *Garth Loch* at Cardigan, during the nineteenth century.

The main shipping place, a sloping beach, was the sheltered Traeth y Llongau, next to which limekilns and warehouses were built. Until the First World War the herring fishery was the principal means of livelihood for the inhabitants of Aberporth.

NEW QUAY

New Quay grew to be a significant centre of ship and boatbuilding. Campbell-Jones (1975) lists over 200 vessels built at New Quay or on the beaches of Cei Bach and Traethgwyn during the period 1779-1878. Of the first thirty-four, thirty-one were sloops. Most of the vessels were employed in the coastal trade, but some of the bigger ones undertook longer voyages. The *Friendship* (92), for example, was built in 1817 for carrying Canadian timber, sometimes taking emigrants on the outward journey. The first barque to be built at New Quay, *Prince Llewelyn* (286), was launched in 1858 and traded to South America for twenty-five years, until wrecked off St Thomas in 1883. The schooner *Gleaner* (97), of 1825, transported salted cod from Newfoundland to the Mediterranean, and carried salt and wine back to Canada, but was lost off Ireland in 1870. Launched in 1835, the schooner *Sylph* (135) was taken to Archangel by a crew of four, to collect a cargo of hemp.

Eliza Mary (43) was a typical coastal trader of the time. Built in 1840, a record of the voyages for the years 1848 to 1859 showed that the vessel went once from Liverpool to Rouen, but more usual journeys involved carrying limestone and coal from Welsh harbours. Other employments included Newport-Liverpool (rails), Liverpool-Chepstow (wheat), Barrow-Cardiff (iron ore) and Swansea-Aberystwyth (coal).

74 The brig *Hetty Ellen* was built by James Bevans at Llanelli in 1860. Owned at New Quay, the brig carried the prefabricated parts of a river steamer to David Livingstone. The illustration shows the components of the steamer being transferred to Livingstone's steamer *Pioneer* at the mouth of the Zambezi in January 1862.

The *Hetty Ellen* (189), built by James Bevans at Llanelli in 1860, was owned at New Quay. The brig was employed on a variety of routes such as, in 1860, an eighteen-day voyage to Gibraltar with a cargo of coal; 1861 Hamburg to Liverpool, then Liverpool to Gibraltar (which took twenty-three days). Later in 1861 came an unusual assignment: to carry the prefabricated parts of a river steamer, *Lady Nyassa*, to David Livingstone's Zambezi expedition, which had set off three years before. Captain David Davies took *Hetty Ellen* to the Clyde, where the components of the *Lady Nyassa* were taken on board. Built by Tod and McGregor the river steamer was, when assembled, 115ft long by 14ft wide, and driven by twin screws. Mrs Livingstone was collected at Cape Town, and everything was delivered to Dr Livingstone at the mouth of the Zambezi on 30 January 1862. Captain Davies then took his vessel to Mauritius to collect a cargo of sugar.

The last voyage of the *Hetty Ellen* was in 1881. The brig left Prince Edward Island for Britain on 2 November, under the command of David Evans, and was last seen in distress in the middle of the North Atlantic, with sails ripped to pieces by a gale, yards carried away, and no rudder.

Clayton lists over a hundred vessels belonging to New Quay in 1865, sixty of them schooners. The managing owners were spread across a variety of occupations; one active owner was the draper Evan Timothy, who operated five schooners. During the 1860s some dozen Prince Edward Island ships were owned at New Quay; usually trading to Newfoundland, most of them were too large to be able visit New Quay.

On 27 August 1885 the brig *Resolven* (143) sailed from Harbour Grace, Newfoundland for Snug Harbour, Labrador to collect a cargo. Two days later the vessel was found abandoned at Trinity Bay, Newfoundland. The sails were set, and a fire burned in the galley stove. There was no one on board, and a boat was missing.

75 Aberaeron harbour in about 1860, painted by Dr J. Albert Evans.

ABERAERON

As with the other fishing villages of Cardigan Bay, cargoes of salt were imported from Ireland and Chester. Salted herrings were sent off by sea or, inland, by packhorse. In 1807 the Revd Alban Thomas Jones-Gwynne was authorised by the Aberaeron Harbour Act to make improvements. The work was completed by 1811, resulting in increased traffic through Aberaeron, especially in trade with Bristol. *Clayton's Register* of 1865 listed over thirty sailing vessels (two-thirds of them schooners) belonging to Aberaeron. J.N. Evans, merchant, was managing owner of six, four of which were schooners.

The Aberayron Steam Navigation Co.
Formed by local shopkeepers in September 1863, taking delivery of the first vessel, *Prince Cadwgan*, in July 1864. This newly built coaster called at harbours in Cardigan Bay, West Wales and the Bristol Channel until 30 September 1876 when, leaving Solva in the dark, she hit the rocks and sank. The company ceased trading.

Aberayron Steam Packet Co.
From 1877 the Aberayron Steam Packet Co. operated *Ianthe* (139), built in 1873. It was a vessel which carried large numbers of pigs from Aberaeron during its career. After April 1894 *Norseman* (194) – built at Paisley in 1883 – was also in service. In December 1895 *Ianthe* was sold, but *Norseman* continued its voyages to Bristol, calling at Fishguard and Solva. The steamer was sold in 1916 and the company was wound up.

The Liverpool & Cardigan Bay Steamship Co.
Formed in July 1900, taking over the *Telephone* from the Aberdovey & Barmouth Steamship Co. The vessel's usual routes were a return trip of Liverpool-Aberaeron-New Quay and in the following week Liverpool-Cardigan-Fishguard. The *Telephone* was joined in 1902 by the small steamer *Margaret* (33), built in 1899. In April 1905 both vessels were transferred to the Liverpool and Menai Straits Shipping Co.

The railway arrived at Aberaeron in 1911, beginning the decline of the coastal trade. Calls by small steamers began again in the 1920s, when regular cargoes of flour were brought from Cardiff and cargoes of stone came in from Porthgain. From the middle of the 1930s the harbour was used only by fishing and pleasure craft.

ABERYSTWYTH

Thomas Phaer observed of sixteenth-century Aberystwyth that it had 'a barred haven of no value... All this is very bare country and mountains. At Aberystwyth is a castle of the King's, decayed, but the hall remains yet, covered in lead'.

Lewis Morris wrote in 1748 that: 'Aberystwyth Bar is often choked up, so the smallest vessel can neither pass nor repass; and all the vessels in the harbour are obliged to lie there, till a land flood from the rivers Rheidol and Ystwyth sets them at liberty'. Lewis Morris also noted that 'this is one of the greatest fisheries of Wales' and that:

> In this bay are employed, during the herring-fishery, fifty-nine small sloops out of Aberystwyth; and between Aberdovey, Borth, Aberaeron and New Quay, thirty-eight more; in all ninety-seven. The fishery generally begins in September, sometimes sooner, and holds three or four months. The rest of the year they are employed in the coast and Irish trade, with some few larger sloops they have to carry lead ore, timber, and bark.

The Cambrian Traveller's Guide (1808) stated:

> The Harbour is deep enough at high water to receive the larger kind of Welsh coasting vessels, but a bar of shifting sand at its mouth is a great annoyance. The town exports lead and calamine, procured from the mines near Plinlimmon, oak bark, and some manufactured goods, such as webs, flannels, and stockings; which are sent chiefly to Bristol and Liverpool. It imports cast iron goods from Coalbrookdale, shipped at Bristol; lime, groceries, and porter, from Bristol; grain from Liverpool and Ireland; and coals from the southern counties of Wales. A considerable fishery is also carried on here. Cod, mackerel, herrings, etc., are sent as far as Shrewsbury.

Samuel Lewis's *A Topographical History of Wales* (1833) stated:

> The harbour is small, and the approach to it is obstructed in some degree by a bar, which prevents the entrance of ships of any considerable burden, except at high water of spring tides. An attempt was made some time since to remedy this inconvenience, by constructing a pier on one of the ridges of rock which stretch from the shore into the bay; but it was designed upon too small a scale to be efficient... The trade is considerable, and, if not obstructed by the insufficiency of the port, would doubtless be much more extensive; it consists principally in the importation of timber, hemp, tar, tallow, wine, spirits and grocery. The number of ships belonging to the port is one hundred and twenty-two, averaging a burden of fifty-three tons each; and during the summer months nearly one hundred vessels are employed in the coasting trade. The herring fishery was formerly carried on to a great extent, and herrings and cod are still taken occasionally.

Lead had been mined in mid-Wales for centuries, but more intensive lead mining developed in the early 1830s, leading to an increase in the number of vessels arriving at Aberystwyth to load ore. Improvements were made to the harbour, including a breakwater over 200 yards long and diversion of the river channels, so that larger vessels could now get in and out. By this time timber was being brought from the Baltic and Canada for local shipbuilding yards, and coal, grain and limestone were also imported. Exports were lead ore (most of which went to the Dee), bark, herrings and wool.

An impression of the sea-borne trade of Aberystwyth may be gained from the 'Shipping Intelligence' published regularly in the *Caernarvon and Denbigh Herald*:

11 January 1840: Arrived at Aberystwyth: *Mary* from Aberdovey (slates), *Equity* from Bristol (general cargo), *Countess of Lisburne* from Liverpool (general cargo), *Mary Anne* from Dublin, *Nancy* from Cardiff (coals), *Sisters* fom Caernarfon (slates).
    Sailed: *Earl of Lisburne* for Bristol (lead ore), *Mary* for Aberdyfi, *Bee* for Neath.
26 December 1840: Arrived: *Anne and Mary* from Bideford (earthenware), *Diligence* from Porthmadog (slates), *Speculation*, *Osprey*, *Eagle* from Liverpool (sundries), *Nelly* from Caernarfon (slates), *Margaret* from Chester (coals and sundries).
    Sailed, all carrying lead ore: *Jane and Elizabeth*, *New Margaretta* for Chester, *Anne and Mary*, *Defiance*, *Mary* for Flint.

Large numbers of people emigrated from the Welsh countryside in the 1840s, with many groups sailing from Liverpool. In May 1840 a Liverpool steam tugboat was sent to Aberystwyth to collect nearly 200 men, women and children who were to travel to New York on the *Orpheus*, on their way to Ohio. The sloop *Pilot* took fifty emigrants to Liverpool on 5 April 1842.

Aberystwyth shipowners soon realised that vessels being sent to collect timber from North America might well (instead of sailing in ballast on the westward voyage) earn revenue by taking emigrants. Thus in April 1842 the brigs *Credo* and *Rhydol* left Aberystwyth for Quebec with over 200 people. In May 1847 the new barque *Anne Jenkins* sailed from Aberystwyth with more than eighty passengers. In the following month the barque *Tamerlaine* left for Quebec with 462 emigrants 'mainly from the eastern parts of Cardiganshire, from the neighbourhood of Lledrod, Mynedd-bach and Taihirion-y-rhos'. The *Credo* and the *Elizabeth* left for Quebec in April 1849 with fifty-eight passengers, mostly 'small farmers from the neighbourhood of Llangaetho and Yspytty Ystwyth'.

Aberystwyth Shipbuilding

From 1830 to the 1870s over a hundred vessels were built at Aberystwyth. One of the most prolific builders was John Evans whose vessels included: *Countess of Lisburne* (30) built in 1836, a smack 40ft by 13ft; 1839's *Earl of Lisburne* (52), a schooner; the 1840 snow, *Truant* (141); the 1846 schooners *Anne* and *Two Brothers*; the 1847 barque *Anne Jenkins* and the schooner *Arcturus* as well as 1850's *Eigen* (135), a barquentine. Other builders at this period were Owen Jones; William and Richard Roberts; Lewis and John Roderick.

Aberystwyth Shipowners

Shares in local vessels were, generally, taken by local people. The shareholders in the schooner *Earl of Lisburne*, as at 9 March 1839, are typical: Thomas Evans (master mariner) owned 18/64 shares; John Evans (shipbuilder) 8/64; Thomas Jones, the younger (timber merchant) 4/64; Thomas Williams (esquire) 8/64; Evan Jones (wine merchant) 8/64; Thomas Jones (rope maker) 4/64; Lewis Jones (grocer) 4/64; John Jones (cabinet maker) 4/64; William Evans (master mariner) 4/64 and Evan Bennett (victualler) 2/64.

Clayton's Register of 1865 lists about 150 vessels (70 per cent of them schooners) owned by people from Aberystwyth and the villages around. *Clayton's Register* shows four steamers at Aberystwyth: *Prince Cadwgan* of the Aberayron Steam Navigation Co.; *Queen of the Isles* (146) built in 1860, managing owner W.S. Crealock, Aberystwyth; *Express* (108) built in 1857 for the Aberystwyth & Cardigan Bay Steam Packet Co. and *Aberllefeni Quarry Maid* (59) built in 1859, whose managing owner was H. Price of Aberystwyth. This was a wooden steamship built by Roger Lewis at Aberdyfi, with engines installed by De Winton's at Caernarfon. The principal shareholder was Robert Davies Jones of Aberystwyth. The vessel's builder, Roger Lewis, also took shares and was the vessel's master. After 1865 the *Quarry Maid* became the *Orcadia* of Kirkwall.

In the summer of 1834 the *Vale of Clwyd* (Cardigan Bay Steam Navigation Co.) ran a steamer service from Pwllheli. Ten years later the local paper noted that tourists had begun arriving at Aberystwyth for the 'season' and the coaches were packed. In addition, the *Caernarvon and Denbigh Herald* of 29 June 1844 stated: 'The first rate steamer *Eclipse* pours in its weekly contribution of visitors'. From 1842 until the late 1860s the *Plynlimon* provided a steamer service on the Liverpool-Aberystwyth-Bristol route.

Cambrian Steam Packet Co. 1856-71

The company ran vessels to Bristol, Liverpool and London. On 5 May 1856, *The Times* carried an advertisement inviting tenders for the supply of 'an iron screw and paddle steamer to be 120ft by 20ft, depth of water 8ft when loaded. Able to do 10 knots, and to carry sixteen cabin passengers. Tenders with plans to be addressed to Mr George Green, Manager of the Cambrian Steam Packet Co., Aberystwyth'.

By the 1860s vessels employed included *Aberystwyth*, *Queen of the Isles*, *Young England* and *Genova*. In January 1863 details of services were advertised: the steamer *Aberystwyth* – under Captain William Hoskins – 'or some other suitable vessel' was operating from Liverpool's Great Landing Stage-Bull Bay Pier-Aberaeron-New Quay-Aberdyfi-Tywyn-Barmouth. The steamer *Cricket* – under Captain Charles Duck – provided a service via Aberystwyth-New Quay-Aberaeron-Aberdyfi-Tywyn-Barmouth, 'with Liverpool and London goods'. The advertisements boasted of 'good accomodation for passengers, and a stewardess on board'. (Lloyd 1994)

Aberystwyth & Cardigan Bay Steam Packet Co.

The seven original shareholders, in 1863, were all from Aberystwyth: the harbour master, a master mariner, a carrier, two grocers and two merchants. The company owned the *Express* (108), built in 1857, and the newly built *Henry E. Taylor* (118) was acquired in June 1868. Its usual voyage was from Aberystwyth to Liverpool with lead ore, returning with shop goods and supplies for the lead mines. The business was wound up in 1885.

Aberystwyth & Aberdovey Steam Packet Co.

The *Henry E. Taylor* was transferred to the new company in 1885, but sold a year later when the new *Countess of Lisburne* (135) was bought. The voyages to Liverpool continued, with calls at other Cardigan Bay harbours. The *Countess* was replaced in 1908 by the steel *Grosvenor* (218), which went to Liverpool once a week. The vessel was sold in 1916.

John Mathias

Born in 1837, Mathias was a grocer. By 1869 he was part-owner of the schooner *Miss Evans*, built at Derwenlas, and in 1875 was managing owner of the brig *Solway*. He acquired the steamship *Glanrheidol* (1005) in 1883 and placed it in a single-ship company. Too large to work out of Aberystwyth, she was employed as a tramp from Cardiff. John Mathias set up further single-ship companies, attracting not only local investors, but local men to sail in them. Other entrepreneurs followed, and by the eve of the First World War 'there were three major shipping companies of Cardiganshire origins operating out of Cardiff' (Jenkins 1987).

From the 1860s there was a drop in the demand for Cardiganshire lead ore, with competition from the cheaper ore of Colorado and New South Wales. In spite of a period of revival in the first decade of the twentieth century, by the First World War many lead mines had closed. In the 1920s and 1930s only half-a-dozen vessels a year entered the Aberystwyth harbour.

Ystwyth Shipping Ltd

Set up by local master mariner Roger Meredith in 1987 with *Sara M.* (211), built in Germany in 1950. The vessel carried steel from Sweden to Aberystwyth, and traded to the Baltic and the east of England. *Sara M.* was sold in 1988.

76 The *Grosvenor* was operated by the Aberystwyth & Aberdovey Steam Packet Co. from October 1908 until June 1916. The illustration shows the steamer when owned by Robert Gardner of Lancaster.

ABERDYFI

A survey in the 1560s reported that:

> Dyfi, being a haven and having no habitation, but only three houses whereunto there is no resort, save only in the time of herring fishing, at which time of fishing there is a wonderful great resort of fishers assembled from all places within this realm, with ships, boats and vessels.

Increasing numbers of boats visited the haven during the seventeenth century to load lead ore, bark and timber, and there were imports of coal, culm and grain.

The river was navigable as far as the wharf at Derwenlas, near Machynlleth, where there were two quays; Cei Ellis and Cei Ward. In the early nineteenth century Machynlleth was described as 'the port of Montgomeryshire, the Dovey being navigable to within a mile-and-a-half of the town'. Pigot's *North Wales Directory* of 1835 notes that: 'The staple manufacture of Machynlleth is flannel, which provides employment for many hands. Slate quarries and lead mines, in the vicinity, are worked extensively, and their produce conveyed to Derwenlas, where it is shipped to various distant parts.'

Vessels arriving at Aberdyfi in January 1840 included: *County of Cork* from Liverpool (coal and rye); *Sincerely* from Newport (coal); *Three Sisters* from London (rye); *Lady Harriet* from Mostyn (coal); *Patriot* from Porthmadog (ballast) and *Anne and Betty* from Liverpool (general cargo). One vessel departed: the *Credo* left for the Dee, with a cargo of slates and brick.

In September 1850 the incoming ships were: *Hirondelle* from Newry; *Catharine* from Nolton; *Eleanor and Betsy* from The Skerries; *Diligence* from Red Wharf; *Countess of Lisburne*,

Brothers, *Margaret and Mary* from Newport; *Laura and Elizabeth* from The Skerries; *Britannic* from Newport; *Mermaid* from Chester; *Francis* from Drogheda and *Amity* from Drogheda. Departures noted were: *Eagle*, *Robust*, *Unity* for the Bristol Channel; *Mariner* for Glasgow; *Hope* for Flint. The *Best* and the *Catharine* left the harbour 'seeking' (looking for a cargo).

Aberdyfi Shipbuilding

Vessels were constructed at any convenient point on the banks of the river, with some concentration at Derwenlas. Lloyd (1996) lists over fifty vessels built on the Dyfi from 1760 to 1840, they were all sloops, apart from three brigs, a brigantine and a snow.

Between 1840 and 1880, although some vessels were built at Derwenlas, the centre of activity moved to Aberdyfi where, over forty years, sixty vessels were built. They were mostly schooners, but there was one steamship.

Some of the local builders were:

John Jones

Most of his vessels were built at Aberdyfi, but some at Llwyn Bwtri, near Pennal and at Derwenlas. During the 1850s and early 1860s he built about thirty schooners, sixteen of them between 1857 and 1864. One witness described a vessel built by Mr Jones thus:

> He did not accurately measure the width of the ship, so in hauling her out of the yard on to the sand, they had to take a corner off the house. Then, after getting her out of the yard, she stuck across the road, and they had to get all the horses and men of Aberdovey to haul her on to the sands. (Lloyd 1996)

Roger Lewis

Vessels built included the 1848 *Dovey Packet* (24), a smack; the 1853 *Koh-i-Noor* (54), a smack; in 1857 two schooners; in 1858 the steamer *Aberllefeni Quarrymaid* was built. *Napoleon* (54) was built in 1866 and Roger Lewis retained a 48/64 share in this schooner, becoming sole owner in 1869.

Thomas Richards

For over two decades from around 1860 to 1880 he built fourteen vessels: a smack, a brig and twelve schooners. Shipbuilding at Aberdyfi came to an end at the beginning of the 1880s.

Some Aberdyfi Vessels

Amity (80): A sloop, launched in 1802 at Derwenlas. The business of 1806 was a typical year, when the vessel's itinerary was: Liverpool-Cork-Kinsale-Rye-London-Milford Haven-Dublin-Waterford-Dublin-Chester-Dublin-Milford Haven-Waterford.

Prosperity (32): A sloop launched by John Lewis in May 1842. Dimensions: 33ft by 14ft. Its shareholders were: Thomas Lloyd (master), Aberdyfi, 8/64; John Parry, Dolyddbychan, Llanwrin, Montgomeryshire, 14/64; Thomas Jones the younger (timber merchant), Aberystwyth, 8/64; Richard Evans (timber merchant), Dinas Mawddwy, 14/64; William Jones (gent), Aberdyfi, 4/64; David Davies (clothier), Aberdyfi, 4/64; David Lloyd (blacksmith), Aberdyfi, 4/64; Thomas Edwards and Richard Griffiths, Treddol, 8/64. The vessel's routine voyage was to carry lead ore to Flint, returning with coal.

Aberllefeni Quarry Maid (58): A steamship launched at Aberdyfi by Roger Lewis in October 1858. Engines and machinery were installed at Thomas and De Winton's Union Foundry at Caernarfon. The maiden voyage to London began from Aberdyfi on 23 April 1859. The *Quarry Maid* was operated by a crew of master plus six men, usually between Aberdyfi and Liverpool, in one six-month period thirteen return voyages were made. In 1865 the *Quarry Maid* was sold to the Orkney Steam Navigation Co. and renamed *Orcadia*.

Martha and Harriet (139): A schooner, built by Thomas Richards, launched 2 January 1874. Dimensions: 95ft by 23ft. Shareholders: Richard Williams (master), Aberdyfi, 20/64; Thomas Richards (shipbuilder), Aberdyfi, 4/64; David Jones (gent), Machynlleth, 12/64; Griffith Griffiths (farmer), Tyhir, 8/64; William Lloyd (draper), Ruthin, 12/64; William Theodore Rowlands, Ruthin 8/64.

In the first year the *Martha and Harriet*'s voyages were: Aberdyfi-Santander-Workington-Rotterdam-Nantes-Santander-Workington-Rotterdam-Middlesbrough-Newport. Lost off Cape Sable, Nova Scotia on 28 October 1882 but all on board were saved.

Glenalvon (456): Built at Parrsboro, Nova Scotia in 1856. A barque bought by J.H. Jones and G.W. Griffiths, timber merchants of Machynlleth, in April 1864. Employed in the timber trade, typical voyages were: 1864 Aberdyfi-Quebec; 1868 Liverpool-St Johns, New Brunswick-Aberdyfi; July 1869 left Pembroke Dock-Miramichi, New Brunswick and arrived at Aberdyfi in October 1869. Later voyages were to Swedish and American ports. The *Cambrian News* of 7 January 1881 reported:

> Aberdovey. Shipping. The barque *Glenalvon* (Captain Richards), notwithstanding very adverse weather, arrived here safely on Sunday. She brings timber for her owners, Messrs. Jones and Griffiths, timber merchants. Her arrival is a great boon to the place, as the shipping trade has been exceptionally bad here for some time.

The vessel was destroyed by fire at Oran on 29 December 1881, when loaded with iron ore and esparto grass. (Lloyd 1996, Vol. II, contains details of many Aberdyfi vessels. Much of the above has been derived from this work.)

The port's most active period came in the years from 1850 to 1870. A tramway was opened from Corris to Machynlleth in 1859, and the Cambrian Railway line was soon to open; the local newspaper reported on 18 January 1862 that at the Cambrian Railways' wharf at Aberdyfi 'a very large accumulation of plant has already been made. About a thousand tons of rails are already in transit, from Ebbw Vale Iron Works'. The railway opened on 2 October 1863, and two months later the last cargo of lead ore to be transported on the river left Derwenlas.

In 1865 Cambrian Railways took over the management of Aberdyfi harbour and in 1866 the Talyllyn narrow-gauge railway was opened to carry slates from quarries to Tywyn. They were then brought by the coastal railway to Aberdyfi, as described in *Slater's Directory*:

> The depot of the Abergynolwyn Slate Co. is situated at Towyn, Large quantities of slates are brought here from the quarries of Abergynolwyn, about six miles distant, by the Talyllyn miniature railway... These slates are reloaded at the depot, and conveyed by the Cambrian Railway to different parts of the kingdom, and to Aberdovey, where large quantities are shipped to various parts.

A jetty, wharf and pier were built at Aberdyfi between 1880-82.

Waterford & Aberdovey Steamship Co.

The *Liverpool* (246) began a service in April 1887 carrying cattle and pigs from Waterford to Aberdyfi. The vessel made the voyage four times in that month, with the livestock being sent on by rail to the English Midlands. There are records of the *Magnetic*, with similar cargoes, making more than a dozen trips from Waterford between November 1887 and March 1888, but the whole venture petered out, as did maritime activity at Aberdyfi, although there was a brief revival of herring fishing:

77 Aberdyfi harbour.

> During the last week some heavy catches of herrings have been made by the local fishing boats. On Friday morning the *Cetawayo*, Captain D. Williams, came in with ninety-four maize of herrings, being the heaviest catch by an Aberdovey boat in the recollection of the oldest fisherman. The fish were so thick that seven of the nets had to be left in the sea. The *Albatross*, Capt. Evan Lewis, was also loaded to the brim. (*Cambrian News* 26 October 1888)

There was virtually no commercial traffic at Aberdyfi quay after the 1920s.

BARMOUTH

Very few people lived at Barmouth. By the middle of the sixteenth century there were only four dwellings, with two small ferry boats. As at other Cardigan Bay settlements fishing for herrings was an important seasonal activity, but the reefs off Barmouth were always a hazard for shipping. The most celebrated wreckage is that discovered in 1978, probably the remains of two ships. One of them sank early in the eighteenth century, with a cargo of large marble blocks. In addition, over twenty cannon have been found at the site and a bronze bell, bearing the date 1677 and with an inscription of words from Psalm 117: *Laudate Dominum omnes gentes* – 'Praise the Lord all nations'.

By 1729 four Barmouth vessels appear in the records: *Hopewell* (master Griffith Evans), *Speedwell* (David Griffith), *Elizabeth and Margaret* (Robert Roberts) and *Catherine* (John Roberts). With a crew of three or four, the vessels sailed locally and, occasionally, as far as Llanelli for coal.

For nearly a quarter of a century, from around 1770, there was an active trade in woollen products from the area around Dolgellau. It was a cottage industry, but with water-powered fulling mills, producing 'webs'– very long pieces of coarse white cloth. The grip of the Shrewsbury drapers had at last been prised open, and cloth began to be routed elsewhere, particularly through Barmouth. A canal was dug from Dolgellau to the Mawddach so that river boats could take webs down to Barmouth, on the way to Chester, Liverpool and London. Thomas Pennant noted in 1773 that 'many of the webs are sold to Spain, and from thence to South America'.

78 Barmouth. On the right is a brig, on the shore are a sloop and a vessel under construction.

Sailing vessels were built on the banks of the Mawddach as far up as Storehouse, close to Dolgellau. In the twenty years from 1770 nearly 150 vessels (i.e. an average of seven or eight a year) were constructed: 80 per cent of these were sloops of 12 to 95 tons. (Lloyd 1993)

Lloyd lists 119 vessels built from 1791 to 1823, of which seventy-one were brigs or snows. Shipbuilders included Ellis Evans, John Evans, Evan Morris and Griffith Thomas. After the ending of the wars with France in 1815 fewer vessels were built annually, perhaps one or two a year, now mostly smacks and schooners.

In 1802 the newly formed Barmouth Harbour Trust tried, in vain, to revive the wool trade by improving the harbour. It was made deeper and a new quay was built. In the years 1845 to 1848 about three or four vessels a week arrived, loading cargoes of bark, timber and ore. By the 1860s trade had diminished still further.

The reef of Sarn Badrig (St Patrick's Causeway) continued to claim vessels, as it had always done. In December 1854 the newly built Baltimore barque *Pride of the Sea*, carrying cotton from New Orleans to Liverpool, ran straight onto the reef. Another vessel – the *Culloden*, making for Liverpool with a cargo of timber – had been following the American clipper and also ran into Sarn Badrig. The crew abandoned their ship, and managed to reach the safety of Barmouth.

The men of *Pride of the Sea* were also ashore, their boats having been towed in by the little river steamer *Victoria*. Crossing the Bar the boats had capsized, but the men were rescued by the lifeboat. Later that night Captain Harp returned to the *Pride of the Sea* to collect food and blankets for his men. Next morning the vessel was seen to be on fire. *The Times* (18 December 1854) described the scene:

The splendid bark *Pride of the Sea* reported as burnt to the water's edge, in Cardigan Bay, 7 miles off Barmouth, presented an awfully grand spectacle. The fire raged, without intermission, for 30 hours, and illuminated the country for miles. The range of the Merionethshire Hills was brilliantly lighted up and presented a wild and beautiful picture. The gale blew so strongly all the time that no boats could put out, and the vessel was one entire sheet of flame fore and aft. The cargo, worth £30,000, is said to be fully insured, partly at Lloyds and partly in Liverpool. Fragments of burnt timbers now strew the coast, and about 120 bales, besides a large quantity of loose cotton, have been washed ashore... Strong suspicions were entertained that the vessel had been set on fire by the crew, but the master, who is the sole owner, said it was his belief that the catastrophe was occasioned by spontaneous combustion. He supposed that the cotton had been mouldering for some time, and that a draught was occasioned by the removal of a hatch, to get at some new rigging to be taken on shore, and that the admission of the air caused the flames to burst forth.

Another big American ship came to grief in December 1859. The *Britannia* (from Savannah to Liverpool, with cotton) was driven aground off Llanddwywe. *The North Wales Chronicle* – on 7 January 1860 – praised the Barmouth lifeboat crew:

Fourteen persons, including the captain's wife, were taken from the vessel; five men preferred remaining on board, who came on shore next morning in one of the ship's boats. The lifeboat filled very often, but soon discharged the water. One of the ship's crew had a very narrow escape of being crushed to pieces between the ship and the boat. He fell in trying to get on board the lifeboat and, but for the activity of some of the boat's crew he must have been killed. It will probably be remembered that this valuable lifeboat was instrumental, a few weeks ago, in saving from destruction another large American ship, the *Troy*, with her valuable cargo of cotton.

Ten days after the wreck of the *Britannia* four Barmouth men drowned when their boat overturned near the stranded vessel. It was reported on 21 January that: 'Innumerable carts are daily employed carting the cotton of the *Britannia* to Barmouth to be then trans-shipped to Liverpool. Many poor and destitute individuals have been earning good wages from their work'.

As a commercial seaport, most activity ended in the early 1880s but some Barmouth residents were still involved in the ownership of vessels, particularly Dr Joseph Herbert Lister, who gave up medicine for shipowning. Guided by his associate Captain Edward Lewis Jones he operated *Billow Crest* (116), *Consul Kaestner* (146), *Jenny Jones* (152), *Cariad* (152) and *Royal Lister* (140). The trading patterns of these vessels, bought between 1890 and 1902, were basically those of the schooners from Porthmadog and Pwllheli, including carrying slates to the Baltic and sailing to the Mediterranean and Newfoundland. In 1903/04 the voyages of Lister's schooner *Jenny Jones* were: Porthmadog-Stettin-Swansea-L'Orient-Cadiz-St John's, Newfoundland-Harbour Grace-Glasgow-Villefranche-Leghorn-Porthmadog. The *Jenny Jones* was sold in 1904 when Dr Lister retired from shipowning. It was lost nine years later off Morocco.

Aberdovey & Barmouth Steamship Co.

Founded in May 1892, the impetus was provided by the wholesale grocers David Jones & Co. of Liverpool, from whose offices the company was managed. The first vessel was the iron-screw steamer *Telephone* (162) built in 1878 by H.M. McIntyre & Co. of Paisley.

The *Telephone* was sold in July 1900 to the Liverpool & Cardigan Bay Steamship Co., to be replaced by another Paisley-built vessel, the steel screw *Dora* (295). The *Dora* was employed on a regular run, leaving Liverpool every Friday for Porthdinllaen, Barmouth and Aberdyfi. Her last call at Barmouth was in October 1915. In November 1916 the *Dora* was commandeered for the Liverpool-Belfast route. On 1 May 1917, the steamer was intercepted by a German submarine and sunk by gunfire, after the crew had been allowed to take to their boat. The Aberdovey and Barmouth Steamship Co. was wound up on 29 June 1918.

On 21 June 1912 well over a thousand people crowded into the Pavilion to honour a Barmouth mariner. He was presented with a 'beautiful gold watch and chain, value £35, suitably inscribed, together with an album containing the names and addresses of the subscribers'. The inscription read 'Presented to Harold G. Lowe, 5th Officer of RMS *Titanic*, by his friends in Barmouth and elsewhere, in appreciation of his gallant services at the foundering of the *Titanic*, 15 April 1912'.

79 Porthmadog harbour and slate quay.

Harold Lowe was in charge of one of the *Titanic*'s boats, launched as the liner was sinking after striking an iceberg. At times he threatened to shoot men who were attempting to overload the boats and he steered his boat back towards the liner, looking for survivors. With boats roped together, he and his charges were picked up next morning by the *Carpathia*. One of those who survived presented him with 'a very high-power binocular', a telescope and a sextant. Each was inscribed: 'To Harold Godfrey Lowe, 5th Officer RMS *Titanic* – The real hero of the *Titanic* – with deepest gratitude from Mrs Henry B. Harris of New York'.

PORTHMADOG

William Alexander Madocks built an embankment in 1800 – earth covered by turf – which enclosed a thousand acres of Traeth Mawr (the 'big beach'). Madocks was authorised by an Act of 1821 to build a new harbour – Port Madoc – which opened in 1825. Up to this time slates had been carried on pack animals or wagons to the River Dwyryd, then by river boat to Ynys Cyngar – a small island in the estuary of the Glaslyn, about a mile-and-a-half from the new harbour – for trans-shipment into sea-going vessels. Slate traffic on the river began to diminish from 1836, when the 23in.-gauge Ffestiniog Railway opened. The slates were transported in horse-drawn wagons until the introduction of steam locomotives in 1863. Most of the slate was sent to destinations in Britain and Ireland, but there was a devastating fire at Hamburg in 1842, which destroyed large areas of the city. Rebuilding led to a big demand for slates, and there were also increasing sales to Australia, France and the United States.

Clayton's Register of 1865 shows that there were seventy vessels belonging to Porthmadog, of which 70 per cent were schooners. The vast majority of managing owners were master mariners, but there were others, including two widows, shipbuilders, a coal merchant, a timber

80 The schooner *M. Lloyd Morris* at Bristol. Built at Porthmadog in 1899 by David Jones, the
managing owner was David Morris of Caernarfon.

81 The end of a Porthmadog schooner. The *Miss Morris* was built in 1896 by David Jones. On a
voyage in ballast from Genoa to Malaga the schooner was intercepted on 11 April 1917 by the German
submarine U-35. The crew were allowed to row away and the vessel was sunk by explosive charges.
The illustration is a still from the German film *Der Mägische Gürtel* of 1917.

merchant, an ironmonger and the harbour master. The *Register* lists ten managing owners called Jones. All were master mariners, and all but two were operating schooners: David Jones operated *Elizabeth Thomas* (103) and *Margaret* (90); Evan Jones, the *Gazelle* (85) and *Glaslyn* (105); Humphrey Jones, the *Isabella* (110); John Jones operated *Betty* (89) and *Nathaniel* (106); Peter Jones, the *Ebenezer* (105); Peter Jones Jnr operated *Margaret and Mary* (61); Richard Jones, the *Agnes* (93); Thomas Jones operated *Louisa* (59) and *Mary and Jane* (96); Elizeus Jones ran the smack *Star* (42), and Morris Jones the brigantine *Edward Windus* (156).

From the 1870s increasing use was made of the rail network to carry slate. This, and the vagaries of the slate market, led to a search for new sources of income for Porthmadog shipowners. Many vessels were being chartered for the Newfoundland fish trade in the 1860s and early 1870s, and Porthmadog vessels began to take part. From the end of the 1870s Porthmadog vessels sailed regularly to Newfoundland, loading cargo either at St John's or in Labrador. The busiest time for this trade was from 1890 up to the First World War, and vessels were built at Porthmadog specifically for the purpose.

Before the embankment was erected, vessels had been constructed at suitable places around Traeth Mawr and Traeth Bach, but later building took place at Porthmadog. The Porthmadog three-masted schooners, built in the two decades before the First World War, have been much admired: 'They were lovely ships. The grace of their hulls and the balance of their tall spars gave them a beauty, both under way and lying at anchor, not exceeded in all the history of sailing vessels.' (Greenhill 1988)

Porthmadog Shipbuilders

Ebenezer Roberts built the 1892 *Consul Kaestner* (146) and *Jenny Jones* (152) in 1893; David Jones built fifteen vessels between 1891 and 1909; David Williams launched seventeen between 1891 and 1913, including *Gestiana* (124), the last vessel to be built at Porthmadog. It was lost on the coast of Newfoundland in October 1913, on its maiden voyage.

An example of the work done by these Porthmadog schooners is described in Greenhill (1995): in March 1906 the *M.A. James* (with a cargo of slate) left Porthmadog for the Elbe, then went to Gröningen, Morlaix and Cadiz, before setting off from there on a four-week voyage to St John's, Newfoundland. A cargo of salt fish was loaded in Labrador. The rest of the voyage was Gibraltar-Leghorn (arrived 4 November)-Genoa-Newport-Porthmadog, where the *M.A. James* arrived, after nearly a year away, on 24 February 1907.

Carnarvonshire & Merionethshire Steamship Co.

The five-year-old steamer *Rebecca* (203) was bought in 1864 by a syndicate of businessmen from Porthmadog and Blaenau Ffestiniog. Managed by David W. Davies & Co. of Liverpool, the vessel ran once a week between Liverpool, Pwllheli and Porthmadog. The steamer was sold in 1896 and replaced by another, *Rebecca* (332). A small vessel, *Celt* (58) – a Clyde puffer, built in 1894 – was acquired in 1906. The vessels were sold during the First World War and the company, after an existence of fifty years, was wound up.

PWLLHELI

In the sixteenth century Pwllheli consisted of about three-dozen dwellings. Some of the vessels recorded there in the 1580s and early 1600s were:

Date	Name	Route	Cargo
28 March 1587	*Matthew* (10) of Milford Haven	Tenby-Pwllheli	Coal and wine.
7 July 1587	*Grace* of Wexford	Tenby-Pwllheli	Coal, malt and salt.
1602 and 1603	*Ellin* (8) of Pwllheli	Beaumaris-Barmouth	Barley malt.

March 1603	*Phillip* (7) of Pwllheli	Beaumaris-Aberystwyth	Salt from France).
22 June 1603	*Trinity* (10) of Milford Haven	Pwllheli-Pembroke	Hides.
22 July 1603	*Mary Fortune* of Wexford	Milford Haven-Pwllheli	Malt and wheat.

By the eighteenth century: 'In this bay are large beds of oysters, and plenty of other fish, and some years they have a good herring fishery here; but the chief commodities of the place are butter and cheese.' (Lewis Morris in 1748).

There was more shipping at Pwllheli in the early nineteenth century, with arrivals and departures being reported in the *North Wales Gazette*:

> February 1812: Arrivals – *Two Friends* from Liverpool for Falmouth; *Unity* from Southampton for Beaumaris. Departures – *Hope* for Liverpool (oatmeal, butter and cheese); *Britannia* for Barmouth (malt, wheat and barley); *Favourite* for Conwy (salt herrings and bacon); *Maria* for Conwy (salt herrings); *Indefatigable*; *Morning Star* for Dublin (salt herrings).
>
> October 1813: Arrivals – *Sisters*; *Speedwell*; *Indefatigable*; *Hope*; *Mary*; *William and Mary* all from Liverpool (coal and sundries); *Mermaid* from Chester (coal and sundries); *Diligence* from Aberystwyth; *Bee* from Barmouth (timber); *Fancy*; *Speedwell*; *Mary* from Llanelli (culm). Departures - *Catherine* for Newnham; *Catherine* for Dublin (slates); *Promptness* for Liverpool (butter and bacon). *Favourite* for Liverpool (paving stones); *Minerva* for Caernarfon (wheat, oatmeal and furniture).

From the 1830s to the 1860s imports consisted of coal, culm, general goods, limestone and timber from North America. Exports were bacon, butter, cheese, granite setts and paving stones.

Pwllheli Shipowners

Cardigan Bay Steam Navigation Co.

Their service from Pwllheli to Aberystwyth began with the *Vale of Clwyd* in June 1834, when a local newspaper reported that 'nearly all the population of the town and the country for several miles around' turned out to watch the steamer's arrival at Aberystwyth. 'The reports of the guns, the music, and the acclamations of the assembled thousands, rendered the scene one of unmingled gratification, and proved how much and how sincerely the undertaking was approved on that side of the Bay.' The *Vale of Clwyd* called at Barmouth and Aberdyfi on both the outward trip and the return. Later on, Aberaeron and New Quay were added. At the end of the summer the vessel was put on the Portdinllaen-Liverpool run, carrying pigs as well as passengers.

Clayton's Register of 1865 lists twenty-nine vessels belonging to Pwllheli, registered at the Port of Caernarfon, of which over 65 per cent were schooners. There were three smacks, a sloop, three brigantines, a barque and a ship.

Some of the managing owners were: Robert Griffith (merchant), operated a schooner and a sloop; John Jones (master mariner), operated a barque, two schooners and a smack; Owen Owens (coal merchant), had two schooners; Evan Prichard (master mariner), owned a schooner; John Prichard (shipbuilder), was the operator of four schooners; Robert Prichard (shipbuilder), had two schooners and Hugh Pugh (banker) operated a ship, a barque, a schooner and a smack. Hugh Pugh, from Dolgellau, became manager of the Pwllheli branch of the North & South Wales Bank. He founded his own bank in 1847 and was later head of the Caernarfon-based banking firm of Pugh, Jones & Co.

Pwllheli Shipbuilding

The brothers John Arthur Prichard and Richard Arthur Prichard had adjoining yards. The *John Arthur Prichard*, a brig, was launched in 1851. Ten years later the vessel arrived at Rio de

Janiero after a rough passage lasting three months. Members of the crew were unhappy, and wanted to leave the ship. Meeting the British consul they alleged 'that spirits have been too freely used in the cabin'. The master had to sign a document declaring that he would 'have all spirituous liquors removed from the cabin and placed below hatches and... that the same shall not be touched during the voyage from this port to Guatemala'. After a stormy voyage around Cape Horn it was found that fever had broken out, and the vessel was quarantined at Guayaqil. There was more drunkenness and discontent.

On the return voyage members of the crew went ashore in Guatamala. A week later the master recorded that: 'All that had been ashore, first having lost their appetite, not able to swallow anything but water.' Two men died, but the rest managed to reach the Falklands, where the sick were discharged. The *John Arthur Prichard* was wrecked in March 1863. (Eames 1973)

John Roberts

Launched the schooner *Joseph Brindley* in April 1849. The *Caernarvon & Denbigh Herald* described it as 'a fine low-built schooner... This vessel being of a very different style to the vessels generally built at this port, has been particularly admired'. By 1853 John Roberts had moved to Holyhead.

William Jones

Jones, a druggist, entered the shipbuilding business by setting up a new yard at Alltfawr. His vessels included: in June 1835 *Ann*, a brig intended for the North American timber trade. The local newspaper gave an account of the launch day:

> In the afternoon the workmen about 50 in number dined in the Guildhall; a select number of Mr. Jones's particular friends were entertained at his own house; and Mrs. Jones had also a party of her friends to tea in the evening, the day was spent in the most pleasant manner.

Three-and-a-half years later the vessel was wrecked. Commanded by Evan Williams, the brig had loaded timber at Quebec and set off for home. On 1 December 1838, in the North Atlantic, the *Ann* was struck by a 'violent sea' which washed overboard three crew members as well as both masts, the boats and superstructure. For five days the seven survivors were marooned on a battered hulk, unable to steer, and with no food or fresh water, until rescued and taken to New York by the *Republic*. Three months later a large floating object was sighted off St Anne's Head, Pembrokeshire. This turned out to be the remains of the *Ann*, from which some of the cargo was salvaged.

The 1837 *Cyrus* (132), a brig, was initially registered at Milford Haven, but by 1851 it was on the Beaumaris register. The owners were: Richard Richards (master mariner, Bangor) 36/64; William Jones (shipbuilder, Pwllheli) 8/64; Thomas Eyre (druggist, Liverpool) 8/64. William Davies (master mariner, Milford Haven) 4/64; John Thomas (mariner, Nefyn) 4/64; Robert Thomas (mariner, Nefyn) 2/64 and Evan Thomas (mariner, Nefyn) 2/64.

In April 1838 the schooner *Salem* was launched: 'She glided into her element in the most beautiful style amidst a numerous concourse of spectators, who manifested their approbation by rending the air with their acclamations.'

The 1844 *Mary Winch* (252), a brig 96ft by 24ft, was named after the wife of Henry Winch, a partner in Peek Bros & Winch, tea brokers of Liverpool. William Jones frequently retained shares in the vessels he built, particularly in partnership with merchants from Liverpool. This was a general trend for the rest of the nineteenth and early twentieth centuries, and a number of Welsh people, particularly from North Wales, owned or invested in large Liverpool vessels. In addition, hundreds of Welshmen served on Liverpool ships.

The 1845 *Elizabeth Grainge* (351) was ship-rigged. William Jones took 16/64 shares. The other two shareholders were both Liverpool merchants, John Stockdale 32/64 and John James Melhuish 16/64.

The 1846 *Henry Winch* (474) was also ship-rigged. This vessel had been laid down in November 1844. It was reported that William Jones 'has two others of the same size now building'. These two, and the *Henry Winch*, 'belong to Messrs Melhuish & Co. of Liverpool and Mr Jones, the builder'. In fact William Jones had 16/64 shares in the *Henry Winch* and John James Melhuish (Liverpool merchant) 18/64. The rest were held by three Liverpool merchants (including Henry Winch) and a man from Cornwall. The maiden voyage was to Hong Kong.

In 1846 *Charles Brownell* (421), a barque, was built for the China trade; in 1847 *Mary Ann Folliott* (408) was a ship-rigged vessel, and owned by James Melhuish. 1848 saw *William Carey* (658) ship-rigged and launched on 15 September, having been built for the China trade. The *Carnarvon & Denbigh Herald*, on 23 September 1848, wrote that it was 'The largest mercantile vessel supposed ever to have been built in Wales'. The owners were William Jones 56/64 and Griffith Jones 8/64. The vessel was named after William Carey (1761-1834) the eighteenth-century Baptist missionary, who spent over forty years in India. William Jones gave free passages to India to missionaries and their families. After the death of William Jones the vessel was acquired by Hugh Pugh. Intended voyages in 1863 were to: 'New Zealand and the west coast of America and the West Indies, and to the British Provinces of North America'. The *William Carey* was wrecked at Bass Harbour on 4 November 1864.

Robert Evans
Another builder who retained a financial interest in his vessels. He owned 48/64 shares in the barque *Gwen Evans*, launched on 26 April 1842 and named after his wife. The *North Wales Herald* stated that the vessel 'will sail for New York with all possible dispatch' and it arrived there on 15 August, with forty-one migrants.

On 17 August 1848 the *Ancient Briton* was launched, built by Robert Evans and Richard Arthur Prichard. A full-rigged ship, the shareholders were Robert Evans 36/64, Richard Arthur Prichard 24/64 and John Roberts (sailmaker of Liverpool) 4/64. The *Ancient Briton* arrived at Swansea from South Australia (with a cargo of copper ore) in December 1849 and *The Cambrian* was impressed:

> She is a thoroughly Welsh craft and pure bred. She is a full-rigged ship built at Pwllheli, and manned entirely by members of the principality. The little port of Pwllheli may now boast of having ships built at and belonging to the place as frequenting the five divisions of the globe.

The *Ancient Briton* was lost two years later off Sumatra.

John and Owen Edwards
In partnership with Hugh Pugh, launched the barque *Margaret Pugh* (693) in 1862, the largest vessel built at Pwllheli. The builders took 20/64 shares each, and Hugh Pugh 24/64. In November 1864 he bought out the others to become sole owner. The *Margaret Pugh* was sold to Bordeaux in June 1878.

In 1880 *Slater's Directory* informed its readers that Pwllheli harbour 'is safe, but, from the shallowness of the water is only fit for coasting vessels of from 200 to 300 tons burden'. An inner harbour was built in 1903, but the outer harbour was silting up.

FOUR

North Wales

STEAMER SERVICES

The Menai Straits and the North Wales resorts were to prove popular destinations for passenger steamers and several companies, often short-lived, were involved. By the 1820s four vessels (two of them belonging to the Liverpool & North Wales Steam Packet Co.) were providing a daily service, usually on the Liverpool-Hoylake-Orme's Head-Beaumaris-Bangor route. A voyage from Liverpool to Bangor was likely to take five to seven hours, depending on the weather. On 12 September 1827 the Revd Joseph Romilly and his brother Cuthbert boarded the L. & N.W. Steam Packet Co.'s *Ormrod* at Liverpool:

> Economical, went in steerage, which was half price. There found four gentleman-like young Irish men and three Welsh women with their nasty black men's hats. The English ladies with us and two of the Welsh vastly sick. The English ladies were no ladies at all, but ugly ill-mannered women, saving one who was prettyish and had a pretty brother. All obliged to cram into the hot stinking fore cabin with Cuthbert, properly called the Black Hole – suffered with heat; people sick right and left.

By 1830 the Liverpool & North Wales Steam Packet Co. had been taken over by the St George Steam Packet Co., operating *Prince Llewelyn*, *St David*, *Ormrod*, *Satellite* and *Snowdon*. Thirteen years later the St George Co. reliquished its services to the City of Dublin Steam Packet Co., which introduced the *Erin-go-Bragh*, the first iron paddle steamer on the North Wales routes. In 1881 the Dublin company handed over its North Wales routes to the Liverpool, Llandudno & Welsh Coast Steamboat Co.

At around the same time, the Liverpool & North Wales Steamship Co. was formed. Three of the well-known steamers owned by this company were *Snowdon*, *La Marguerite* and *St Tudno*.

Snowdon (338), was built in 1892 by Laird Bros for the Snowdon Passenger Steamship Co. The company, and the paddle steamer, were taken over by the L. & N.W. Steam Packet Co. in 1899. After running between Liverpool, Llandudno, Beaumaris and Menai Bridge, the vessel was requisitioned in 1915 as a minesweeper, based at Dover and Harwich, returning to civilian duties in April 1919. The steamer continued in service until 1931.

La Marguerite (1,554), was built by Fairfield's, and bought by the company in 1904. The vessel, much larger than *Snowdon*, was intended to carry 2,000 passengers on a new daily return service between Tilbury and Boulogne, calling at Margate. The inaugural voyage was on 23 June 1894 with *La Marguerite* arriving at the French port to cheering crowds, bands playing and a civic reception. From 1904 the steamer was employed on the Liverpool to North Wales coast service, until requisitioned as a transport in the First World War. After the war the steamer spent a year with the Isle of Man Steam Packet Co., before returning to Liverpool in May 1920.

82 The two bays at Nefyn.

La Marguerite's last voyage came in 1925 – at Menai Bridge there were flags, rockets, gunfire and crowds; at Llandudno thousands thronged the pier, promenade and beach, cheering and singing 'Auld Lang Syne'. The steamer was broken up by Thomas Ward at Briton Ferry.

  St Tudno (2,326) – the third of that name – was launched for the company in February 1926 and licensed to carry 2,493 passengers. The vessel spent the Second World War as a depot ship for minesweepers and then resumed its peacetime sailings from Liverpool to Menai Bridge, until the service was withdrawn in 1962.

NEFYN AND PORTHDINLLAEN

Porthdinllaen has a natural harbour and was a base for herring fishing. A few local vessels, and details of cargo, appear in surviving records: in 1620 the *Matthew* (8) and the *Mary* (20) took herrings to Chester. The *Speedwell* of Porthdinllaen brought a general cargo from Chester in 1623, including cloth, hops, pepper and tobacco pipes. The vessels at this time, and in the eighteenth century, were mostly sloops, seasonally employed in fishing. Lewis Morris noted that in the middle years of the eighteenth century at Nefyn and Porthdinllaen, 'There were near five thousand barrels of salt herrings disposed of here besides the country's consumption'.

  One or two sloops were built each year with, occasionally, something larger such as *Maria* (95), a brigantine launched in 1786 and still sailing in the middle years of the nineteenth century. Most vessels were engaged in the coastwise trade, but the larger ships might be seen at South American ports, or in the Caribbean.

  Suggestions arose, to resurface from time to time, to establish a packet station for the Irish mail and in 1806 an Act of Parliament authorised the new Porthdinllaen Harbour Co. to issue shares 'for erecting a pier and other works for the improvement of the harbour of Porthdinllaen in Carnarvon Bay'. At this time the number of vessels putting into Porthdinllaen in one year (1804) was 656, with a minimum of nine in January and a maximum of 122 in June. It is not known how many came for trade and how many for refuge.

83 Porthdinllaen.

There were to be various proposals, discussions, claims and counter-claims concerning the merits of Porthdinllaen as a packet station but, in the end, the prize went to Holyhead; this was confirmed in 1810, when improvements to Holyhead harbour were authorised and a Select Committee recommended that a bridge should be built across the Menai Straits. Edmund Hyde Hall wrote of his visit to Porthdinllaen in 1810: 'There were half-a-dozen carpenters at work laying down the flooring of an inn, what was to be the new pier was already a sort of ruin, and the beneficial effects of the old one were said to have been materially abridged.'

Although denied the Irish mail trade, Porthdinllaen continued as a trading harbour. Two hundred vessels discharged cargo in 1863, but there were only twenty-eight recorded outward cargoes in that year. The number taking refuge from wind and weather was far higher: 645. (Elis-Williams 1984)

Clayton's Register of 1865 lists eighty-six vessels owned at Edern, Nefyn and Porthdinllaen; over 70 per cent of them were schooners. The oldest, more than half-a-century old, was the brig *Alert* (101), built in 1812 and now owned by William Ellis, master mariner, of Nefyn. The largest vessels were four brigs: *Simon* (224), built in 1860 and owned by Owen Griffiths, master mariner; *Volunteer* (207) of 1861, and run by John Thomas, master mariner; *Linus* (189) built in 1857 and owned by Daniel Evans, master mariner and *Glanavon* (184) built in 1862 and owned by J.B. Jarrett, shipbuilder. In addition to Mr Jarrett there were other shipbuilders with shipowning interests: Hugh Hughes of Penrhos owned *Jane Hughes* (99), a schooner built in 1861; Robert Thomas with *Surprize* (126), a schooner built in 1839. William Roberts managed the largest fleet, a smack and five schooners.

A typical local two-masted schooner was the *Eleanor and Jane* – 67ft long by 21ft by 11ft deep – built at Porthdinllaen in 1856 and named after the mother and the wife of John Griffiths. The initial shareholders were: John Griffiths (56/64) and William Griffiths (his father), Sydney Evans (his widowed sister) and David Rice Hughes (sailmaker). A voyage of 1867 was typical: 26 September left Porthmadog, 10 October arrived London. 20 October left London, 12 November arrived Bristol. 22 November left Bristol, 23 November arrived Cardiff. 10 December left Cardiff, 20 December arrived Dublin.

84 Shipbuilding at Nefyn in 1880.

The Aberdovey & Barmouth Steamship Co.'s steamers made regular calls at Porthdinllaen, where a warehouse was built and freight brought ashore by lighter until the jetty was lengthened and vessels could berth alongside. In the twentieth century vessels continued to call, often bringing coal, which small vessels discharged into carts on the beach and larger ones into lighters or on to a platform from which loads were taken ashore by an aerial ropeway.

CAERNARFON

The Segontium Roman fort was founded in AD 77 to protect the coast from sea-raiders, to secure the Menai Straits and to control the local people. Over a thousand years later Caernarfon Castle was built for much the same reasons. As at other locations in Wales an English town, intended to develop as a market place, was 'planted' alongside the castle. The castle itself was built on the shore of the estuary, with a ready-made shipping place and, later, a stone quay. Building materials came by sea, including timber from Liverpool, Rhuddlan and Conwy.

By the early seventeenth century there were over a hundred households at Caernarfon and a few local vessels began to appear in the records. For example:

25 October 1602. The *Jesus* (20) of Caernarfon, master Jerman Hill, took a cargo from Beaumaris to Bristol on behalf of the merchant Robert Williams of Caernarfon: French wines, butter, cheese, beef, leather, calfskins and wool.

4 November 1602. The *Jesus*, master Jerman Hill, merchant Robert Williams. To Bristol: butter, cheese and wool.

15 February 1603. The *Mary* (20) of Caernarfon, master Rees ap Richard, merchant Thomas Williams of Pwllheli. To Bristol: butter and cheese.

22 March 1603. The *Mary*, master Rees ap Richard, carried a cargo from Bristol to Caernarfon, merchant: Nicholas Brogins of Bristol: sack, Gascony wine, iron, alum, figs, hops, pepper, aniseed, tobacco, sugar, sack and Malaga wine.

85 Caernarfon Castle and quay in the early twentieth century.

6 September 1603. The *Mary*, master Rees ap Richard, merchant Nicholas Brogins. Arrived at Caernarfon from Bristol with butter, cheese, cloth, leather and wool.

An Act of 1793 set up a new Harbour Trust for the purpose of 'enlarging, deepening, cleansing, improving, and regulating the harbour of Carnarvon'. Forty years later Samuel Lewis described Caernarfon in his *Topographical Dictionary of Wales* (1833):

> The port… carries on an extensive coasting trade with Liverpool, Bristol and Dublin: the principal exports are slates, of which about 30,000 tons are annually shipped from this place, and copper-ore; and the principal imports are timber from the American colonies, and coal and other commodities from the neighbouring coasts: the coal is deposited on wharfs for the supply of the town and adjacent country.

Lewis went on to note that a breakwater had been built at Llanddwyn Point, seven miles to the north-west, and that 'a patent slip is now being constructed in the harbour, to facilitate the repairing of vessels' and 'a railroad has been formed from the town to the slate quarries in the vale of Nantlle, extending for nine miles into the parishes of Llanllynvi and Llandwrog, and the slates and copper ore are conveyed in wagons, and deposited on wharfs built on the banks of the river Seiont'.

The slate trade from Caernarfon was largely coastwise, with return cargoes of coal from Preston and the shipping places on the Dee and Mersey: an advertisement in the *Caernarvon & Denbigh Herald* on the last day of 1831 informed readers that the sloop *Trafalgar* had just arrived with a cargo of 'the best Orrell coals, obtained from the celebrated strata near Wigan'.

The longest-lasting timber business at Caernarfon was that of Humphrey Owen (later Humphrey Owen & Sons) which was in existence from the 1830s to the 1930s, during

86 The slate quay and harbour at Caernarfon.

which time they added shipowning to their timber trading. Starting off at Turkey Shore they had moved by 1850, via the Patent Slip, to the Bank Quay. Thomas and De Winton's timber business operated from the Slate Quay. Caernarfon timber merchants, like those elsewhere, became shipowners, acquiring vessels from North America, including the brig *Belle Isle* (built in 1825 at New Brunswick), the ship *Royal William* (1831, Montreal) and the barques *Hindoo* (1830, Nova Scotia), *Lady Mary* (1838, New Brunswick), *Alan Keir* (1836, New Brunswick), *Beta* (1853, Prince Edward Island), *Volant* (1853, Quebec) and *Henrietta* (1865, Quebec). Emigrants were carried to North America, although the majority sailed from Liverpool. The *Caernarvon & Denbigh Herald* of 24 April 1841 reported that several families (sixty men, women and children) had left Llanbedr in Merionethshire, to travel to Liverpool and then on to New York: 'The families above referred to passed through Carnarvon on the morning of Thursday last, and embarked on the *Vale of Clwyd*, steamer, for Liverpool.'

Some sailed from Welsh ports: The *Caernarvon & Denbigh Herald* of 3 April 1850 reported:

> Departure of the *Higginson* and *Hindoo*. These fine vessels, the property of Messrs H. Owen & Son, of this port, sailed for the United States on Tuesday last. The *Higginson* left the river in the evening with 141 Welsh emigrants on board, the majority of whom were from Merionethshire, and the county of Anglesey. A parting cheer echoed by the numerous passengers who thronged the decks as she slowly glided from her moorings, was given by the townsfolk who had congregated on the pier head. Her place of destination is New York. The *Hindoo* was bound with a ballast of slates for Boston, and had but a few passengers on board.

The *Hindoo* arrived at Boston on 15 May, and the *Higginson* (with its 141 passengers) reached New York on 18 May.

Clayton's Register of 1865 lists sixty-three vessels (65 per cent of them schooners) with managing owners resident in Caernarfon town. The two largest ships, both built in 1853, were owned by Thomas & De Winton (ironfounders): the barques *Beta* (502) built at New London, Prince Edward Island, and *Volant* (459), built in Quebec. They also owned the schooner *Heroine* (87). J.T. Jones managed the barque *Culdee* (364), and John Evans (master mariner) the brig *Hannah* (205). *Pioneer* (190), a brig, was owned by the draper Thomas Hobley. (He invested in several other vessels, including the *Princess of Wales* (844), built for him at Neyland by James Warlow.)

Almost half of the vessels listed were managed by master mariners and often they – or a family member – sailed as master of their ship. Other owners included: John Thomas, shipbuilder, owned the schooners *Arethusa* (71), *Frances Anne* (99), *George Dundas* (75) and the smack *Menai Packet* (44). The *George Dundas* had been launched in 1861 at Wheatly River, Prince Edward Island. Another shipbuilder, Thomas Williams, had two vessels listed in the register, the schooner *Aurore* (42) and the sloop *Jane* (41), which was over fifty years old.

Several local businessmen operated one or two vessels; drapers, flour and corn merchants, a fishmonger, an accountant, a banker, a spirit dealer and a coal merchant. Humphrey Owen and his sons John, Thomas and William were iron and timber merchants, brass and iron founders, shipowners and quarry owners. Several of their vessels were registered at Liverpool, but those at Caernarfon included *Higginson*, *Hindoo* and *Royal William*.

Late in 1871 John Owen's ship *Ireland* was on its way from Rangoon to Liverpool with a cargo of cotton and rice. After being hit by a storm in the Western Approaches the *Ireland* lost a mast and the hold was filling with water. Ten of the crew were rescued by the *Altair*, of Prince Edward Island, and taken to Cardiff. The Cork vessel *Cormorant* landed the rest of the crew at Newport, Monmouthshire. On 6 January 1872 the *Ireland* was sighted in Cardigan Bay, drifting towards Sarn Badrig; the steamer *Rebecca* managed to get a line on board, and began a tow to St Tudwal's Road (off Abersoch), where a steam tug took over for the journey to Liverpool.

Caernarfon Shipbuilders

During the nineteenth century perhaps two vessels a year were launched at Caernarfon. Roughly until 1820 they were mostly sloops, but from the 1840s schooners predominated. Half the vessels built by Thomas Williams were schooners: his first vessel was launched in 1821 and his last, the schooner *Clare*, in 1868.

William Jones

Constructed seven schooners and three smacks, building the later craft on the Slate Quay. When the schooner *Unicorn* was launched, in August 1840, it was estimated that well over 3,000 people watched. Seventy-two years later the *Unicorn* was to be lost in the Pacific. William Jones prepared to launch another schooner in 1847, the *Prince Edward* (60). The *Caernarvon & Denbigh Herald* of 19 June described the events:

> All things being ready at nine o'clock, the bridles were loosened, and as our worthy Mayor washed the majestic bow, by striking it with a bottle of wine, she glided stately into the briny element. She is ornamented with a figurehead of the Prince, bearing a sceptre in his hand. She has the appearance of a fast-sailing craft.

Proceedings continued with dinner at the Fleur-de-lis for some friends of the owner and 'all the hands employed upon the vessel'. As was customary at Caernarfon *englynion* were spoken in praise of the new vessel.

Just over a year later the *Arethusa* (80) was named by Llewelyn Turner 'throwing a bottle of wine plump on her stern'. The dinner and *englynion* were at the Royal Oak. The vessel was destined to come to grief on Caernarfon Bar in March 1876.

Owen Barlow

Rented the Patent Slip for some years and built: 1846's *Industry* (20), a smack; the 1856 *Catherine Williams*, owned by William Williams, flour merchant of Palace Street, with his brother Robert as master; the 1858 schooner *Aneurin* (82); the 1860 *Prince Llewelyn* (111), a schooner; in 1862 *Mary Jenkins* (91) was launched from the Patent Slip, owner David Jenkins, with his son John as master; the 1865 *Ann and Jane* (71), launched fully rigged and three smacks: the 1864 *Ann and Charlotte* (25); the 1870 *Letty Ann* (28) and *Virtue* (16) of 1874. In the 1861 census, Owen Barlow is shown as employing ten men and four boys.

Richard Price
Apart from his other vessels, he launched Caernarfon's only locally built barque, the *Princess Royal*, on 17 July 1852. Built on the Slate Quay, the vessel was sold to Liverpool owners by the end of the year.

Richard Edwards
Built five vessels over the quarter-of-a-century from 1846: three schooners, one smack and one cutter.

The Liverpool, Carnarvon & Menai Straits Steam Ship Co.
Founded in December 1873 in Liverpool, the directors were David Richards, shipowner and broker, W.S. Caine, iron merchant, and Jeffrey Parry De Winton. In 1874 they bought the four-year-old *King Ja Ja* (203). The *Caernarvon & Denbigh Herald* of 4 April 1885 carried an advertisement for the vessel's services:

> Liverpool, Carnarvon & Menai Straits Steamship Co.; the quickest and cheapest goods transit between Liverpool and North Wales. The steamer *King Ja Ja* leaves the West Side, Trafalgar Dock, Liverpool, every Wednesday, with goods for Beaumaris, Carnarvon, and Bangor. Every Saturday for Menai Bridge and Carnarvon. For freights, etc, apply at the company's offices, Messrs Richards, Mills & Co., 17 James Street, Liverpool or at Carnarvon; John Roberts, Co.'s Warehouse, New Harbour. NB. To insure shipment, all goods should be delivered by noon on the day of sailing.

King Ja Ja was sold in 1891, after the arrival of the *Prince Ja Ja*, a new steamer completed by William Thomas & Sons of Amlwch, with engines installed by De Winton's at Caernarfon.

Carnarvon & Liverpool Steam Ship Co.
Of the seven original shareholders, five were grocers. By November 1893 there were sixty investors, the majority shareholder being John Jones Griffith of Barmouth. The company bought *Ibis* (171), a twelve-year-old steamer built at Bristol for Henry Burton of Newport (Monmouthshire). *The Times* of 16 November 1895 carried the news that: 'A disastrous collision occurred off New Brighton, at the mouth of the Mersey, about 7 o'clock last night'. The *Ibis*, from Caernarfon with general cargo and one passenger, was in collision with the steam vessel *Alarm* and, according to the press report, sank in five minutes. Five people were lost. The vessel was not insured, and the company was forced to suspend its activities. A new vessel, *Christiana* (295), ordered by the company, was taken into the ownership of William O. Roberts, and run in competition with the *Prince Ja Ja*.

Liverpool & Menai Straits Shipping Co.
This was an amalgamation of the Liverpool, Carnarvon & Menai Straits Co. and the Carnarvon & Liverpool Co. In 1901 the merged business began to operate the *Christiana* and the *Prince Ja Ja*, and took over warehouses at Bangor and Caernarfon. The *Prince Ja Ja* was sold a year later, leaving the *Christiana* to make two voyages a week between Liverpool and the Menai Straits towns. In 1905 the *Telephone* and the *Margaret* joined the company. The enterprise was wound up in 1920.

87 At the Caernarfon landing stage is the paddle steamer *Snowdon*, built in 1892 by Laird's at Birkenhead. It was in service until 1931. The other steamer is the *Rhos Trevor*, built in 1876 and bought thirty years later by the Colwyn Bay & Liverpool Steamship Co. By May 1909 it belonged to the Liverpool & North Wales Steamship Co., who renamed it *St Trillo*.

The Victoria Dock had opened in 1876, having taken eight years to complete. By 1900 slate shipments through Caernarfon totalled just under 15,000 tons; by 1913 they were around half that quantity, and in 1917 were negligible. An oil depot was opened in 1913 by the Anglo-American Oil Co. The last dry cargoes were discharged at the Victoria Dock in the early 1960s.

The construction of Landerne Pier was completed in June 1996, for use by both commercial and pleasure boats. Victoria Dock was re-opened in 1997, with nearly fifty berths at pontoons for leisure craft.

PORT DINORWIC

A quay and tidal dock were constructed in 1797, later to be extended up the narrow inlet. The purpose of the dock was to ship slate from the Dinorwic quarries and what was once Y Felinheli became known as Port Dinorwic. In the early years lighters had taken the slate out to anchored vessels, so to eliminate this time-consuming process (and to cut down on slate breakages) quays had been built, with lock gates and a dry dock added later.

From 1824 the slate was brought to the dock by means of a tramway; twenty years on this was superseded by the 4ft gauge Padarn Railway. George Borrow visited in the 1850s: 'Port Dyn Norwig seems to consist of a creek, a staithe, and around a hundred houses; a few small vessels were lying at the staithe.' He thought that it was 'one of the most thoroughly Welsh places I had seen, for during the whole time I was in it, I heard no words of English spoken, except the two or three spoken by myself'. Two years after Borrow's visit the Chester & Holyhead Railway line reached Port Dinorwic. Demand grew, and in the 1880s around 400 vessels a year loaded slate. The dock facilities were completed from 1897 to 1900 by the construction of another basin and lock and, in 1905, a sea wall.

Small vessels had been built at Dinas (later part of Port Dinorwic) during the eighteenth century, and the trade was continued at Dinas shipyard from 1849 to 1897 by the Revd Rees Jones (a Methodist minister) and his son, William Edward Jones. Altogether they launched about twenty-nine vessels, including the *Ordovic* (825) in 1877. After loading coal at Cardiff the vessel left on her maiden voyage to Batavia. The *Ordovic* was wrecked at Cape Horn in 1894.

Lewis Lloyd (1986) provides an account of the career of the brig *Atalanta* (227) from 1864 to 1891. The *Atalanta* (104ft by 25ft by 14ft) was launched by Rees Jones on 9 February 1864, the shareholders being Griffith Griffiths, master mariner, Llanbedr (28/64); his son William Griffiths, master mariner, Llanbedr (8/64); Rees Jones, shipbuilder, Port Dinorwic (16/64); Catherine Roberts, widow, Llanfairisgair (4/64); John Evans, schoolmaster, Caernarfon (4/64) and John Jones, painter, Caernarfon (4/64).

Early voyages were to Ceylon (Sri Lanka) and to Egypt. On 11 September 1865 the *Atalanta* – master William Griffiths – left London, arriving at Point de Galle (Ceylon) on 2 January 1866. The brig was back at London by July.

Twelve days later the vessel began her next voyage (this time commanded by Griffith Griffiths), leaving for Middlesbrough on 11 August 1866, arriving at Alexandria on 2 November and at Bristol on 25 February 1867. Lewis Lloyd reproduces some entries from the Official Log of this voyage:

> 8 September 1866 (off Margate) the sixty-year-old cook/steward was drunk, and a bottle of rum was missing from the cabin. 24 October (in the eastern Mediterranean) the cook refused 'to lend a hand to pump ship... the men having worked all day, the vessel making a great deal of water'.
>
> 29 November (at Alexandria) the cook, drunk, 'came down in the cabin and struck the cabin table with his hand and said he was the best man on board the vessel, having found just before the keg of spirits'.
>
> 17 January 1867 (eastern Mediterranean) the cook was 'put off duty for filthyness, the men cannot eat the food he cooked'.

The *Atalanta* sailed the world for twenty-seven years, visiting ports such as Stettin, Naples, Smyrna, Madeira, Cape Town, Bahia and Pernambuco. On 6 October 1891 the brig sailed from Aruba with a cargo of phosphate and was not seen again. Those on board were the master, Hugh Jones (fifty) of Nefyn; mate, Richard Parry (twenty-three), of Nefyn; boatswain, Joseph Lawrance (thirty), of Falmouth; cook/steward, J.H. Mitchell (twenty-eight), of Porthleven; John Thomas, Joseph Gibbens (twenty-two), Thomas Thomas (twenty-three), all able seamen, from Falmouth and ordinary seaman Robert Roberts (nineteen) of Caernarfon.

At around the time that the *Atalanta* was sinking in the North Atlantic, the owner of the Dinorwic Quarry – G.W.D. Assheton-Smith – was deciding that his enterprise should own its own coasting steamers, the first five being ordered from the yard of S. McKnight & Co. at Ayr: *Dinorwic* (276) was bought in 1892 and sold in 1919. *Vaynol* (233) was also bought in 1892; ten years later the vessel sank after a collision while on passage from Glasgow to Port Dinorwic; *Velinheli* (126) was completed in 1892, acquired by Assheton-Smith two years later and was in service for over fifty years. *Enid* (267) was bought in 1903 and sold for scrap in 1954; *Elidir* (423) joined the fleet in 1903 and was sold in 1942 to Coppack Brothers of Connah's Quay. These were followed by half-a-dozen other vessels, the final purchase being *Sybil-Mary* (270), acquired from Penrhyn Quarries in 1954 and sold for scrap just four months later.

Commercial traffic at Port Dinorwic ended with the closure of the Dinorwic quarry in 1969.

BANGOR

There had been sporadic shipments of slate from Abercegin during the eighteenth century, but trade began to increase after Richard Pennant asserted his control over the quarrying on

88 The *Velinheli* was built at Ayr in 1892. Two years later it was bought by G.W.D. Assheton-Smith to carry slate from the Dinorwic quarries. The vessel was sold in 1941.

his estate. Pennant appointed Benjamin Wyatt as his agent in 1786, and improvements in the transport arrangements followed. Up to this point slate had been carried by packhorse, but now Wyatt built a new road which could cope with horse-drawn wagons. By 1790 new quays were in use at Abercegin. On the west bank of the river a warehouse was erected, and on the east bank quay there were, later, offices and a factory for producing writing slates. The whole became known as Port Penrhyn, built to export slate from the Penrhyn quarries, with only occasional incoming cargoes.

In 1800 a tramway was laid down to Port Penrhyn, and the quays were lengthened in 1803 and 1830. In 1855 a new quay and a breakwater were built, forming a new dock.

The Chester & Holyhead Railway arrived at Bangor in 1848, and four years later a line opened to Port Penrhyn but, in spite of this competition, the 1850s and 1860s were a busy time for the port; in 1862, for example, an average of about fifty vessels arrived and departed in each month. Larger vessels had to stay outside the dock, with the slates being ferried out by small craft.

A steam service from Liverpool to the Menai Straits began in the 1820s, but passengers for Bangor had to come ashore by boat. By 1828 there were sailings three times a week in each direction in winter and a daily service (not Sundays) in summer. In May 1896 a pier, a-third-of-a-mile long, was opened.

Bangor Shipowners

In 1787 Benjamin Wyatt and his sub-agent William Williams owned shares in the new brigantine *Albion* (71), built at Kidwelly, and in the sloop *Lord Bulkeley* (52). The *Albion* went regularly to London, carrying slate for Benjamin's architect brother Samuel, who promoted the use of Penrhyn slate in London.

There were sixty vessels belonging to Bangor listed in 1865's *Clayton's Register*: over 70 per cent were schooners and about 20 per cent sloops. The two oldest vessels, dating back to the eighteenth century, were the sloop *Robert*, of 1784, and the schooner *Raven*, of 1788; the managing owner of both was 'J. Lloyd, accountant, Port Penrhyn'.

89 Slate schooners at Port Penrhyn in 1890.

Some of the vessels listed in *Clayton's Register*:

Albion (477), a barque, and the largest vessel. Built at Jarrow in 1854, the managing owner was the slate merchant William Pritchard of Tan-y-coed.

Cambria (56), a schooner, built at Bangor in 1860 by Thomas Thomas Parry. Owned by Thomas Thomas Parry, shipbuilder (30/64); John Jones, innkeeper, Samuel Roberts and William Parry, brazier. The vessel was lost in 1903.

City of Bangor (99) a schooner, built at Bangor in 1857. The initial shareholders were: Meshach Roberts, druggist (20/64); John Thomas, master mariner (12/64); Henry Parry, slate dresser (8/64); John Williams, slate dresser (8/64); Mary Willoughby, hotel keeper (6/64); Owen Morris, assistant overseer (4/64); Robert Thomas, carter (4/64); Hugh Pritchard, butcher (2/64). Sank after a collision off the South Devon coast.

Emily (88), launched as a brig at Harbour Grace, Newfoundland, in 1826 and bought fourteen years later by Richard Williams (mariner) and Zacharias Roberts. Re-rigged as a schooner in 1852 and recorded as 'condemned not worth repairing' twenty years later.

Gazelle (85), built at Berwick-on-Tweed in 1845. Until October 1863 the sole owner of the schooner was Edward Owen, but in that month he sold four of his sixty-four shares to Robert Hughes of Gaerwen, four to Owen Thomas of Islington (both Hughes and Thomas were ministers of religion), three to T.T. Parry, three to Richard Threlfall Power (merchant of Liverpool) and two to Samuel Roberts. (*Clayton's Register* lists the managing owners as Parry & Co.). The *Gazelle* was lost in the Pentland Firth in October 1866.

Glanogwen (131), a brigantine, built by John Parry in 1855 and was owned by three generations of the Parry family: John Parry, his sons Robert Thomas Parry and Thomas Thomas Parry and his daughter Anne (widow of William Thomas); then by Anne's sons Robert Parry Thomas and John Parry Thomas. (Elis-Williams 1988). The vessel became a hulk in 1915.

Idwal (69), on 2 May 1857 it was reported (in the *Caernarvon & Denbigh Herald*) that, on 24 April a schooner, 'the *Idwal* was launched from the building yard of Mr Edward Ellis, Garth,

Bangor, in the presence of a large concourse. The lines of this elegant vessel were drawn by Mr Ellis's foreman'. The length of keel was given as 64½ft, breadth 19¾ft and depth of hold 9ft:

> She is to be commanded by Captain Thomas Jones, of Ysgubor Fawr, Llanfairmathafarneithaf, who is the principal owner. The other shares are distributed amongst several tradesmen at Bangor. An excellent dinner was subsequently given by the owners at the Vaynol Arms Inn, of which upwards of a hundred persons partook.

In July 1864 the *Idwal* left Garston with a cargo of iron for Saundersfoot, then to Youghal (culm); Youghal-Briton Ferry (grain); Neath-Red Wharf (culm); Bangor-London (slates); London-Newcastle (ballast); Newcastle-Milford Haven (coal): arrived January 1865. Three years later the schooner left Sligo, only to be wrecked at Mullaghmore. Those lost were the master Thomas Jones, the mate Thomas Jones (aged twenty-two) and William Rowlands (nineteen). Hugh Roberts (twenty-four) survived.

Sarah Jane (73) was a schooner built in 1861 by Henry Owens. The managing owner was John Simon (described as a tanner) who owned twenty shares; the other investors were Robert Roberts, postmaster; Richard Jones, master mariner; Ellis Roberts, accountant; Henry Owens, shipbuilder and Thomas Byewater, shipbuilder.

The largest fleet in 1865 was that of Parry & Co., the shipbuilding/shipowning firm of Thomas Thomas Parry, Richard Threlfall Power and Samuel Roberts. They managed a brigantine, nine schooners and three sloops.

John Lloyd, accountant, Port Penrhyn, controlled five schooners and three sloops. They were owned by Penrhyn Quarry managers and Lloyd was a minority shareholder in the vessels – the schooner *Talacre* will serve as an example: Arthur Wyatt (40/64), James Wyatt (16/64), John Lloyd (8/64).

William Pritchard, slate merchant, of Tan-y-coed operated four vessels, including the two largest at the port: the barque *Albion* (477) and the brig *Caradoc* (224), his other two were sloops.

Evans & Co. (coal merchants) managed two schooners and a sloop.

Owen Owens, farmer, was managing owner of three sloops. Other Bangor vessels were managed by an innkeeper, a surgeon, a painter and a druggist. Meshach Roberts came from Holyhead to Bangor in 1833, at the age of fourteen, to become an apprentice to a druggist. From his late twenties, he invested in several vessels and became a director of the Bangor Mutual Ship Assurance Society. His later interests were in large ocean-going ships. Other local investors included the master mariner Humphrey Williams who was part-owner of, among other vessels, the barque *Helen* (252), built at Prince Edward Island in 1865 (the other part-owner was W.A. Darbishire, one of the owners of the Penrorsedd Quarry in the Nantlle Valley). The coal merchants Robert and Richard Williams began with part-ownership and later became sole owners of sloops and schooners, as did the wine merchant Evan Evans.

Bangor Shipbuilding

John Parry
Built vessels on Hirael beach, five in the 1830s and four in the 1840s: the smack *Mary Grace*; the 1843 brig, *Three Susans*; the 1844 smack *Port Penrhyn*; in 1847 the *Lady Louisa Pennant*. In 1855 he launched the brig *Glanogwen*.

T.T. Parry
John Parry died in 1855, when the shipbuilding business was taken over by his son Thomas Thomas Parry, together with Richard Threlfall Power (John Parry's son-in-law). Over the next twenty-four years they were to build eight vessels, the first of which was a schooner, *Arthur Wyatt* (96).

Edward Ellis
Built twelve vessels, in a yard rented from R.H. Dawkins Pennant. The yard was advertised for sale in June 1856, when it included a steam-powered saw mill, a blacksmith's shop, stores and a patent slip. The yard was taken over in the 1860s by T.T.Parry & Co.

John Roberts
Built seven vessels between 1846 and 1864. The *Victoria* (11), launched in 1854, was a river paddle steamer (55ft long) built for a syndicate from Barmouth and Dolgellau. The *Victoria* carried freight and passengers on the Mawddach for a decade.

The schooner *City of Bangor* (99), launched in September 1857, celebrated the eighty-four-year-old Right Revd Christopher Bethell, MA, DD, Bishop of Bangor, the figurehead representing 'in striking manner, the likeness of the present Bishop of Bangor in his episcopal robes and in an attitude of preaching'. At the dinner in the Union Hotel, Garth, forty people (including the eight owners and their friends) were in one room and 120 workmen in another.

Thomas Lewis & Co.
Thomas Lewis learned his profession from Meshach Roberts, before going into business on his own account as druggist and grocer in the 1850s. He was to become a magistrate, Chairman of the Board of Health, Mayor of Bangor, High Sheriff of Caernarfonshire and a chapel deacon. He died, at the age of ninety-two, in 1922. He set up the steam-driven Snowdon Flake Flour Mills and – to bring in supplies for his businesses – built a jetty at Garth in 1878. In the same year Thomas Lewis bought the steamer *Medway* (60), built at London in 1866. His other vessels were: in 1886 the newly built *Saint Seiriol* (140), sold in 1905; in 1895 the new *Saint Tudwal* (198), sold to the Bristol & Cardigan Trading Co. in 1909. The larger vessels were employed not only to collect Thomas Lewis's goods, but could sometimes be seen further afield, trading to South Wales ports.

The Anglesey Shipping Co.
Formed by two businessmen from the north of England, William Henry Preston of Lleiniog Castle and Samuel Taylor Chadwick of Haulfre. The vessels were managed by Owen Thomas Jones of Bangor. They bought the steamer *Anglesey*, newly built at Carrickfergus, in 1891, and were joined in the company by Sir R.H. Williams Bulkeley. For the next vessel they turned to sail, the three-masted steel schooner *Mary B. Mitchell*, which was bought from the same Carrickfergus yard as the *Anglesey*. During the First World War the vessel, by then owned by Lord Penrhyn, was hired by the Admiralty for employment as a Q-ship. Equipped with three hidden guns and posing as a merchant vessel, the object was to lure an enemy submarine to the surface, when it might be destroyed by gunfire. The *Mary B. Mitchell* was sold in 1919 to Job Tyrrell of Arklow, and in 1935 took the title role in the film *Mystery of the Mary Celeste* (Hammer Film Productions). Wrecked on a voyage from Dublin to Silloth in 1944, when the two crew members were rescued by the Kirkcudbright lifeboat.

Subsequent vessels owned by the company included: *Harrier*, bought in 1894; *Bangor* (bought in 1894); *Penrhyn* (bought in 1895) and *Pennant* (bought in 1897).

In 1898 the four steamers and the *Mary B. Mitchell* were acquired by the agent of the Penrhyn Quarries, Emilius Alexander Young. On his death in 1910 the fleet was bought by Lord Penrhyn. During the 1920s and 1930s, the steamers were often employed carrying cargoes other than slate, and some Penrhyn vessels sailed on until the 1940s and one, *Sybil-Mary*, until 1954.

In the Second World War the Bangor yard of A.M. Dickie built prefabricated coastal craft (such as motor torpedo boats and motor gun boats) designed by the Fairfield Marine Co. After the war there were few shipments of slate through the port, but there were some imports of construction materials. The Penrhyn Quarries, but not the port, were acquired by McAlpine's in 1964.

The largest commercial vessel to dock at Port Penrhyn took on its cargo on 31 August 2001, when the *Ocean Hanne* (an offshore windfarm installation vessel) loaded sections of nine windfarm towers made by Cambrian Engineering. The towers were conveyed to Campbeltown.

The Training Ship Clio

In 1877 the Training Ship *Clio* arrived at her permanent anchorage, 300 yards off Bangor Pier. The former Royal Naval vessel had been launched at Sheerness in 1838, and was now, like the *Havannah* at Cardiff, to house up to 200 boys, under the age of fourteen, who were thought to need residential care, and who would be trained as seamen. Boys with a criminal record were not eligible.

On 7 August 1877 *The North Wales Chronicle* reported that the *Clio* had arrived in the Menai Straits 'in the charge of Captain Moger RN with whom the proposal for such a ship originated, and has been carried out, and who has been appointed Captain-Superintendent'. For the official opening the band of the training ship *Indefatigable* was brought from Liverpool, and hundreds of visitors took the opportunity to visit the *Clio*. An Eisteddfod was being held in Caernarfon, and one of the competitions was for the best essay, in English or Welsh, on the subject of 'The Industrial Training Ship for North Wales and the Border Counties, moored in the Menai Straits: its physical, social and moral advantages'. The first prize of ten guineas was won by Owen Parry, of the *Bristol Daily Press*.

Although described as being for boys from North Wales and the border counties, the 1881 census shows that many came from Lancashire towns. Of the total listed (246) about 40 per cent originated in Manchester or Salford, and over 20 per cent from London. Only 15 per cent were born in Wales.

The *Clio* was broken up in 1919.

HMS Conway

The Mercantile Marine Service Association, formed at Liverpool in 1857, asked the Admiralty for a vessel which could be used to train boys for a career at sea. The frigate HMS *Conway* arrived in 1859, to be moored in the Mersey off Rock Ferry. The *Liverpool Daily Post* (14 May 1859) reported that Mr Dobson, a Cambridge graduate, had been appointed headmaster and Captain Powell was to be commander of the ship:

> The boys to be admitted so far as funds permit, are the sons of deceased and destitute Masters, Officers and Seamen of the merchant service whose circumstances will not enable them to pay for their education; and boys of any class, intended for sea service, whose friends pay the whole or part of their maintenance and education. The general course of tuition will embrace a sound English education and such boys that are capable will be taught trigonometry, navigation, nautical Astronomy, etc.

The vessel proved to be too small, so the larger HMS *Winchester* (renamed *Conway*) was provided instead. In 1876 this was replaced by an even larger and final *Conway*, formerly HMS *Nile*, which had been launched at Plymouth in 1839.

During an air raid on 13 March 1941 parachute mines fell near the *Conway* and the 200 cadets and staff had to evacuate the ship. The *Tacoma City*, near at hand, was sunk. It was decided that the *Conway* would have to be moved from the Mersey, and it was towed to the Menai Straits, to a position off Bangor Pier. Arriving on 22 May 1941 the ship stayed there for eight years, before being moved to a mooring off Plas Newydd, where access to playing fields was easier and part of the mansion could be used by the school.

The *Conway* had to go into dry dock at Birkenhead in 1953. It was planned that the voyage would take place in two stages: the first, in April, to the former moorings off Glyn Garth and then, after the summer term, on to Birkenhead. Moving such a vessel was always likely to be

90 The loss of HMS *Conway* in 1953.

difficult: it was very big, could not be steered and had no engine and no anchors. Everything depended on the tugs, *Dongarth* and *Minegarth*.

The operation, on 14 April 1953, did not go well. At 9.40 a.m. the *Conway* was being pushed by a strong wind towards the shore. The *Dongarth* was towing, but against a strong tide. Around 10.30 a.m. wind and tide forced the *Conway* on to the Platters Rocks, near the Suspension Bridge, where it became a total loss. An investigating Sub-Committee of the Mercantile Marine Service Association concluded that the grounding was due to the unusual 10-knot tide. The cadet training continued, based on shore at Plas Newydd, until the school closed in 1974.

MENAI BRIDGE

Towards the end of the eighteenth century there was a daily coach to Holyhead from both Chester and Shrewsbury. The ferry crossing to Anglesey could be hazardous; in one accident in 1785, more than fifty people were drowned. Traffic to and from Ireland via Holyhead increased after the Act of Union of 1800, and it became necessary to improve not only the means of crossing the straits, but the whole route from London. Construction of the Menai Suspension Bridge began in 1818 and the first Royal Mail coach was able to cross at the end of January 1826. Building the bridge had brought a large number of people to the area, and the town of Menai Bridge began to develop.

Two years after the bridge opened, Richard Davies of Llangefni secured a lease on some land, a timber yard and a warehouse at Menai Bridge. The Davies family later built a wharf between Porth y Wrach and Porth Daniel. Richard Davies's eldest son John, aged twenty-one, was made manager in 1830, and the family members began to invest in small vessels, such as the *Eliza Catherine*, built at Bangor by Edward Ellis. Larger vessels were bought during the 1840s, the first being *Chieftain* (795), a ship-rigged vessel built at St John's, New Brunswick. Two years old, the ship was intended for the North Atlantic routes, carrying slate and emigrants westwards and timber on the homeward voyage. During the five years after 1843 the *Chieftain* sailed from Menai Bridge or Liverpool to Quebec (eight times), taking three to four months, New Orleans (three times), taking four to five months and once to Mobile.

The first voyage of the *Enterprise* was from Liverpool on 3 July 1844. The vessel was wrecked in the following year, after setting out from New Orleans for Menai Bridge. *Agnes* was built at Miramichi, New Brunswick, in 1844, bought in 1845 and wrecked in 1846. *Courtenay*, built at St John's, New Brunswick, was bought at Liverpool in June 1845. The vessel left St John's on 24 January 1846 but did not arrive at Menai Bridge until 17 June. Taking in water, and with sails carried away, the *Courtenay* had drifted for forty-one days before reaching Donegal Bay. After some weeks at Killybegs a steam tug towed her to the Menai Straits.

In April 1846 the *Chieftain* was towed out to sea from Menai Bridge carrying slates and seventy passengers; four months later the ship was again leaving the Straits, this time with 200 people, nearly all from north-west Wales, most of them making for Wisconsin. In October 1847 Davies & Sons announced:

> To Emigrants, to sail about the fifteenth November from the Menai Straits, the following fast-sailing ships: *Tamarac*, new ship, 1,400 tons burden; *Peltoma*, new ship, 850 tons burden; *Northumberland*, 700 tons burden. To persons emigrating to the United States, the above offers a most desirable opportunity, as steamers proceed directly from New Orleans to Wisconsin, Missouri, Iowa, Indiana, Illinois and Ohio, which makes the expense less than from any other port in the States.
>
> The Commanders being well known Welshmen, is a guarantee that their comforts will be attended to.

From 1851 there was more trade with Australia (following the discovery of gold), Chile (nitrates) and Peru (guano; in the 1860s Davies ships made more than a hundred voyages to Callao). Voyages to these places took a year to eighteen months and began, not from Menai Bridge, but from the larger ports of Britain and Europe.

John Davies had died at Torquay in 1848, at the age of thirty-nine. His shares were inherited by his father and the two brothers, Richard and Robert, who managed the business with their cousin Richard Hughes. By the mid-1880s the company was operating eighteen vessels, controlled by Charles Pierce, nephew of Richard Davies Snr. When he retired Henry Rees Davies, Richard Davies's son, took on the task.

In 1866 the first iron ship was bought, *Dolbadarn Castle*, built at Sunderland in 1863. Eight years later *Malleny* was acquired, the first of eight Davies vessels built by T. Royden & Sons of Liverpool. They were all of iron, and ship-rigged: built in 1875 *Anglesey* and *Merioneth*; built in 1876 *Carnarvonshire*, *Denbighshire* and *Flintshire*; built in 1877 *Cardiganshire* and *Montgomeryshire*. The *Merioneth* turned out to be a record-breaker, leaving Cardiff with coal on 16 October 1887 and arriving at San Francisco on 20 January 1888, a passage of ninety-six days. The *Merioneth* left San Francisco on 4 April, reaching Cardiff on 8 July 1888, a record passage of ninety-four days. In the same year other vessels of the Davies fleet made swift voyages to the west coast of the United States.

The last ships to be bought by the firm were two four-masted steel barques, both built by Alexander Stephen & Sons at Glasgow: the *Afon Alaw* (2,052) of 1891 and the *Afon Cefni* (2,066), which was towed from the builder's yard to Barry in April 1892. On 5 January 1894 the vessel left Swansea and was never seen again, although wreckage was found on the Cornish coast.

By the final years of the nineteenth century nearly all the Davies ships were engaged on the long voyages to San Francisco, but there were increasing periods of unemployment. Five ships were sold in 1903, including the *Afon Alaw*, which had been at San Francisco for more than a year. The last two vessels were sold in 1905.

The Davies's first large vessel had been acquired in 1843, the last in 1892. Altogether there were seventy, of which forty-eight had been built in New Brunswick, Nova Scotia or Quebec. (For the full story of the Davies family's ships see Eames 1973.)

91 *Afon Cefni.* A four-masted steel barque launched on the Clyde in March 1892 for the Davies family, Menai Bridge. The *Afon Cefni* left Swansea for San Francisco on 5 January 1894 and was not seen again. Wreckage was washed up on the Cornish coast.

The Indefatigable

The sea training school *Indefatigable* was at Llanfair P.G. on Anglesey for over fifty years. Founded in 1864, the original *Indefatigable* (with a complement of 200 boys) was moored at Rock Ferry on the Mersey. In 1914 the vessel was replaced by HMS *Phaeton*, a thirty-year-old steam cruiser, renamed *Indefatigable*.

The school moved in 1941, spending three years at a former holiday camp, before settling at Plas Llanfair, near the Britannia Bridge. There were new buildings and a parade ground and a new name: the school joined with the Liverpool Sea Training Homes to become the '*Indefatigable* and National Sea Training School for Boys'. By 1994 recruitment had fallen off so much that the school had to be closed.

HOLYHEAD

Charles II's yacht, the *Mary*, was wrecked near Holyhead. The vessel was a gift to the King at the Restoration, but it turned out to be unsuitable and spent fifteen years carrying officials and the well-connected between Dublin and Chester or Holyhead. The *Mary* ran into The Skerries in fog in the early hours of 25 March 1675, drowning thirty-five people. Thirty-nine managed to get ashore, but were not rescued for two days. During this time they made a fire from the wood of the wrecked boat, roasted meat, and drank wine. Finds from the wreck have included cannon, coins, gold lockets, rings, silver candlesticks and the master's pewter plates, silver spoon and fork. To prevent accidents such as this a lighthouse was built on The Skerries in 1714, and another in 1809 on South Stack, at the southern entrance to Holyhead harbour which Lewis Morris had called in 1748 'only one of the rough drafts of nature'.

The Act of Union of 1800, with Irish members attending the House of Commons, and officials travelling back and forth, generated considerably more traffic between London and Dublin. A Report of a Parliamentary committee described the London to Dublin mail service of 1815:

> The Irish mail is despatched from the General Post Office at 8 p.m. The coach which carries it passes through the towns of Oxford, Birmingham and Shrewsbury, and arrives at Holyhead at 1 o'clock on the second day, travelling over 276½ miles in forty-one hours, being at the rate of 6¾ miles an hour. The mail is sent off one hour after its arrival at Holyhead on board a Post Office packet for Dublin, where it commonly arrives in the course of the following day, being the third from the day of its leaving London.

The sea crossing was made in privately owned sailing packets, chartered to the Post Office. In addition to carrying the mails the vessel's owner could take paying passengers, carriages and horses, but not freight. The increasing number of travellers led to a demand for better facilities at Holyhead, and new piers and a dry dock were completed in 1824. Telford's Suspension Bridge across the Menai Straits opened on 31 January 1826 and now, with an improved road all the way from London, the mail coach took only thirty hours to reach Holyhead.

The first contract for a new harbour at Holyhead was signed on Christmas Eve 1847. Construction was still going on when the works were battered by the great storm of 24/25 October 1859. Many vessels had sought refuge at Holyhead, including the *Great Eastern*, which had come from Weymouth. Too large to get into harbour, it managed to avoid major damage by using the paddles and screw to steer clear of danger. (A few miles along the coast the *Royal Charter* was less fortunate. See pages 152-154.)

More than a quarter of a century after the contract was signed the work was completed. Some kind of ceremony was, obviously, in order, and on the morning of Saturday 16 August 1873 five battleships steamed into the outer anchorage: HMS *Agincourt*, *Devastation*, *Hercules*, *Northumberland* and *Sultan*. *The Times* sent its Special Correspondent, who reported the arrival of the dispatch boat *Lively*, the yacht *Vivid*, bearing Admiral Sir Harry Keppel, GCB, 'who was received with the usual salute', the *Galatea* – with the Deputy Master of Trinity House – and six training brigs. The *Princess Alexandra* brought the Commissioners of Irish Lights

At 1 a.m. on Tuesday 19 August the Royal Yacht *Victoria and Albert* – the captain His Highness Ernest Leopold, Prince of Leiningen – entered the harbour. On board with the Prince of Wales, the future King Edward VII, was his brother, the Duke of Edinburgh. At 8 a.m. a royal salute boomed out from the warships' guns. The Prince went ashore later in the morning, when he was greeted by a guard of honour from the 101st Regiment, around two-dozen gentry, and naval and military officers.

> I must not omit to mention the goat, which opposite the landing place was hoisted upon a small platform surrounded by evergreens, a national emblem, meant probably to remind the Prince that he was now in the land which gives him his title, though hereabouts it certainly does not speak his tongue.

Thus wrote the man from *The Times*.

The Prince's party sat in small brightly painted carriages, which were then pulled by a steam locomotive to the end of the breakwater. The wagons were those which had been used for carrying rock during the construction work. Standing on a dais the Prince of Wales said, 'I now declare this breakwater complete, and the Harbour of Refuge open' and then unveiled a plaque, before going off to a private luncheon and garden party at Penrhos, followed by a large dinner party on the yacht, which left harbour at about midnight. *The Times* correspondent observed that few of the local people had turned out to watch proceedings at the harbour although, he wrote, the route through Holyhead was decorated with flags and the streets were 'fairly filled' by what he perceived to be 'a loyal but undemonstrative crowd'.

92 The new Holyhead Dock from the hotel, 1880.

Seven years later the Prince of Wales was back, to declare open more harbour improvements. *The Times* correspondent was there:

> Hitherto the traffic has been carried on at a one-sided station and quay, but what is now provided will give separate and distinct passenger platforms, quay walls, goods sheds and sidings for the export and import traffic of the harbour and the up and down traffic of the railway. The water area of the old harbour has been increased from 10½ acres to 24 acres'

There was a new, larger, graving dock (which was to remain in use until 1980) and a hotel.

The Prince came by special train and on arrival, reported *The Times*, 'remained within the limits of the railway company's jurisdiction, and these were strictly guarded at all points against the intrusion of the general public by a body of the Metropolitan Police drafted to the town for that purpose'. There were bands playing, a guard of honour from the local militia and 700 guests invited by the directors of the London & North Western Railway. The heir to the throne and 'a select company' went for a short sea trip on the *Lily*, to be saluted outside the harbour by the guns of the warships *Belleisle*, *Bacchante* and *Hercules*, with sailors manning the yards. Then there was luncheon in the new (decorated) goods shed, speeches and toasts, before the Prince rejoined his special train to travel to Trentham, where he was to be the guest of the Duke of Sutherland.

Steamship services

The *Talbot* (150) – newly built at Port Glasgow by John Wood, with engines by David Napier – began a service from Howth to Holyhead in 1819, followed by the *Ivanhoe* (170) in 1820. The Steam Packet Co. was not awarded a mail contract and so in April 1821 the Post Office agent at Holyhead, Richard Griffith, went to Ireland to see if he could buy or charter the two vessels. Failing in this, he continued looking for suitable ships at Liverpool and in Scotland, but had no success. The Post Office decided to order two new vessels from William Evans of Rotherhithe: the paddle vessels *Meteor* (189) and *Lightning* (205). In 1821

93 The official opening of the new harbour at Holyhead, 19 August 1880. View from the clock tower. The vessel making her way out of harbour is the LNWR's new steamer *Lily*, taking the Prince of Wales and party on a short sea trip.

King George IV made the crossing in the *Lightning*, which was promptly renamed *Royal Sovereign*.

The Committee of Inquiry into the Management of the Post Office Department recommended in 1836 that the Packet Service should be taken over by the Admiralty. This was done within twelve months, and twenty-six vessels were transferred and renamed. There was then a significant development in the carriage of mail on land: by the Conveyance of Mails by Railway Act of 1838 the Post Office was able to insist that mail be carried by the railway companies. Letters sent from London to Dublin by rail, via Liverpool, took twenty-two hours. By road, via Holyhead, they took five hours longer. In January 1839 the Royal Mail coaches from London to Holyhead were withdrawn, and two of the Admiralty packet boats were transferred to Liverpool. Four were left at Holyhead to carry mail originating in North Wales.

The situation changed in August 1848 when the railway track arrived at Bangor, and passengers and mail began to return to Holyhead: they left the train at Bangor, crossing the Suspension Bridge by coach. In 1850 the rail bridge over the Menai Straits opened and the first through train from London arrived at Holyhead. The mail service was switched from Liverpool back to Holyhead, and four new ships of the Admiralty Packet Service arrived: *Banshee* (653), *Caradoc* (676), *Llewellyn* (671) and *St Columba* (720). The new mail contract was awarded to the City of Dublin Steam Packet Co. (CDSPC), which had been founded in 1822 as Charles Wye Williams & Co. (In January 1839 the company had won a contract to operate a night-mail service, on behalf of the Post Office, from the Admiralty Pier at Holyhead.) With the new contract secured, the company bought *Llewellyn* and *St Columba* from the Admiralty and had two new steamers built: *Eblana* and *Prince Arthur*. Ten years later the CDSPC bought four new vessels: *Connaught*, *Leinster*, *Munster* and *Ulster*.

There were also the paddle steamers of the Chester & Holyhead Railway: *Anglia*, *Cambria*, *Hibernia* and *Scotia*, each with a speed of around 14 knots, which took passengers, livestock and freight to Kingstown, and freight and livestock to North Wall, Dublin. In 1859 the company was taken over by the London & North Western Railway (LNWR), which gradually brought in new, faster vessels: 1868's *Countess of Erne*, the 1869-built *Duchess of Sutherland*, and in 1870 *Edith*. From 1873 the LNWR began a service from Holyhead to Greenore and in 1876 to Newry. Some of the ships in service with the LNWR were: 1876 *Shamrock* and *Rose*; 1880 *Lily and Violet*, which was built for the company's express service to Dublin.

In 1897, after their contract was renewed for twenty-one years, the CDSPC bought four identical ships from Cammell Laird: *Connaught*, *Leinster*, *Munster* and *Ulster*. These were twin-

94 The Holyhead steamer *Violet*, built in 1880 by Laird's at Birkenhead.

screw steel vessels, each of 2,646 gross registered tons, with a service speed of around 20 knots, making the crossing in under three hours.

In the same year the LNWR brought *Cambria* into service followed, from 1900 to 1902, by *Anglia, Scotia* and *Hibernia*. This latter vessel was a steel, twin-screw vessel, launched in August 1900 by Denny of Dumbarton, and capable of 22 knots. It was employed on the express passenger service to Dublin, and later to Kingstown. By now, in addition to the passenger services, the LNWR had developed a considerable cargo trade with Dublin and Greenore.

Liverpool-bound White Star liners began calls on 20 June 1909, when passengers and mails from New York were landed by the *Cedric* (21,035). Other transatlantic liners which stopped at Holyhead included the *Arabic, Baltic* and *Celtic*. They came between 1 April and 30 September, and only if they were able to arrive between 8 a.m. and 7 p.m. (6 p.m. in August and September). Passengers were landed by tender, and transferred to special trains. All calls by White Star liners at Holyhead finished in October 1910 because 'the management have come to the conclusion that passengers have not appreciated the facility of getting to London a little earlier and that the larger number preferred that the steamers should go straight to Liverpool'.

THE FIRST WORLD WAR

The CDSPC's *Leinster, Munster* and *Ulster* continued as ferries, carrying troops as well as civilians. During the Easter Rising of 1916 the *Ulster* carried reinforcements for the British Army and on 25/26/27 April took a total of nearly 3,000 soldiers to Kingstown.

The LNWR steamer *Hibernia* was requisitioned by the Admiralty, becoming HM Armed Boarding Steamer *Tara*. On the morning of the 5 November 1915, patrolling off the Egyptian coast near Salum, the vessel was torpedoed by a German submarine and sank in five minutes. Eleven men were killed in the engine room, but the rest managed to get into three boats, which the submarine towed to land. One man died on the way, and another died after his injured leg was amputated.

The ninety or so survivors were now prisoners of the Senussi, who were fighting a guerilla war against the Allies. J.H. Swaine gave an account to the *The Times* of the prisoners' ordeal. He began by pointing out that 'we were all Holyhead men...'.

95 The *Rosstrevor*, built at Dumbarton in 1895 and employed by the LNWR on their Holyhead to Greenore route. The vessel was broken up in 1926.

96 The White Star Line's *Cedric* was the first transatlantic liner to call at Holyhead, on 20 June 1909. Passengers and mail were landed by tender. A few more White Star liners came, but the experiment finished in October 1910.

HOLYHEAD HARBOUR & STATION HOTEL.
S. S. HIBERNIA LEAVING FOR DUBLIN.

97 The LNWR's *Hibernia*. In the First World War it became HM Armed Boarding Vessel *Tara*. Torpedoed and sunk off the Egyptian coast on 5 November 1915, the surviving crew members were held prisoner by the Senussi until rescued by an armoured car column in March 1916.

> The Senussi started to march us to where they said we should find a beautiful flowing river with plenty of fish in it and delicious dates growing in abundance by the river side. They marched us for twelve days and nights in the clothing that we came ashore in… On arrival they gave us some native clothing and some blankets.

By now the *Tara's* crew had been joined by men from another vessel, the *Moorina*, which had been sunk by gunfire.

The prisoners, malnourished and suffering from dysentery, were set to work clearing out wells, walking about eight miles a day in the process. Four more men died:

> Thus, cold, starving, beaten and hopeless, we went along until March seventeenth. About 2.30 in the afternoon of that day we saw some motor cars in the distance, but could not make out what they were. Our chief officer and the interpreter had gone to… try to get some food for us, and we thought that the cars might be them returning. But when we saw the Red Cross we knew the cars were English, and our feelings overwhelmed us. After attacking and killing our guards, who numbered about thirty, the Duke of Westminster and his party picked us up and took us off to the British camp. So overjoyed were we that we shed tears and put our arms round the necks of our deliverers and kissed them.

There were around forty vehicles, including ambulances, in the armoured column, which had driven well over a hundred miles in search of the prisoners. The former captives were taken to Alexandria by the hospital ship *Raschid*. Among the rescued was the *Tara's* dog, which became a mascot of the armoured car crews.

Anglia became a hospital ship. On 17 November 1915 the vessel was on passage from Calais to Dover with sixty crew and nearly 400 hospital staff and patients. The *Anglia* sank after hitting a mine off Folkestone. Estimates of the number of lives lost vary from 120 to 160, including twenty-five of the crew.

98 The crew of the *Hibernia*.

Connaught was requisitioned in 1915, and employed as a troopship until torpedoed in the afternoon of 3 March 1917, on the way from Le Havre to Southampton. Three men were killed, but the captain and the rest of the crew, seventy-four altogether, were able to get away in lifeboats.

Connemara left Greenore for Holyhead at 8 p.m. on 3 November 1917 with thirty crew members and fifty-one passengers. Half an hour later the *Connemara* was hit amidships by the steamer *Retriever* (483), with a crew of nine, carrying coal from Garston to Newry. *Connemara* sank in five minutes, the *Retriever* in fifteen. The only person to survive, from both vessels, was James Boyle of the *Retriever*, who scrambled ashore from a capsized boat.

One month before the Armistice in 1918 the *Leinster* left Kingstown harbour for Holyhead. The vessel was painted in dazzle camouflage and a twelve-pounder gun, manned by naval gunners, was installed on a platform at the stern. The crew was largely from Dun Laoghaire and Holyhead and most of the passengers were military: from the British Isles, Australia, Canada, New Zealand and the United States. Soon after leaving harbour the *Leinster* was torpedoed by a German submarine. Survivors were rescued by HM Ships *Lively*, *Mallard* and *Seal* and the Armed Patrol Yacht *Helga* (the vessel which had shelled Dublin in 1916). Of the 775 people who set off from Kingstown, 532 died.

The CDSPC lost two vessels in the war, and in 1920 the contract to carry the Irish mail went at last to the LNWR. Four years later the CDSPSC was wound up.

The LNWR was absorbed into the London Midland & Scottish Railway in 1921, and new vessels came into service: *Anglia*, *Cambria*, *Hibernia* and *Scotia*.

Scotia was sunk after being dive-bombed at Dunkirk in 1940: thirty of the crew died, as did about 300 of the French soldiers on board. After the war, ferries were operated by B+I Line and by Sealink (British Rail). Existing vessels were gradually replaced by roll-on, roll-off ferries and in 1991 Stena Line took over the operation. Ferries today take about 3½ hours, and the 'superferries' only 1½ hours.

99 Amlwch harbour, 1994.

AMLWCH

Copper had been mined on Parys Mountain since the Bronze Age, but it began to be exploited on a large scale only from the 1760s. Within twenty years the output from the Mona and Parys Mines sent out through Amlwch dominated the world copper market and an Anglesey solicitor, Thomas Williams, became the 'Copper King' and a millionaire. Some of the ore could be smelted locally, but enormous quantities were sent to the Dee, to Lancashire, or to South Wales.

Amlwch harbour was, as Lewis Morris observed in 1748, 'no more than a cove between two steep rocks', but if necessary a vessel might seek refuge there 'provided the mouth of the harbour can be discovered which is now difficult for a stranger'. Another writer described the port as 'no more than a chasm between two rocks, running far into the land and dry at low water'.

The Amlwch Shipping Co., formed in the 1780s, was managed by the Mine Agents of the Mona and Parys Mines. By 1786 the company had invested in five brigs and three sloops, built at Beaumaris, Caernarfon, Pwllheli (two), Liverpool (two), Red Wharf and Rhuddlan.

Amlwch harbour was too small, and an Act of Parliament was obtained in 1793 authorising the 'enlargement, deepening, cleansing, improvement and regulation of the harbour'. The rock was cut away, making a new quay 400ft long and 60ft wide. Large storage bins were built, filled by ore tipped down wooden chutes from a new roadway. At a later date two short piers were built at the harbour entrance; the space between them could be closed by a number of large timbers, one on top of the other, protecting the vessels in harbour from northerly winds.

The *Wales Register and Guide* of 1878 pictured the town:

One hundred years ago it only consisted of six houses, the residents of which were fishermen; but owing to the valuable mines in the neighbourhood, it has now become one of the most important towns in the country, and has railway communication with Bangor and Holyhead. The harbour, cut out of slate rock, and protected by a small breakwater, is capable of holding forty moderate-sized vessels, many of which belong to and trade with the port.

Clayton's Register for 1865 lists fifty-four vessels belonging to Amlwch, about 75 per cent of them schooners. Fourteen vessels were listed as being managed in the name of 'J.H. Treweek', and 'Treweek, Son & Co.' managed six, including the *N.E.V.A.* (146), a schooner built at Newport in 1855: the initials stood for 'Napoleon Eugénie Victoria Albert'.

James Treweek
Originally from Cornwall, between 1825 and 1844 he and his sons built fourteen vessels, eleven of them sloops or smacks. His son Francis died in 1832. Another son, Nicholas, acted as an agent in Liverpool for Amlwch copper, but maintained his interest in the repair and building of vessels, setting up a yard at Hirael, Bangor, in the 1840s. Ten years later he had investments in three full-rigged ships, seven barques, six brigs, five brigantines, twelve schooners, three snows, nine sloops and three smacks. The 1861 census listed forty-five people working at his Amlwch shipbuilding yard, which had moved from a site west of the harbour to one on the eastern side, at the same time creating a dry dock. Six schooners were built between 1858 and 1866, two of them of iron.

William Cox Paynter
Used Treweek's old yard, mostly for ship-repairing, but he also built eight schooners, the first, *Charles Edwin* (94) in 1859 for Dyer & Co. of Amlwch, who were involved in the management of the Parys Mine. Paynter died in 1884, but the yard carried on, under the management of Captain Thomas Morgan (Thomas Morgan & Co. were also substantial investors in shipping). Over fourteen years the only vessels launched were the three-masted schooners: the 1884

100 The entrance to Amlwch harbour, from William Daniell's *A Voyage around Great Britain*, 1815. On the left are the large bins for storing copper ore, which was tipped into them from the road above.

Camborne (118), 1892 *Ailsie* (130) and in 1897 *Donald and Doris* (142) a vessel which, for years, carried cargoes for the Hodbarrow Mining Co. of Cumberland. *Ailslie*, in its first year, took slates from Port Dinorwic to Germany, Portland stone to London, oilcake from the Elbe to Great Yarmouth, firebricks from Sunderland to London and herrings from Lowestoft to Dublin.

Aled Eames studied the Crew Agreements of the *Camborne* for the years 1886 to 1898, finding that of the 150 signatures, or marks, 120 were of men from Amlwch. The masters, both from Amlwch, were Owen Owens (1886-93) and Owen Thomas (1893-98). The schooner went to British Isles ports, and to Hamburg, but there were two longer voyages: Hamburg to Morocco in 1888 and Lerwick to Bilbao in 1889. (Eames 1973)

William Thomas & Sons

Born near Amlwch in 1822, by 1849 William Thomas was master and part-owner, with his father and brother, of the brigantine *Clyde* (123) built in Nova Scotia in 1842. William Thomas was an associate of another Anglesey-born William Thomas, now a ship-broker and owner in Liverpool. They acquired a full-rigged ship, the *William Melhuish* (680), in 1859, giving command to yet another William Thomas of Anglesey. William Thomas (Liverpool) was kept busy supervising the large ocean-going sailing vessels, while William Thomas (Amlwch) concentrated on his business at Amlwch and at the yard he had acquired at Duddon in Cumberland, although he also invested in, and managed, large vessels trading to the Far East and South America.

By 1865 William Thomas & Sons were managing six vessels from Amlwch: five schooners and a brigantine. Fifteen vessels belonging to William Thomas entered the port of Amlwch in the year 1870; of their thirty-two visits fourteen brought in coal from Lancashire or Wales. There were forty outward voyages to Duddon.

101 The steamship *Liverpool* was on the way from London to Liverpool after a voyage from Calcutta. The barque *La Plata* left Liverpool for Lima on 6 January 1863. They collided in the dark off Point Lynas. Both vessels were lost.

In their yard at Amlwch several vessels were built for Cumberland owners, including *Holy Wath*, a schooner, in 1872; *Cumberland Lassie*, a three-masted schooner, in 1874 and *Baron Hill*, a three-masted schooner in 1876. In the autumn of 1875 the nineteen vessels managed by Captain William Thomas were at harbours in France, Ireland and Spain as well as at Liverpool, Ayr, Ramsey, Duddon, Runcorn and Red Wharf. Larger ships visited ports such as Montevideo, Pondicherry, Callao and Iquique.

From the 1880s Captain Thomas's sons began to play more important roles in the business: Lewis Thomas was a master mariner, William Thomas had trained as a naval architect. In the twenty-five years between 1883 to 1908 the firm built twenty-three vessels of which eleven were of iron and five of steel. The first iron vessel, and their first steamship, was the *W.S Caine* (180) built in 1883, and towed to Caernarfon for De Winton's to install the engines. 122ft long by 21ft, it could carry 'about 200 tons on 8ft of water, being thus practically of the most suitable dimensions for the coasting trade'.

Further steam vessels were launched: in 1884 *Exchange* and *Anglesea*; in 1890 *Prince Ja Ja* (their first steel vessel, built for the Liverpool, Caernarfon & Menai Straits Steamship Co.) and the *New St George* (24), the only paddle steamer to be built by the yard. Launched for P. & H. Lewis of Conwy, it was intended for trips up the river to Trefriw; in 1902 *Walton* (82) a steam flat, and during 1908 *Eilian*, a steel auxiliary-screw steamer.

'The elite of all the schooners built at Amlwch were those designed by the younger William Thomas in the 1890s' (Eames 1973). The sailing vessels launched in those years were: the 1891 *Detlef Wagner* (264), a barquentine, built for N.N. Nielsen of Denmark (to be sunk by a submarine in 1917); 1892 *Maggie Williams*, a three-masted schooner; and three almost identical barquentines: 1893 *Cymric* (226), 1894 *Celtic* (226) and 1898 *Gaelic* (224). In the First World War *Cymric* became a Q-ship, fitted with concealed guns, and on 15 October 1918 sank the British submarine J6 in the North Sea, killing fourteen men.

102 The paddle steamer *St George* was built in 1890 by William Thomas & Sons of Amlwch for P. & H. Lewis of Conwy. Renamed *Prince George* in 1910, it ran between Conwy and Trefriw. Canvas awnings could be fitted and the funnel could be lowered to pass under a bridge. The vessel was scrapped in 1926.

The use of the port diminished after the First World War, and responsibility for it was eventually transferred to the Amlwch Urban District Council.

MOELFRE

The *Royal Charter* was driven on to rocks near Moelfre in the early hours of Wednesday 26 October 1859. Launched at Sandycroft on the Dee in 1854 the *Royal Charter* (2,719) was bought while under construction by Gibbs, Bright & Co. (who also owned the *Great Britain*) and sailed on her maiden voyage as a ship of the Liverpool & Australian Navigation Co. The *Royal Charter* got as far as the Portuguese coast but after being hit by heavy weather had to make for Plymouth, where it was found that the hull needed to be repaired. The vessel set off again on 17 February 1856, arriving at Melbourne after a record passage of fifty-nine days, which enabled her owners to advertise that:

> This noble steam clipper built expressly for the company, one of the finest models yet constructed, combines all the advantages of a steamer with those of a clipper sailing ship, and offers the only opportunity yet presented to the public of certainty in the time required for a voyage. She has just made the extraordinary passage of fifty-nine days to Melbourne – a performance never before accomplished. On this voyage she ran one day of 358 miles, during which she attained the astonishing speed of 18 knots. Her daily average for the whole distance to Melbourne was 224 miles or 10.5 knots. Her accomodations for all classes of passengers are unrivalled.

In August 1859 the *Royal Charter* left Melbourne on her final voyage, with some passengers carrying considerable quantities of gold, and sailed directly from Australia to Queenstown in fifty-eight days. After disembarking some passengers, the vessel left for Liverpool on 24 October.

103 The Dic Evans Memorial Sculpture. The sculpture, by Sam Holland, is cast in bronze and stands 7ft high on a 6ft granite plinth at the Seawatch Centre, Moelfre. It was unveiled by the Prince of Wales on 23 November 2004. Richard Evans (who died in 2001 at the age of ninety-six) was Coxswain of the Moelfre lifeboat and was awarded two RNLI Gold Medals. In addition to commemorating Richard Evans, the intention was 'to celebrate the bravery and sense of duty of all lifeboat men and crews past and present'.

The storm which hit the area was exceptional, around 130 vessels were sunk, hundreds badly damaged and many people were killed. Winds of more than 100mph veered around from the east to the north, forcing the *Royal Charter* towards the north coast of Anglesey. Distress rockets were fired, the masts were cut down to provide less wind resistance, but the ship was now out of control, 'like a log of wood', and was battered to pieces on the rocks. It is thought that there were 500 men, women and children on board. Only about forty survived.

For some months the local press continued to report the finding of gold: 31 December 1859, sovereigns and bars of gold valued at £5,700. 1 January 1860, loose sovereigns, dust and one bar of gold valued at £1,000. 3 January, sovereigns, gold dust and bars valued at £1,006. 5 January, loose sovereigns, bars and gold dust valued at £12,000. (*North Wales Chronicle* 7 January 1860)

Two months after the disaster Charles Dickens made the journey to Anglesey, and described the scene in *The Uncommercial Traveller*:

> Cast up among the stones and boulders of the beach were great spars of the lost vessel, and masses of iron twisted by the fury of the sea into the strangest forms. The timber was already bleached and the iron rusted.

Dickens wrote of the Rector of Llanallgo, the Revd Stephen Roose Hughes:

> I had heard of that clergyman, as having buried many scores of the shipwrecked people; of his having opened his house and heart to their agonised friends; of his having used a most sweet and patient diligence for weeks and weeks, in the performance of the forlornest offices that Man can render to his kind; of his having most tenderly and thoroughly devoted himself

to the dead, and to those who were sorrowing for the dead. I had said to myself, 'In the Christmas season of the year, I should like to see that man!'

One hundred and forty of the victims are buried at Llanallgo.

The submarine *Thetis*, built by Cammell Laird, left Birkenhead on the morning of 1 June 1939 to undergo diving trials. The normal complement was fifty-three, but on this occasion there were fifty extra people on board: nine naval personnel and forty-one civilians (among whom were twenty-six employees of Cammell Laird and two caterers). Accompanied by the tug *Grebecock* the *Thetis* proceeded to the diving position, about fifteen miles off the Great Orme. At this point it had been expected that most of the supernumeries would be transferred to the tug, but they were allowed to remain on board.

The submarine submerged, slowly, at 3 p.m. It did not surface at the arranged time, and the destroyer *Brazen* was diverted to the scene, arriving at about 9 p.m. by which time other vessels and aircraft were on their way. The *Thetis* was found at 8 a.m. the next day, with about 20ft of the hull sticking up out of the water. Four men got out through the escape chamber, but the other ninety-nine did not survive. A member of the rescue team also died. *Thetis* was raised at last on 3 September 1939, the day the Second World War began, and was taken to Moelfre Bay, resting there for over two months while the bodies were removed, a task finally completed by Mines Rescue workers from Cannock Chase. On 16 November the funeral of fourteen men took place at Holyhead. Buried with full naval honours, the bodies were placed in a grave already containing thirty others from the *Thetis*.

The submarine was removed to dry dock at Holyhead, before being returned to Birkenhead. After rebuilding, the former *Thetis* took part in the war as HMS *Thunderbolt*, until sunk in the Mediterranean four years later. There were no survivors.

BEAUMARIS

Vessels from Llanfaes sailed to the Mersey in the thirteenth century, wine arrived from France and dairy produce was sent in return. Beaumaris Castle, begun in 1295, was planned so that vessels could come up to the main gate to unload supplies.

More extensive records are available for the sixteenth century when most trade was with Chester, although foreign vessels did visit Beaumaris, for example in 1562 the *Saint Maire* and the *Loche* came from Bilbao with iron, pitch and resin. In 1565 there were fifty-six visits by eight vessels: three from Brittany, two from Chester, two from Waterford and one from Scotland.

Two busy Beaumaris vessels were the *George* (12) and the *Mary* (10).

The George

24 April 1563. Master: Rolland Hamson, arrived with 100 pieces of calico, 6 hundredweights of sugar and three pounds of cloves.

15 February 1583. Master and merchant Richard Hampson, brought 300 'Newfoundland or Cod fishe' from Dublin.

14 May 1583. Master: Rowland Hampson, carried twenty barrels of salt from Ireland to Beaumaris for the merchant John Wigges of Altrincham.

20 September 1583. Master and merchant Rowland Hampson, eight barrels of 'bay salt' from Ireland.

7 November 1583. Master: Richard Hampson, merchant: George Beverley, gent. To Dublin, butter and salted cheese, 'provision for the realm of Ireland'.

7 January 1584. Master: Richard Hampson, merchant: Rowland Hampson. From Ireland, three barrels of 'shotten herrings', and a butt of sack for Thomas Rowland of Beaumaris.

104 The submarine HMS *Thetis* was lost during diving trials in June 1939. Ninety-nine people on board died. On 3 September 1939 the submarine was taken to Moelfre Bay, where it stayed for two months.

The Mary

21 March 1584. Master: Richard Hampson, merchant: George Beverley, gent, by Richard Dobbe, butter and cheese, 'provision for the realm of Ireland'.

19 June 1584. Master: Richard Hampson, Gascony wine from Ireland for Hugh Woodes and Rowland Williams.

1 April 1585. Master: Richard Hampson, two hogsheads of Gascony wine from Ireland for William Arrowsmith of Caernarfon.

The Port Books for the period December 1680 to December 1681 show an average of one inward coastal cargo a week, and a total of thirty-one outward in the year. A regular visitor was the *Wheel of Fortune* of Chester; on one voyage from Chester in April 1681 the cargo consisted of window glass, glass bottles, hardware, forty tanned hides, hops, 4 tons of iron, starch, tobacco, a trunk of books and vinegar.

In July of the same year the *Wheel of Fortune* brought tobacco, four-dozen frying pans, four-dozen hand bellows, 300 tanned hides, four boxes of tobacco pipes, two boxes for the apothecary, and a parcel of 'linen paper'. On the return voyages cargoes included bacon, barley, rye, malt, skins and herrings.

Lewis Morris (1701-65) was brought up on a farm near Dulas, Anglesey. From 1724 he was engaged to survey the estate of Owen Meyrick of Bodorgan, before being appointed a customs official at Beaumaris and Holyhead. In 1734 he tried to interest the Admiralty in his proposal to make accurate marine charts of the Welsh coast, but the response was lukewarm, and Lewis Morris had to charter a boat at his own expense, beginning the survey at Beaumaris.

The folio of eleven maps and sailing directions – *Cambria's Coasting Pilot* – was sent to the Admiralty in 1737, and the survey went on, at intervals, until 1744. Four years later the coastal chart and harbour plans were published to great acclaim, as they were a considerable improvement on any earlier ones. William Morris (Lewis's son) brought out a revised edition in 1801. Beaumaris was described as 'a place of good trade formerly, and might be so still, if its inhabitants pursued it, it being an excellent harbour, well situated and well supplied with the gifts of nature'. At Penmon 'there are several quarries of millstones, of the grit kind, of which great quantities are shipped off there'. Red Wharf was 'a noted place for the limestone trade... black and grey marble in abundance, which bears a good polish ... here is a rich sand for manuring, which is carried in small sloops to all parts of Anglesey'.

Steamboats

Beaumaris was to become a popular stop for steamboat passengers, but one early voyage was to end in tragedy. *The North Wales Chronicle* of 12 July 1831 announced that the wooden paddle vessel *Rothesay Castle* would sail from Liverpool to the Menai Straits on Monday, Wednesday and Friday mornings, returning on alternate days. The steamer is:

> Superbly fitted up for the accommodation and comfort of passengers; and from her easy drift of water she is enabled to go close in-shore, thereby insuring a smooth passage and an opportunity of viewing the beautiful scenery along the Welsh coast. Her speed is unequalled, the average length of passage being only five hours.

On 17 August 1831 the *Rothesay Castle* left Liverpool Pier Head. The *Liverpool Journal* later reported that many of the passengers were from Bradford, Leeds, York and the Lancashire towns of Bolton, Bury, Oldham and Manchester. During the voyage:

> …the wind being a little fresh, some of the passengers became alarmed, and their fears were increased by the tremulous motion of the steamer, which even in calm weather and smooth water was anything but firm. She appeared at this time crazy and weak, and the captain, it is reported on the authority of a surviving passenger, was importuned to put back.

It took ten hours to reach the Great Orme but the steamer ploughed on. A little after midnight the *Rothesay Castle* hit Dutchman's Bank, off Puffin Island. Of the 130 passengers, only twenty-one were saved. The inquest jury wished it to be recorded that:

> From the evidence brought before them, the jury, on this inquest, cannot separate without expressing their firm conviction, that had the *Rothesay Castle* been a seaworthy vessel, this awful calamity might have been averted. They therefore cannot disguise their indignation at the conduct of those who could place such a vessel on this station, and under the conduct of a captain and mate who have been proved by the evidence before them to have been in a state of intoxication.

In spite of the wreck of the *Rothesay Castle*, people flocked to take pleasure trips on the steamers, and Beaumaris Pier was opened in 1846. George Borrow in *Wild Wales* (1862) enthused over the view: "'What a bay!' said I "for beauty it is superior to the far-famed one of Naples. A proper place for the keels to start from, which unguided by the compass found their way over the mighty and mysterious Western Ocean!'"

Two cargo steamers were owned at Beaumaris in the early twentieth century by Sir Richard Williams Bulkeley. He was already involved in shipping in various ways, including investments in the Anglesey Shipping Co., whose vessels carried slate for the Penrhyn quarries. The Bulkeley Estate at Baron Hill made its own gas, which was also supplied to tenants in Beaumaris, and in 1908 a Clyde 'puffer' – *Mary* (98) – was bought to bring coal for the gasworks from Mersey ports. The vessel was sold in 1911 and, a year later, the *Tern* (158) was acquired from R. & W. Paul of Ipswich. The *Tern*, and the gasworks, were sold in 1919.

The demand for steamer services declined in the 1950s, and the landing stage at the pier was taken down.

CONWY

There were about sixty households at Conwy in the 1560s. The only local vessel appears to have been the *Katheryn* (40), owned by William Holland, William ap Richard and Robert Wynn. On 28 November 1565 the *Katherine*, master John Colley, brought home from La

105 *Conwy* in winter during the late nineteenth century.

Rochelle: 6 tuns of wine for William ap Richard; 3 tuns for Robert Wynne; 14 tuns of wine and eight pieces of 'poole Devias' for John Londall of London; 2 tuns of wine, 6 barrels of tar, 9 hundredweights of pitch and 7.5 hundredweights of iron for Henry Cardye of Beaumaris and 4 tuns of wine for Richard Holland of Conwy.

A later vessel, the *Mary* (12) of Conwy, Master David ap Hugh, arrived at Beaumaris on 17 March 1585 with cargo from the Isle of Man: barley, tallow, Manx wool, malt, Gascony wine.

Conwy Castle had been built by Edward I at the end of the thirteenth century to dominate the area, and to guard the river ferry. Over 300 years later the ferry was still important, and when the route for the new Royal Mail service was decided in 1599, its latter stages were Chester-Rhuddlan-ferry at Conwy-Beaumaris-Holyhead. Crossing at Conwy could be dangerous, one of the worst accidents being in 1806:

> A melancholy accident happened on Christmas Day. In consequence of a heavy swell in the River Conway, the boat which carried the Irish mail, with eight passengers, the coachman, the guard, and a youth of about fifteen years of age, in all fifteen in number, including the boatman, was upset, and all except two perished (*The Times* 29 December 1806)

A quay, built in 1835, handled slates from Blaenau Ffestiniog, but on a much smaller scale than other slate ports. Up to the end of the nineteenth century products from Llanrwst were taken to Trefriw before being brought down the river and trans-shipped at Conwy.

Conwy Shipbuilders

Carnarvon & Denbigh Herald 3 September 1836: 'The *Conway Castle* steam packet now building at Conway will be launched on Wed fourteenth instant.' It has been built 'under the superintendence of the most experienced Liverpool shipwright' and is intended for the Conway-Liverpool route. Local builders included John Roberts, Robert Roberts, Thomas Roberts, John Jones and Richard Thomas. Robert Roberts built schooners of up to 80 tons upriver at Caerhun between 1819 and 1855. Robert and Thomas Roberts launched the small steamer *Temple* (77) at Trefriw in 1874.

Top: 106 *The Three Janes* (101), a topsail schooner built in 1858 at Conwy. The managing owner was Morris Roberts, master mariner, of Porthmadog. The vessel was lost in 1895 after a collision off Land's End.

Above: 107 Conwy.

Left: 108 The quay at Trefriw in the late 1850s.

Clayton's Register of 1865 shows the following vessels belonging to Conwy, and their managing owners: *Alfred* (54), a schooner, built 1845, managing owner: the master, R. Edwards; *Conway's Pride* (49) a sloop built in 1859 owned by T. Jones, timber merchant; *Gwydir Castle* (41), a sloop built in 1834, the master, H. Hughes; *Hectorine* (40), a schooner built in 1840, owned by M. Edwards, timber merchant; *Jane Tudor* (393), a barque built in 1847, owned by T. Jones, timber merchant; *Janet* (70), a schooner built in 1862, and owned by H. Jones, Bodedda; *Lord Willoughby* (62) a schooner built in 1841, R. Davies, draper; *Margaret* (56) a schooner built in 1862, owned by R. Thomas, shipbuilder; *Penelope* (87), a schooner from 1855, owned by R. Davies, draper and the sloop *Sarah* (44) owned by the farmer, T. Jones.

The barque *Jane Tudor* is an obvious anomaly among the sloops and schooners. This vessel – on its maiden voyage from Bath, Maine to Liverpool – was wrecked at the Great Orme in 1847. The crew saved themselves by cutting down the mainmast, and then struggling along it to reach the shore. The wreck of the *Jane Tudor* was bought by T. Jones of Conwy, salvaged, repaired and then employed in carrying timber from North America.

Passenger steamboat services between Conwy and Trefriw began around the middle of the nineteenth century, the trip taking 1½ hours. In the 1880s Trefriw became known as a spa, complete with hotel, pump room and baths, and the quay was refurbished. The principal vessels, making trips only in summer, were the *Prince George* and the *King George*. The *Prince George*, built at Amlwch in 1890, began life as the *New S. George*, just over 70ft long and with a loaded draught of 3ft and 7in., it could carry up to 120 people. Canvas awnings could be fitted and the funnel was hinged, folding down to pass under a bridge. The vessel became *Prince George* in 1910. The other boat, *King George* (built at Northwich by W.H. Yarwood and Sons), was 80ft long and could carry 225 passengers.

LLANDUDNO

Copper was mined at the Great Orme during the Bronze Age. In later times ore was carried by sea to smelters in Lancashire or South Wales, and by the middle of the nineteenth century about 400 men were employed at the workings. The ore was hauled by horse and cart onto the beach at low tide, where it was loaded into grounded vessels.

At this time the only dwellings at Llandudno were miners' cottages. In the 1830s there was a plan to make a packet port at Orme's Bay, connected by rail with Chester, but it was soon realised that the sea journey to Dublin would be much longer than that from Holyhead, so nothing came of the idea.

The Great Orme was a notorious hazard for shipping, and innumerable vessels have been wrecked there, for example on New Year's Day 1824, when the brig *Hornby* was lost and only one man managed to scramble ashore. He decided to change his occupation, becoming a miner at the Great Orme.

Llandudno was developed as a Victorian seaside resort, complete with a pier, opened in 1877 and extended seven years later. The town became a popular call for pleasure steamers; at high water passengers could be embarked at the old wooden pier, but at low water they had to use small boats until a landing stage was built at the new pier in 1891.

RHUDDLAN

Construction of the castle at Rhuddlan began in the thirteenth century. The river was canalised for three miles so that vessels supplying the garrison could be brought up to the castle walls. During King Edward's second campaign Rhuddlan was the base for his naval force of about forty vessels and over a thousand men.

109 *La Marguerite* was a frequent visitor to Llandudno and other North Wales resorts from 1904 to 1925.

The bridge at Rhuddlan was rebuilt during the sixteenth century, preventing larger vessels from continuing upstream. Thomas Pennant wrote in 1788 that: 'The tides flow very little higher than this place, and bring up to the bridge flats or vessels of about 70 tons.' By then the town was the commercial centre for the Vale of Clwyd, and vessels loaded cargoes of coal and lead, grain and timber. In the *Handbook to the Vale of Clwyd* William Davies wrote that:

> Near the bridge the tide rises sufficiently to bring up flats and other vessels of considerable tonnage, and a commodious harbour has been formed which is accessible at all states of the tide for vessels of 100 tons burden. Spacious quays and wharves have been constructed and warehouses erected for facilitating the trade of the place, which more recently has become a depot for supplying the several towns of the Vale of Clwyd, and adjacent ports of North Wales.

Hughes (in Roberts 1991) produced a list of vessels built on the River Clwyd, indicating that twenty-eight were built at Rhuddlan between 1767 and 1863, twelve of them schooners. The principal builder was Robert Jones, who launched the schooner *Lord Mostyn* in 1845, partly owned by John Roberts (Robert Jones's foreman). The *Lord Mostyn* was acquired by William Thomas of Amlwch in 1863 and was wrecked there in 1890. Vessels built by Jones and Roberts in the 1850s included *Joshua*, a schooner; *Margaret and Elizabeth*, a schooner and *Pennington*, a flat.

In the 1881 census four small vessels were noted at Rhuddlan: *Hannah*, *Lizzie*, *Milton* and *William Henry*.

RHYL

There was a well-established shipping place at the Foryd long before Lord Mostyn ordered his fertiliser:

110 Rhuddlan.

Guano: Lord Mostyn has ordered a ship-load of this valuable manure to be consigned to him at the Foryd. The noble Lord has taken every precaution to ensure its being delivered in a pure state; and we understand that his friends and neighbours, as well as tenants, will be allowed to purchase on easy terms. (*Caernarvon & Denbigh Herald* 30 November 1844)

More usual loads handled at the small harbour were mixed cargoes, timber and slate. The Chester & Holyhead Railway arrived in 1847 and in the following year traffic began to cross the River Clwyd on a new railway bridge, which could be opened in the middle to allow vessels to pass.

Ships had been built at the Foryd for some time, but it can be difficult to distinguish in the records between those built at Rhuddlan and those built at Foryd. Thirty-four craft are listed as being built at the Foryd between 1842 and 1878, nearly half of them schooners. These tended to be larger than those built upriver; the Rhuddlan vessels were 61 to 75ft long; those at Rhyl were 71 to 110ft long.

Robert Jones moved his shipbuilding downriver from Rhuddlan to the Foryd in 1857, but the first launch at the new site did not go smoothly, according to the *Rhyl Record*: 'Owing to some mismanagement, the workmen failed in inducing her to take to her native element, and there she had to be left as before standing bold and erect on *terra firma*.' A later edition of the newpaper carried an account of a case heard by the local magistrates on 30 June 1857, when the complainant John Jones, shipwright, accused William White of assault. John Jones's solicitor stated that the assault took place when a ship was about to be launched. John Jones was on the slipway, trying to make sure that everything was in order. A dog appeared, which scampered about on the slip, peppering the grease with sand and pebbles. Jones shouted for the owner, who did not appear, so he threw some stones to frighten the dog away: 'He kicked the dog as it again passed him through the cradle, on which the dog turned and seized him by the leg, and while disengaging it with his foot he was struck from behind by the defendant and thrown with great force into the trough'. If the vessel had begun to move John Jones would have been killed.

The defendant, William White, said that:

RHYL.HARBOUR.

111 The Foryd harbour, Rhyl.

…his little dog was swimming in the water and he whistled it out fearing that the tide might carry it away, but the dog crossed the track of the ship and the complainant, who was drunk at the time, threw immense stones at the dog… He feared that the dog would be killed and he told the complainant that if he hit the dog again he would knock him down. The dog was only playing with the complainant's leg and did him no harm. He admitted that he gave him a push but then went away.

He was chased by Jones and 'a great number of ships' carpenters' so he jumped into the river to escape. James Harding, a witness for the defence, 'noticed the little dog, a small thing like a spaniel, playing and jumping around, but he could have done no harm. Large stones were unnecessarily thrown by the complainant which he thought was very cruel'. John Jones 'here requested that the dog might be sent for, when it proved to be a fierce-looking bull-terrier bitch'. William White was fined 7s and 6d, with £1, 2s costs.

The brigantine *Neophyte* was launched on 22 August 1857, when 'an excellent band of music was stationed on board and there was a profuse display of flags… A party of about seventy sat down to an excellent luncheon prepared in a spacious tent in the immediate vicinity'.

The vessel was to be wrecked, a year later, off Sierra Leone.

There were other builders at Foryd, including Owain Hughes and James Patterson who launched the *Queen of the Vale* in 1862 (it was to be lost at sea a year later) from the west bank of the river. In the same year, 1862, a new Act of Parliament permitted a branch of the railway to be laid to the west bank, opposite Robert Jones's yard. Rails from South Wales came in by sea, to be discharged at the Foryd harbour.

The *Rhyl Record* of 6 April 1865 noted that Robert Jones had just finished another vessel, the purchasers being Brayne & Co. of Liverpool: 'This is the thirteenth vessel which has been built by Mr. Jones in a few years, and another vessel is on the stocks for Messrs William Morris & Co, Rhyl'. A year later the schooner *City of St Asaph* (230), 110ft long, came down the slipway, the largest vessel launched on the Clwyd. Next day, it was towed to Liverpool for fitting out.

112 The paddle steamer *Denbigh*, which went from plying between Liverpool and Rhyl to running the blockade in the American Civil War.

After Robert Jones died, in May 1871, the business was carried on by his son, another Robert Jones. He built: 1872 *Annie Jones*, a schooner, owned by John Jones of Chester; 1873 *Sarah Elizabeth*, a schooner; in 1875 two flats, launched on the same day, *Minnie* and *Tryfan*.

William and George (151), a three-masted schooner, was sunk by a submarine in 1916 while carrying coal from Swansea to St Valery-en-Caux. Two flats were launched in 1877, as was the schooner *Burgedin* (161), which was to be lost after a collision with a steamer in Liverpool Bay. Two schooners came down the slipway in 1878, ending shipbuilding on the Clwyd (apart from a small pleasure boat built in 1911). Robert Jones concentrated on his dredging business, while the timber business of brother Charles Jones was sustained by timber-carrying vessels which discharged their cargoes at the Foryd.

By the late 1820s there was a daily service from Liverpool to Rhyl by paddle steamers, including the *Gulliver* and the *Hercules*, vessels which arrived after having called, usually, at Hoylake and Mostyn Quay. Services had developed considerably by the 1890s, when there were calls by vessels such as the *Elwy*, *St Tudno* and the *Vale of Clwyd*. John J. Hughes of Rhyl was manager of the Rhyl & Vale of Clwyd Steam Ship Co. which ran the *Fawn* between Liverpool and the Menai Straits from 1891 until the vessel was sold in 1893 to the Orkney Steam Navigation Co.

The paddle steamer *Denbigh* was built by John Laird & Sons at Birkenhead, with an overall length of 180ft and a breadth between paddle boxes of 22ft. Launched in August 1860, the vessel was acquired in order 'to connect the flourishing watering-place Rhyl with Liverpool by sea'. The *Denbigh* was employed on this route for three years until sold to the 'European Trading Co.', a syndicate of people from Britain, France and Alabama. President Lincoln had imposed a blockade on the Confederate States of America in April 1861, enforced by United States naval vessels, and the *Denbigh* was bought for use as a blockade runner, carrying supplies from Havana to Galveston and Mobile.

The steamer sailed from Liverpool, with a master and crew of eighteen, on 19 October 1863, and became one of the most effective blockade runners, making thirteen successful runs.

113 The first powered submarine, *Resurgam*, which sank off Rhyl in February 1880. The wreck was
not found until 1955.

The end came on the night of 23/24 May 1865, when the former Rhyl steamer ran aground
on Bird Quay, a sandbank near Galveston. The *Denbigh* was shattered by gunfire from Union
vessels and then burned by boarding parties. The remains of the vessel were found in 1997 and
there is now a project to study and preserve the wreck, undertaken by the Institute of Nautical
Archaeology of Texas A. & M. University.

Resurgam

Rhyl had grown considerably by 1880. *The Wales Register and Guide* noted that:

> Rhyl, one of the most flourishing towns in the county, is an excellent bathing place at the
> mouth of the Clwyd. During the last ten years it has made wonderful progress, and from a
> small village has now become a fashionable town, much frequented by English visitors... A
> little commercial trade is carried on with the town, and steamers ply to Liverpool. Population
> about 8000.

From the harbour of this 'fashionable town' a strangely shaped object departed at 10 p.m. on
24 February 1880 - this was the *Resurgam*, the first submarine which could travel underwater
using its own power. Designed by the Revd George William Littler Garrett it was 42ft long by
12ft wide (at its maximum) and built of steel by J.T. Cochrane & Co. at Birkenhead. The vessel
was powered by steam and the crew of three had to stand up all the time; when the submarine
was on the surface they could look out of the top hatch by standing on the boiler.

The maiden voyage began on 10 December 1879 when the *Resurgam* set off down the
Mersey, on the way to Admiralty trials at Portsmouth. On board were Garrett, George Price
(the engineer) and Captain W.E. Jackson. The vessel spent thirty hours submerged before

114 The 'tubular' lifeboat was patented by Henry Richardson, of Aberhirnant, near Bala. This is the Liverpool boat, launched in 1863, but the first was stationed at Rhyl in 1856.

berthing at Foryd harbour. Modifications needed to be made to the propeller, so it was decided to break off the voyage and have new castings made.

Ten weeks later the *Resurgam* resumed the journey to Portsmouth, towed by the steamer *Elphin*. Next day, in a gale, the *Elphin's* boiler began to give trouble, and the three men from the submarine transferred to the other vessel to see if they could help. At 10 a.m. on 26 February the towing hawser broke. The weather was getting worse and the steamer had to make for the shelter of the Dee Estuary, anchoring off Mostyn. Next morning its anchor chains broke, and the vessel began to drift. The *Iron King*, coming to help, rammed the *Elphin*, which was lost. Meanwhile, the *Resurgam* had disappeared, and was not found until October 1995, when a local fishing boat snagged its nets on the wreckage.

Richardson's Patent Tubular Lifeboat

Three successive tubular lifeboats were stationed at Rhyl from 1856. The boats, designed by Henry Richardson of Aberhirnant near Bala, were made of iron (except for gunwhales and strake). Two iron tubes ran from stem to stern, with fourteen water-tight bulkheads, and any water shipped into the boat could drain away through gratings. The crew had no protection from the weather, and quickly became soaked.

FIVE

The Dee Estuary

Chester had been a port from Roman times, but was always badly affected by the difficulties of navigating the notorious Dee Estuary, where the sands shifted constantly. There were various proposals, and a few attempts, to improve matters. In 1737 the Dee was canalised between Golftyn and Chester, diverting the river from the northern to the southern side, and leading to the demise of Parkgate as a port. An Act of Parliament in 1740 established a joint-stock company: the 'Co. of Proprietors of the Undertaking and Preserving the Navigation of the River Dee', usually known as the River Dee Co.

Coal was an important commodity on the Welsh side of the estuary, supplied to those building Edward I's castles and later for local domestic use. By the seventeenth century coal was being exported, mostly to Dublin, and along Deeside were several creeks used to ship the coal. A petition to Parliament stated that there were 'about ten harbours and several docks upon the said river'.

POINT OF AYR

A tragedy in October 1775 led to the building of a lighthouse at Point of Ayr. The *Nonpareil* and the *Trevor* sailed regularly from Parkgate to Howth. On 19 October they left at the same time, but the *Trevor* was forced by the storm on to the Lancashire coast (only one man was saved) and the *Nonpareil* was lost on the Hoyle Bank. In the two wrecks over 200 people died.

A committee was formed which concluded that lighthouses were needed at Point of Ayr, and that the channels needed to be better marked because 'the banks shift so often that the pilots are obliged to fix empty casks as temporary buoys before they dare venture to bring up any large vessels'. The Mayor of Liverpool objected, on the grounds that the lighthouses 'would be of great prejudice to the Navigation of Liverpool because these lights would be taken for the lighthouses they had already erected and would lead their pilots into many errors'. The River Dee Co. refused to provide any money. In spite of these difficulties the light began to shine on 30 September 1777.

The Point of Ayr lifeboat was launched in a gale at 10 a.m. on Sunday 7 January 1857, on its way to help a brigantine in distress. The boat was 42ft long and was propelled by ten oars, although there were also sails. The crew was led by two fishermen, Robert Beck (in charge) and John Sherlock (mate). The rest of the men in the boat were three miners, three labourers, two gardeners, a coachman, a shopkeeper and a sawyer. The lifeboat capsized off Rhyl, and all the men died. In the meantime the Rhyl tubular lifeboat had managed to rescue the men from the brigantine.

Coal began to be mined by the Point of Ayr Colliery Co. in 1883. The workings went under the estuary of the Dee, and there was an existing quay (formerly used for exporting stone)

115 A model of the *Talacre*. This small steamer was launched in 1917 at Great Yarmouth for Point of Ayr Collieries Ltd. It was in service until 1959.

where a good deal of the mine's output could be loaded into coasters and taken to Ireland and the Isle of Man.

In 1916 the colliery company bought the *Clwyd* (289) from the Clwyd Steamship Co. of Liverpool; just before Christmas, a year later, the vessel sank, with the loss of one man, after a collision with the steamer *Paragon* off Anglesey. In August 1917 the *Talacre* (301) was launched for the company by Crabtree & Co. of Southtown, Great Yarmouth. Two other coasters followed in 1922 and 1923. On 1 January 1947 the Point of Ayr enterprise was taken over by the new National Coal Board. The vessels were scrapped in the late 1950s, and coal was sent out by rail until the colliery closed in 1997.

MOSTYN

There was some trade and a little shipbuilding at Mostyn from medieval times. Coal was mined but the treacherous sandbanks hampered its shipment, until a channel was cut by Sir Thomas Mostyn.

There are occasional records of Mostyn vessels and their trade; for example on 10 October 1602 the *Mary* (20) of Mostyn, master John Hodson, carried from Chester to Beaumaris: salt, iron, hardware, candles, cloth, leather, forty empty casks, a cupboard, a table, five-dozen stools, five chairs, a bed, soap, flax, hops, glass, madder and alum. In the next month the same vessel and master took iron, salt, raisins, sugar, currants, prunes and vinegar from Chester to Beaumaris for Hugh Arthur.

By the 1840s timber from North America and the Baltic was being unloaded at Mostyn and floated, or carried by barge, up to Chester.

116 The Liverpool to Mostyn packet, 1829.

The impetus for the growth of the town came with the arrival of the Chester & Holyhead Railway, followed by the establishment of the ironworks in 1865. The Mostyn Coal & Iron Co. took over the docks, importing iron ore and exporting such coal as was not used in their works. In 1877 the firm merged with a Lancashire concern to become the Darwen & Mostyn Iron Co. Seven years later the workings of the Mostyn Colliery flooded, and the colliery was closed, which meant that coal for the ironworks had to be brought in by sea. Iron ore came from France, Portugal, Spain and even further afield.

There were occasional steamer services from Mostyn to Liverpool, including those provided by the *Hercules*. Later, freight and passengers were carried by the Coal & Iron Co.'s vessels: the paddle steamer *Swiftsure* was advertised in 1875 as willing to carry goods, carriages and horses to Liverpool. The *Wales Register and Guide* of 1878 noted, 'Water conveyance – To Liverpool, the *Swiftsure* from Mostyn Quay, occasionally'. Details of sailings could be had from the Mostyn Colliery storekeeper. The *Swiftsure* (115) was an iron paddle steamer – 125ft by 19ft – built at Chester in 1861. Until 1894 it left Liverpool for Mostyn on two or three days a week.

In the 1890s the *Flying Falcon* (154) was employed in a similar manner. Owned by the Star Steam Tug Co., the vessel had been built at South Shields in 1878 as the *Lord Bandon*. It went daily in summer from Liverpool to Mostyn, except on Sundays, when it took trippers to Southport.

The tug *Taliesin*, built at Cardiff in 1883, was employed (other duties permitting) on Sunday trips to Llandudno, carrying up to a hundred passengers at a time.

The Mostyn Iron Co. owned six small steamers between 1866 and 1940, three of them built in Wales: *Temple* (77) launched in 1874 by Robert and Thomas Roberts, Trefriw, and bought in 1894; *Honor Storey* (129) completed for the company in 1915 by Abdela and Mitchell at Queensferry; *Fer* (151), built for the company in 1921 by J. Crichton & Co., Saltney. The company's last ship was the *Lady Mostyn*, sunk by a mine near the Formby Lightship on 23 July 1940. All seven of the crew died.

The Lewis family owned seven vessels (five of them built by Readheads of South Shields) between 1876 and 1898. Each was owned on the 64th system by family members including Enoch Lewis and John Herbert Lewis.

The last cargo of ore was discharged at Mostyn in the early 1950s. After that, coal and ore were transported by rail. The docks managed to continue, handling general cargo, and Mostyn received a boost in November 2001 when P&O decided to move its Dublin ferry service from Liverpool to Mostyn, cutting 1½ hours from the crossing. A roll-on, roll-off terminal was built, and the dock was dredged. Bad news came eighteen months later, when P&O sold its ferry vessels to Stena Line, and Mostyn was abandoned.

The wings (each one 148ft long) for the A380 Airbus aircraft were built at Broughton, Flintshire, where over 6,000 people were employed. Components of the aircraft were made at Hamburg, Puerto Real and St Nazaire, as well as at Broughton, and were then transported to be assembled at Toulouse. In April 2004 the first wing began its journey from Broughton to the Dee, a distance of about a mile, on a ninety-five-wheeled trailer. It was then loaded into a purpose-built self-propelled barge, the *Afon Dyfrdwy*, which had a normal service speed of about 6 knots. Operated by the Holyhead Transportation Co. the barge carried the wing to Mostyn, where it was transferred to the *Ville de Paris*, a roll-on, roll-off vessel built in China specifically for this task. The maiden flight of the A380, the world's largest passenger aircraft, took place a year later.

HOLYWELL

The holy well of St Winefride, celebrated as one of the 'Seven Wonders of Wales', became a place of pilgrimage in the twelfth century, and it still is today. The well and the pilgrims were, until the Dissolution, looked after by the monks of Basingwerk Abbey who also, in the Cistercian way, engaged in the production of wool.

The first industrial enterprises to be established at Holywell were cotton, wool and metal-working. Cotton factories were operating from the 1770s until about 1850. The first copper and brass works was set up in 1755 and in 1787 the Parys Mine Co.'s works began production, specialising in making the copper sheathing which protected wooden vessels against the Teredo worm, and copper bolts for shipbuilding.

Lead was mined at the Holywell level. A directory published in 1878 informed readers that:

Lead is found in [the] Halkyn mountains and the vicinity of Holywell, Mold and Prestatyn. These mines give employment to hundreds of workmen, and to numbers who are afterwards

117 A wing for the Airbus 380 is brought down the Dee by barge to be loaded on to the *Ville de Paris*, which will take it to Pauillac, near Toulouse.

engaged in smelting it at Bagillt, Mold, Holywell and Flint. The Talacre lead mines, near Llanasa, are some of the richest in Wales, producing annually several thousands of tons of the ore. The ore is also shipped at Holywell and Mostyn for Chester, where it is smelted.

Sales of lead ore were held once a fortnight, alternately at Holywell and Flint.

BAGILLT

Edward I's castles were built in the late thirteenth and early fourteenth centuries, and during this period up to thirty ships a day sailed from Bagillt carrying stone and coal to the workforce. The lead industry grew to be important, and in the late eighteenth century there was a large rope-making facility, and a soap works.

With the steamer *Ancient Briton* (Mersey & Dee Packet Co.) running between Parkgate and Bagillt in 1817 it was possible to shorten the journey from Liverpool to North Wales by crossing the Mersey to Tranmere, then by coach to Parkgate, and on by the paddle steamer to Bagillt. Soon there were direct services between Liverpool and Bagillt: 'The newly built steam packet *Cambria* will be sailing to Bagillt fitted out with every convenience, with accomodation for horses and carriages' announced the *North Wales Gazette* on 10 May 1821. The first passage to Bagillt was made on 4 June 1821. By 1824 it was being advertised as leaving Liverpool every day at 8 a.m. carrying passengers and freight. At Bagillt coaches were waiting to take passengers on to Denbigh, Holywell and St Asaph. The *Albion* and the *Druid* were also used on this route, and five years later the service had been extended to Rhyl, departing from Liverpool and calling at Hoylake and Mostyn Quay, rather than at Bagillt.

The main traffic across the Dee Bank Wharf continued to be lead ore, and in the year 1840 about 40,000 tons were landed for the Bagillt Lead Works.

FLINT

By the mid-sixteenth century Flint was 'a small town with a fair castle having a creek for small boats' and a quay was in use by the end of the seventeenth century.

In the 1820s the steamer *Black Diamond* – owned by Eyton & Co. – ran between Flint and Liverpool. Commercial traffic to Chester was declining in the 1830s, to the benefit of Flint, which began to function as 'the port for Chester'. In the year 1833, a total of 683 vessels with cargoes cleared coastwise from Flint, and 141 arrived carrying cargo.

Coal was hauled to the shipping places by cart or pack animal but, later, tramways connected pits to the sea. There were two quays, one for the mines of the Eyton family, the other for those of Pickering and Ormiston. By 1886 coal production had dwindled to the point where only one pit was being worked.

The smelting of lead was an ancient occupation at Flint, and in the 1820s there were seven furnaces, five slag hearths and two silver refineries, with sales of lead ore being held fortnightly. Thirty years later there was no local smelting.

An alkali works was set up in 1852 and the wharves handled manganese imported for Smith and Maudsley's chemical works. In 1887 John Bartholomew's *Gazetteer of the British Isles* lists the imports at Flint as sulphur and other chemicals; the exports included coal, soda and potash. The alkali works closed in 1919 and after that the dock was little used by commercial vessels.

Shipbuilders at Flint included Edward Evans, David McCartney, Andrew Green, William Patton and, for a short period, Ferguson and Baird. The *Mary Jones* (118), a three-masted schooner launched by David Jones in 1863, was probably the last vessel to be built at Flint. It was wrecked off Ramsgate in 1932.

CONNAH'S QUAY

Up to the 1860s there was only a small quay, but the port began to develop with the opening of the Wrexham, Mold & Connah's Quay Railway in 1862. In 1886 a new wharf was added by the railway company. The Great Central Railway acquired the port in 1904, when it was serving the needs of chemical works, engineering firms and shipbuilders. Nearly 300 vessels arrived in 1900 and about 200 in 1912. Exports included earthenware, bricks from Buckley and tiles from Ruabon, all cargoes which needed careful handling and loading.

Connah's Quay Shipbuilding
Ferguson & Baird moved from Flint to Golftyn in 1858. They were to build over fifty vessels, including:

In 1858, *Edward* (65), a schooner, joint owners Daniel Ferguson, John McCallum and James Baird.

In 1881, *Hawarden Castle*, a steamer for the Connah's Quay Alkali Co.

In 1890, *Windermere* (174), a three-masted schooner, 104ft by 24ft by 11ft, launched in August, for a Barrow owner.

In 1900, *Lizzie May* (136), a three-masted schooner launched for John Coppack, and named after his daughters. Sold to a Youghal owner in 1908 and traded from there, usually carrying coal from the Severn ports to Ireland, as the *Kathleen and May*. Sold to Appledore owners in 1931, when an engine was fitted. Continued trading to 1960, but eventually fell into disuse. After lengthy periods of restoration, the vessel is sailing again, from a base at Bideford, and is a popular attraction.

In 1901, *J. & A. Coppack*, a ketch, lost off Cornwall in November 1909, on passage to Mousehole; *Catherine Reney*, a ketch, wrecked in December 1905 at Donaghadee, with the loss of all on board.

In 1903, *Sarah Latham*, a ketch.

118 This triple-masted schooner was built in 1900, as the *Lizzie May*, by Ferguson & Baird at Connah's Quay. It was sold to a Youghal owner in 1908, when the name was changed to *Kathleen and May*. The illustration shows the vessel, over a century old, in her current restored condition.

By the 1890s there were three builders at Connah's Quay: Ferguson & Baird, W. Butler & Son and T. W. Toby.

J. Crichton & Co. followed on from Ferguson & Baird in 1918, having opened a yard at Saltney five years before. Their yard at Connah's Quay was next to the docks and covered ten acres. In 1920 Crichton's launched the steam coasters *Kinnaird Head* (415) – for the General Steam Navigation Co. – and *Wearside* (420), for the Wear Steam Shipping Co. These were followed by the small motor coasters *Georgita, Jonita, Marcita* and *Wilita* for John Summers & Sons, Shotton.

In the following year, on 12 April 1921, the oil tanker *Allegheny* (856) was launched for the Anglo-American Oil Co. and was towed to Saltney for installation of machinery. This was the first oil-burning steamer to be built on the Dee. Apart from four dumb barges in 1924, all other building by Crichton's was done at Saltney, with vessels being towed to Connah's Quay for finishing until that yard closed in 1932.

Vessels belonging to Connah's Quay were usually registered at Chester. In the 1865 *Clayton's Register* there were nineteen vessels (thirteen of them schooners) with managing owners at Connah's Quay. Eleven were owned by 'J. Davison, merchant' and four by 'J. Reney, sailmaker'. By the 1880s members of the Reney family were managing ten vessels.

Lloyd's Register of 1891/92 lists owners at Connah's Quay as: Coppack, Carter & Co., five vessels; James Coppack, one; Samuel Coppack, two; James Reney, three; John Reney, two; William Reney, one; Joseph Vickers, three; Samuel Vickers, four; William Vickers, one; Thomas Mathias, two; Christopher Bennett, one and John Hughes, one.

At the outbreak of the First World War the Reneys operated fourteen schooners.

119 The *Allegheny* was launched at Connah's Quay in 1921 by J. Crichton & Co. for the Anglo-American Oil Co. The largest vessel built by Crichton's, it was taken to Saltney for fitting out.

The Coppack Family

Members of the Coppack family managed twenty-three vessels between 1882 and 1971, their first steamship being the *Aston* (132), launched on the Tyne in 1867, and acquired in 1882. Only three of their vessels were bought directly from the builder: *Rosalind* (681) in 1884, *Shotton* (300) in 1909 and *Fairfield* (468) in 1921. Most were around 250grt (gross registered tons), with only four over 400grt. Three came from local yards; *Hawarden Castle* (95) built by Ferguson and Baird in 1881 for the the Connah's Quay Alkali Co., and two motor vessels built by Abdela & Mitchell at Queensferry for John Summers & Sons: *Fleurita* (170) and *Indorita* (201). The longest-serving ship was the *Mourne* (221), which was in the fleet for thirty-two years. Built at Paisley in 1894 for Irish owners, it sank in December 1898 after a collision in Penarth Roads. The vessel was salvaged, and acquired by another Irish firm, before being bought by Coppack's in 1901. The *Mourne* foundered in 1933 while carrying China clay from Par to Runcorn.

The *Moss Rose*, a three-masted schooner built in 1888 at Ardrossan, was sunk by gunfire in the First World War, but the crew were saved.

During the Second World War the *Farfield* was carrying granite from Penmaenmawr to Gloucester when it was bombed and machine-gunned off the South Stack, Holyhead. Seven men died, but one survived by clinging to a hatch cover in the sea for twelve hours. The firm bought *Elidir* from the Dinorwic Quarry Co. in 1942. Requisitioned by the Admiralty it sailed in support of the Normandy landings to the Mulberry harbour and French ports. The *Watergate* was damaged on the beach at Arromanches, and repaired at Sunderland.

After the war the company bought the motor vessels *Fleurita* (built by Abdela & Mitchell in 1913 for John Summers) and *Indorita* (built in 1920, also for John Summers). *Indorita* was 109ft by 22ft, and was operated by a master, a mate, two engineers and two seamen, usually to Belfast, Cork, Dublin, Manchester and Swansea. Stone was loaded at places such as Penmaenmawr and taken to Liverpool or Preston. The last Coppack vessel, *Vauban* (370), was bought in 1968 and sold in 1971.

There was a reduction in the traffic of the port in the years immediately before the First World War, 450 vessels had entered or left the port in 1905/06 (total registered tonnage: 35,000). By 1912/13 there were 276 vessel movements (less than 22,000 registered tonnage). It was a port used by small coasting vessels, 80 per cent of them sailing. Bricks accounted for 60 per cent of the cargoes, and half of all outgoing cargoes were taken to Belfast, Dublin or Liverpool. The principal import was grain for the Cobden Mills at Wrexham. By the 1930s there were still five schooners owned at Connah's Quay, including the sister vessels *Isabella* and *Useful*.

120 *Rosabelle* was completed at Carrickfergus in 1893. Acquired by Coppack Brothers at Connah's Quay in 1906 she remained with the company until 1934.

In the 1950s bricks were still being exported, as well as chemicals, and timber was being imported. A marina was opened in 1981.

SHOTTON

The Summers family, nail manufacturers at Stalybridge in Cheshire, began building their Hawarden Bridge Iron Works in 1896. The size of the workforce was to grow to about 13,000. The company bought its first vessels, used to carry supplies from Liverpool, in 1897. They were all second-hand: *Sunflower* (69), *Buffalo* (118) and *Rio Formoso* (163). Altogether John Summers & Sons were to own a total of twenty-seven vessels, ten of them built locally: six by Abdela and Mitchell at Queensferry and four by J. Crichton & Co. at Connah's Quay.

At the wharves owned by John Summers & Sons vessels discharged such cargoes as iron ore, pig iron, iron bars and steel bars. The exports were the steel products of the works, as well as basic slag (a by-product, used as a fertiliser) to the south-west of Scotland.

The company was taken into public ownership in 1967, when the remaining two Summers vessels were sold. The wharf remained in occasional use until the 1980s.

QUEENSFERRY

James Boydell launched a vessel a year at Queensferry from 1836 to 1843. He was followed by George K. Smith, who launched three small iron vessels between 1889 and 1892; *Alerta*, *Daisy* and *Nora*, all around 50ft long. Wilson & Co. built *Reliance* in 1892 and the Queensferry Shipbuilding & Engineering Co. launched a tug and two ferries (1894-97), and then a number of lighters for use on the Mersey.

The steamer *Aston* (132) was built on the Tyne in 1867 for J. and F. Thompson of Queensferry. Among the investors were William Gladstone of Hawarden (who was to become Prime Minister in February 1868), Alexander Ward (a local mining engineer), James Wilson (a Belfast merchant) and the Mack family of Liverpool. A second vessel, the fourteen-year-old *Shark* (176), was bought in 1880. Both were sold in 1882, the *Aston* to John Coppack of Connah's Quay.

The Dee Shipbuilding Co. built small steam vessels and motor boats, unloading raw materials at their own wharf.

In 1908 Abdela & Mitchell took over the Dee Shipbuilding yard. They had gone into shipbuilding at Brimscombe, near Stroud, seven years earlier, when they acquired the business of Edwin Clark & Co. From 1908 to 1931 the firm built thirty vessels at Queensferry, five of them for John Summers & Sons: in 1913, the *Carita* (141) and *Fleurita* (170); in 1915, *Warita* (305); in 1920 *Indorita* (201) and *Eldorita* (201). *Sir William* (170) was completed in November 1914 for John H. Vernon of Liverpool, and bought by Summers six months later.

Several tugs were built including, in 1909, the *Provencal 17* and *Provencal 19* for the port of Marseilles and two small canal tugs in 1912 – the *Birmingham* and the *Worcester* – for use on English waterways. Abdela & Mitchell's largest vessel was the river steamer *Lobão* (534) launched at Queensferry in 1911, and destined for Brazil. The engines, and her steam launch, were built at Brimscombe. Four small oil tankers were constructed, three in 1921 - *Shell Mex 4*, *Shell Mex 5* and *Aurora* – followed by *Energy*.

SANDYCROFT

As well as a few sailing craft, John Rigby built a series of paddle steamers at Sandycroft: the 1827 *Dairy Maid* (43); in 1830, the *Kingfisher* (120); *Lapwing* (33) was built in 1832; in 1835, *Alexandra* (83); in 1841, the Amazon river steamer *Guapiaçu*; in 1843 the *Prince of Wales* (38); the *Star* (92) built in 1845 and in 1846 *Forth* and *Birkenhead* (132).

George Cramm set up at Sandycroft in 1852 and launched *Amelia* (350) and *Winefred* (1,359), an iron full-rigged ship for Sharples & Co. of Liverpool. The *Royal Charter* was laid down by George Cramm, but completed under the supervision of William Patterson, who had built Brunel's *Great Western* and *Great Britain*. The *Royal Charter* was bought before completion by Gibbs, Bright & Co. and finished as a full-rigged ship with an auxiliary engine. (Gibbs, Bright & Co. of Liverpool also owned the *Great Britain*.)

Northern Daily Times of 1 August 1855 stated:

> Yesterday was fixed for the launch of the magnificent screw steamer *Royal Charter*, built for Messrs Gibbs Bright and Co. of the Australian Steam Navigation Co. The vessel was built at Sandicroft Works on the Dee… Much interest was felt in the launch of the vessel, great numbers travelled yesterday from Liverpool and Chester to be present. From 9 a.m. till 4 p.m. the rain poured down, yet despite this fact, both banks of the Dee were crowded with spectators, and boats gaily decked with flags passed up and down the river. Precisely at 1 p.m. the great vessel moved in its place and the wine bottle, which consecrates its 'christening', was flung by Mrs S. Bright, who performed the ceremony. The vessel glided on gracefully, amid the cheers and waving but, just after entering the water, met with a sudden check, and rested motionless as before. Every effort was made to free her by the tug boats, but without effect. She was propped up firmly to wait for the next tide.

The *Royal Charter* was launched, at last, on 30 August 1855. Just over four years later it was to be demolished on the rocks of Anglesey (see pages 152-154).

121 Abdela & Mitchell's shipyard at Queensferry. They built thirty vessels here between 1908 and 1931.

122 This vessel, which had an overall length of 80ft, was built by Abdela & Mitchell in 1923. It had a crew of four and could carry 200 people. After service on the Caernarfon to Foel ferry it was sold to the operators of the Neyland-Hobbs Point ferry, who gave it the name *Alum Chine*. It was scrapped in 1956.

123 The steamer *Lobão*, launched at Queensferry in 1911, was built for service on Brazilian rivers. It was the largest vessel constructed by Abdela & Mitchell.

124 The *Royal Charter* was launched at Sandycroft on 30 August 1855. Its maiden voyage to Australia was done in record time, but the *Royal Charter* was wrecked on the rocks of Anglesey in October 1859, when nearly 500 people died.

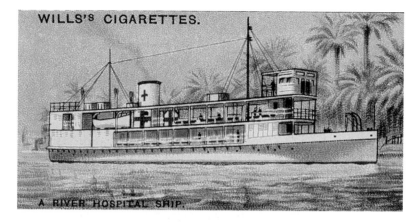

125 Cigarette cards from the series 'Strange Craft'. These craft were built by J. Crichton & Co. at Saltney:

Above: A hospital ship built during the First World War for service on the River Tigris.

Left: A floating grain elevator built in 1924. 100ft high, it was used in Liverpool Docks.

Opposite above: The *Beta*, a floating beacon built in 1925. It was 40ft long, with a 30ft-high lattice tower. The *Beta* was stationed on the Crosby Channel at the mouth of the Mersey.

Opposite below: An oil-separator barge built in 1926. Working in docks, polluted water was taken in and clean water pumped out. Up to 50 tons of recovered oil could be stored on board.

126 The *Lurgerena* was a vehicle/passenger ferry built for the government of Tasmania. The photograph shows the hull soon after launch in 1925. Crichton's yard may be seen in the background.

127 The small motor coaster *D.B. Crane*, launched in 1935, was the last vessel to leave the yard of J. Crichton & Co.

SALTNEY

The Dee Iron Works was established in 1847 by Henry Wood & Co. to make anchors, cables and chains, and at the Great Exhibition of 1851 the company was awarded a prize for its chain cables. Six years later the firm made three anchors for the *Great Eastern*. In 1964 the company was taken over, and production was moved to Cradley Heath.

Saltney Wharf was erected in 1906 by the Shrewsbury & Chester Railway Co., which was later taken over by the Great Western Railway (GWR). Imported iron ore was discharged at the wharf, and coal loaded. To encourage use of their wharf the GWR bought a tug and offered vessels a free tow for the extra distance between Connah's Quay and Saltney.

J. Crichton & Co. opened their shipyard in 1913, on land owned by the GWR. Five years later they took over the former yard of A. Ferguson & Son – formerly Ferguson & Baird – at Connah's Quay, while continuing at Saltney. In a letter of May 1913 James Crichton stated that the intention was to undertake 'high-class light-draft shipbuilding'. For the next twenty-two years Crichton's built an astonishing variety of vessels, including tugs, barges, ferries, coasters, oil tankers, launches, stern-wheelers, yachts and a hospital ship. Not to mention railway locomotives and a grandstand for a football club! Crichton's products went to Europe, Africa, the Americas, Borneo, Australia, South Georgia, Burma, Ceylon and India.(A full account of the firm, including a list of vessels built, may be found in Dixon and Pickard 2002.)

Some Examples of Crichton's Vessels
The *British Journal of Nursing* on 23 June 1917 reveals the exotic destination of one of Crichton's ships:

The river hospital ship *Nabha* has reached Basra... having successfully made the passage from Bombay under her own power. This shallow-draught vessel was specially built for service on the Tigris by the British Red Cross Society and the Order of St John, the cost being met from a donation sent to sent to the United Provinces India Fund by the Maharaja of Nabha, whose name it bears.

The accommodation included 'a fully equipped operating room which was designed under the advice and supervision of Sir Frederick Treves'. The *Nabha* could carry sixty bed cases and a large number of 'sitting cases'. An ice-making plant could make 2 tons of ice every two hours.

In 1920: Two teak launches for West Africa.

In 1921/22: Four steam tugs for the Argentine Navigation Co.

In 1924: Two identical vessels were launched at Saltney for the Portuguese State Railways: *Traz-os-Montes* and *Alentejo*. They sailed for Lisbon in June 1924 and were in service until 1960.

In 1925: A vehicle ferry for the Tasmanian government. The *Lurgerena* was 199ft long by 35ft broad by 14ft draft, and could carry thirty vehicles and 120 passengers. It arrived in Tasmania on 5 October 1925, after a journey of 14,000 miles.

In May 1930: The *Sir Charles Orr* was launched for Elemthera Shipping Ltd. The vessel (which was 116ft long by 21ft) was intended for a mail-carrying contract in the Bahamas and for trading between Nassau and Miami. There was a crew of eight and thirty-two passengers could be carried. The voyage across the Atlantic took nineteen days.

In 1931 Chester Football Club was admitted to the Football League, Division III (North). Their new stand was built by Crichton's.

J. Crichton & Co. closed down in October 1935, when the business was taken over National Shipbuilders Securities, a company set up by the government to close uneconomic shipyards. The Motor Vessel *D.B. Crane* (139) was the last ship to leave the Saltney yard.

Sources and Bibliography

General

Clayton's Register of Shipping 1865, Facsimile: National Museums & Galleries on Merseyside.

Davidson, A. (Ed.) (2002), *The Coastal Archaeology of Wales*, Council for British Archaeology, York.

Fenton, R. (1989), 'Steam packet to Wales: a chronological survey of operators and services', *Maritime Wales* 12, pp.54-65.

Greenhill, B. (1988), *The Merchant Schooners*, Conway Maritime Press, Conway.

Gruffydd, K.L. (1987), 'Sea power and the Anglo-Welsh wars, 1210-1410', *Maritime Wales* 11, pp.28-53

Gruffydd, K.L. (1992), 'Wales's maritime trade in wine during the later Middle Ages', *Maritime Wales* 15, pp.7-42.

Gruffydd, K.L. (1996), 'Maritime defence and Wales during the later Middle Ages', *Maritime Wales* 18, pp. 10-32.

Gruffydd, K.L. (1998), 'Royal impressment and maritime Wales during the later Middle Ages', *Maritime Wales* 19, pp.30-49.

Gruffydd, K.L.(2000), 'Maritime Wales' export trade in the late Middle Ages', *Maritime Wales* 21, pp.23-44.

Gruffydd, K.L. (2002), 'Wrecks and wreckers in Welsh waters during the later Middle Ages', *Maritime Wales* 23, pp.55-70.

Gruffydd, K.L. (2003) Piracy, privateering and maritime Wales during the later Middle Ages (part 1) *Maritime Wales* 24, pp.24-40

Gruffydd, K.L. (2004), 'Piracy, privateering and maritime Wales during the later Middle Ages (Part 2)', *Maritime Wales* 25, pp.10-20.

Hawkes, G.I. (1986), 'Illicit trading in Wales in the eighteenth century', *Maritime Wales* 10, pp.89-107.

Jenkins, J.G. (1979), 'Herring fishing in Wales', *Maritime Wales* 4, pp.5-32.

Jenkins, J.G. (1987), 'The fishing ports of Wales', *Maritime Wales* 11, pp.74-96.

Jordan, R.W. (1999), *The World's Merchant Fleets 1939*, Chatham Publishing, London.

Lewis E.A. (1927), *The Welsh Port Books (1550-1603)*, Honourable Society of Cymmrodorion.

Loomie, A.J. (1963), 'An armada pilot's survey of the English coastline, October 1597', *The Mariner's Mirror* 49 (4), pp.288-300.

Owen, J.R. (2002), 'The post office packet service, 1821-37: development of a steam-powered fleet', *The Mariner's Mirror* 88 (2), pp.155-175.

Robinson, W.R.B. (1972), 'Dr Thomas Phaer's report on the harbours and customs administration of Wales under Edward VI', *Bulletin of the Board of Celtic Studies* 24 (IV), pp.585-503.

Schofield, H.M. (1989), 'The Liverpool plantation registers and wool registers 1740-1786', *Maritime Wales* 12, pp.38-53.

Stammers, M.K. (2000), 'The Welsh sloop', *Maritime Wales* 21, pp.55-58.

Thomas, P.N. (1992), *British Ocean Tramps, Volume 2. Owners and Their Ships*, Waine Research Publications.

South Wales

Andrews, J.H. (1955), 'Chepstow: a defunct seaport of the Severn Estuary', *Geography* XI, pp.97-107.

Bennett, P. and Jenkins D. (1994), *Welsh Ports of the Great Western Railway*, National Museum of Wales, Cardiff.

Blundell, J. (1995), 'A Tudor wreck near Aberavon', *Maritime Wales* 17, pp.7-22.

Bullen, M. (1998), 'The Newport customs house', *Maritime Wales* 19, pp.56-69.

Craig, R. (1980), *The Ports and Shipping, c.1750-1850*, in John, A.H. and Williams, G. (Eds), *Glamorgan County History Volume V, Industrial Glamorgan from 1700 to 1970*, Cardiff.

Davies, J.D. (2000), 'The 'revenge' of Llanelli; a Welsh privateer in the seventeenth century', *Maritime Wales* 21, pp.45-51.

Davis, H. (1998), *The History of the Borough of Newport*, Pennyfarthing, Newport.

Dawson, J.W. (1932), *Commerce and Customs – a History of the Ports of Newport and Caerleon*, Newport, Mon: R.H. Johns.

Farr, G.E. (1954), *Chepstow Ships*, The Chepstow Society.

Farr, G.E. (1956), *West Country Passenger Steamers*, Richard Tilling, London.

Greenlaw, J. (2000), *The Swansea Copper Barques and Cape Horners*, Published by the Author.

Heaton, P.W. (1982), *The 'Usk' Ships*, Starling Press, Monmouthshire.

Higgins L.S. (1964), 'The rise and decline of Porthcawl dock', *The Mariner's Mirror* 50 (4), pp.319-327.

Higgins, L.S. 'The parish of Newton Nottage in the seventeenth century', *Morgannwg* VII, pp.57-70.

Hobbs, J.S. (1859), *The Bristol Channel Pilot*, Charles Wilson.

Hughes, S. (2000) *Copperopolis: Landscapes of the Early Industrial Period in Swansea*, Royal Commission on the Ancient and Historical Monuments of Wales.

Jones, G.M. and Scourfield, E. (1986), *Sully: A Village and Parish in the Vale of Glamorgan*

Jones, W.H. (1922), *History of the Port of Swansea*, W. Spurrell & Son, Carmarthen.

Kennerley, E. (1979), 'River trade and shipping in Caerleon from the sixteenth to the nineteenth century', *Gwent Local History*, 47.

Knight, J.K. (1991), 'Newport Castle', *The Monmouthshire Antiquary* VII, pp.17-42.

Redknap, M. (1998), 'An archaeological and historical context for the medieval Magor pill boat', *Maritime Wales* 19, pp.9-29.

Richards, J. (2005), *Cardiff: A Maritime History*. Tempus Publishing Ltd, Stroud.

Roberts, O., McGrail, S. (2002), 'A Romano-British boat recovered from a site in Gwent', *Maritime Wales* 23, pp.32-36.

Roberts, S.K. (1999), *The Letter-Book of John Byrd, Customs Collector in South-East Wales 1648-80*, South Wales Record Society, Cardiff.

Robinson, W.R.B. (1970), 'The establishment of the royal customs in Glamorgan and Monmouthshire under Elizabeth I', *Bulletin of the Board of Celtic Studies* 23 (IV), pp.347-396.

Smith, D. (2004), 'Walker, Thomas Andrew (1828 - 1889)', *Oxford Dictionary of National Biography*, Oxford University Press, Oxford.

Stammers, M.K. (2003), 'Turnbull's 'register of shipping', a snapshot of South Welsh shipowning in 1885', *Maritime Wales* 24, pp.115-132.

Waters, I. (1989), *The Port of Chepstow*, Moss Rose Press, Chepstow.

Williams, M.I. (1962), 'Aberthaw: the Port of the Vale', in Williams, S. (Ed.) *Saints and Sailing Ships*, D. Brown, *Cowbridge*.

West Wales

Bowen, R.E. (2001), *The Burry Port and Gwendraeth Valley Railway and its Antecedent Canals. Volume One: The Canals*, The Oakwood Press, Usk.

Craig, R. (1958), 'W.H. Nevill and the Llanelly Iron Shipping Co.', *National Library of Wales Journal* X (3) pp.265-280.

Craig, R.S. (1989-90), 'The brig *Concord*', *National Library of Wales Journal*, XXVI, pp.397-400.

Craig, R.S, Jones, R.P. Symons, M.V. (2002), *The Industrial and Maritime History of Llanelli and Burry Port 1750 to 2000*, Carmarthenshire County Council.

Craig, R. (1959), 'The emergence of a ship-owning community at Llanelly, 1800-1850, *Carmarthenshire Antiquary* III, pp.17-26.

Craig, R. (1985), 'Carmarthenshire shipping in the eighteen forties', *Carmarthenshire Antiquary* XXI, pp.49-57.

Evans, J. (1993) 'Military aviation', in Howell, D.W. (Ed.) *Pembrokeshire County History. Volume IV. Modern Pembrokeshire 1815-1974*, Pembrokeshire Historical Society, Pembroke.

Evans, M.C.S. (1960), 'History of the port of Carmarthen 1550-1603', *Carmarthenshire Antiquary* 1960, pp.72-87.

Edwards, G. (1963), 'The coal industry in Pembrokeshire', *Field Studies* 1 (5), pp.33-64.

Evans, M.C.S. (1960), 'Carmarthen and the Welsh port books', *Carmarthenshire Antiquary* III, pp.72-87.

Galvin, A.H. (2003), 'The Tenby lugger', *Maritime Wales* 24, pp.77-96.

George, B.J. (1964), 'Pembrokeshire sea-trading before 1900', *Field Studies* 2 (1), pp.1-39.

Goddard, T. (1993), 'Naval activity', in Howell, David W. (Ed.), *Pembrokeshire County History. Volume IV. Modern Pembrokeshire 1815-1974*, Pembrokeshire Historical Society, Pembroke.

Howells, Brian (Ed.) (1987) *Pembrokeshire County History. Volume III: Early Modern Pembrokeshire, 1536 - 1815* (Pembrokeshire Historical Society).

James, David (2005) 'The construction of the shipbuilding sheds at Pembroke Naval Dockyard',

Maritime Wales 26, pp.46-53.

James, T. (1983), 'The logbook of the brig *Priscilla* of Carmarthen: April to October 1820', *Carmarthenshire Antiquary* XIX, pp.43-51.

James, T. (1986), 'Shipping on the River Towey: problems of navigation', *Carmarthenshire Antiquary* 22, pp.27-37.

Jenkins, D., Jenkins, J.G., Evans S. (1982), *The Maritime Heritage of Dyfed*, National Museum of Wales, Cardiff.

Lewis, R. (1993), 'The towns of Pembrokeshire, 1815-1974', in Howell, D.W. (Ed.), *Pembrokeshire County History. Volume IV. Modern Pembrokeshire 1815-1974*, Pembrokeshire Historical Society, Haverfordwest.

Lewis, R. (2002), 'Abereiddi and Porthgain', *Maritime Wales* 23, pp.7-19.

Lewis, R. (2003), 'Abercastle', *Maritime Wales* 24, pp.74–76.

Lynch, J. (1998), 'Bristol shipping and Royalist naval power during the English civil war', *The Mariner's Mirror* 84 (3) pp.260-266.

Matthews, M.D. (1999), Mercantile shipbuilding activity in South-West Wales, 1740 – 1829', *Welsh History Review*, XIX (3), pp.400-404.

Matthews, M.D. (2004), 'Coastal communities: aspects of the economic and social impact of coastal shipping in south-west Wales, *c.*1700-1820', *Maritime Wales* 25, pp.56-71.

McKay, K.D. (1989), *A Vision of Greatness: the History of Milford 1790-1990*, Haverfordwest.

McKay, K.D. (1993 a), 'The port of Milford: the fishing industry', in Howell, D.W. (Ed.), *Pembrokeshire County History, Volume IV, Modern Pembrokeshire 1815-1974*, Pembrokeshire Historical Society.

McKay, K.D. (1993 b), 'The port of Milford: oil in the twentieth century', in Howell, D.W. (Ed.), *Pembrokeshire County History. Volume IV. Modern Pembrokeshire 1815-1974*, Pembrokeshire Historical Society.

Morgan, G. (1992), 'Aspects of West Wales shipping in the eighteenth century', *Maritime Wales* 15, pp.43-50.

Morgan, G. (1996), 'Three nineteenth century Dyfed shipping accounts', *Maritime Wales* 18, pp.36-39.

Pepler, J. (1989) 'Milford Haven shipping, 1881', *Maritime Wales* 9, pp.122-133.

Phillips, L. (1985), 'Captain Sir Thomas Sabine Paisley Bt. R.N. and Pembroke Dock 1849-1856', *The Mariners Mirror* 71 (2), pp.159-165.

Phillips, L. (1993), 'Pembroke Dockyard', in Howell, D.W. (Ed.), *Pembrokeshire County History. Volume IV. Modern Pembrokeshire 1815-1974*, Pembrokeshire Historical Society, Pembroke.

Price, M.R.C. (1982), *Industrial Saundersfoot*, Gomer, Llandysul.

Rees, J.F. (1954), *The Story of Milford*, Cardiff.

Thomas, F. (1920), *The Builders of Milford*, The Pembrokeshire Telegraph, Haverfordwest.

Walker, R.F. (Ed.) (2002), *Pembrokeshire County History Volume 2: Medieval Pembrokeshire*, Pembrokeshire Historical Society.

Williams, E. (1984), 'The Carmarthenshire butter trade', *Carmarthenshire Antiquary* XX, pp.69-75.

Williams M.I. (1978), 'Carmarthenshire's maritime trade in the sixteenth and seventeenth centuries', *Carmarthenshire Antiquary* XIV, pp.61-70.

Cardigan Bay

Campbell-Jones, S. (1975), 'Shipbuilding at New Quay, Cardiganshire 1779-1878', *Ceredigion* VII, 273-306.

Eames, A. and Stammers, M. (1979), 'The *Fleetwing* of Porthmadog', *Maritime Wales* 4, pp.119-122.

Fenton, R.S. (1989), *Cambrian Coasters: Steam and Motor Coaster Owners in North and West Wales*, World Ship Society.

Greenhill, B. (1995), 'Some memories of the famous Porthmadog schooner '*M.A. James*'', *Maritime Wales* 17, pp.80-89.

Hughes, E. and Eames, A. (1975), *Porthmadog Ships*, Gwynedd Archives Service.

Jenkins, D. (1987), 'Cardiff tramps, Cardi crews: Cardiganshire shipowners and seamen in Cardiff, *c.*1870-1950', *Ceredigion* X (1984-87), pp.405 - 430.

Jenkins, J.G. (1981), 'The *Elizabeth-Ann* of Aber-Porth, Ceredigion', *Maritime Wales* 6, pp.28-37.

Jenkins, J.G. (1982), *Maritime Heritage: the Ships and Seamen of Southern Ceredigion*, Gomer, Llandysul.

Jenkins, J.G. (1984), 'The Port of Cardigan', *Maritime Wales* 8, pp.76-93.

Jones, D. L. (1969) 'Aberaeron: the community and seafaring 1800-1900', *Ceredigion* VI, pp.201-242.

Lloyd, L. (1977), *The Unity of Barmouth*, Gwynedd Archives Service.

Lloyd, L. (1979), 'The ports of Cardigan Bay', *Maritime Wales* 4, pp.33-41.

Lloyd, L. (1987), 'William Jones, druggist, and the expansion of shipbuilding at Pwllheli', *Maritime Wales* 11, pp.54-73.

Lloyd, L. (1991), *Pwllheli: the Port and Mart of Llyn*.

Lloyd, L. (1992), 'The *Titanic*'s gallant Welsh officer, 1912. Harold G. Lowe of Penballt, Barmouth', *Maritime Wales* 15, pp.109-122.

Lloyd, L. (1993), *Wherever Freights May Offer: the Maritime Community of Abermaw/Barmouth 1565 to 1920*.

Lloyd, L. (1994), 'Early steamers, the railways and the Port of Aberystwyth', *Maritime Wales* 16, pp.31-51.
Lloyd, L.(1996), *A Real Little Seaport: the Port of Aberdyfi and its People 1565-1920.*
Morgan, G. (1991), 'Aberystwyth herring tithes and boat names in 1730', *Maritime Wales* 14, pp.7-15.
Morgan, G. (1994), 'Wrecking of some Aberystwyth ships', *Maritime Wales* 16, pp.9-19.
Morgan, G. (1993), 'The trading life of the brig *Renown*', *National Library of Wales Journal* XXVIII (3)
    pp.291 – 298.
Morgan, G. (1995), 'Thomas Jones of Aberystwyth, shipowner', *Maritime Wales* 17, pp.28-50.
Morgan, T. (1989), 'Notes on Porthmadog ships', *Maritime Wales* 12, pp.165-168.
Morris, L. (1748 republished 1987), *Plans of the Harbours, Bars, Bays and Roads in St George's Channel*,
    Lewis Morris Productions.
Scott, R.S.L. (1987), 'The Port of Fishguard', *Journal of the Pembrokeshire History Society* 2 (1986/87),
    pp.58-67.
Stammers, M.K. (1990), 'Irish Sea wherries, schooners or shallops', *Maritime Wales* 13, pp.78-83.
Thomas, P. (1986), *Strangers from a Secret Land. The Voyages of the Brig* Albion *and the Founding of the First
    Welsh Settlements in Canada*, Gomer, Llandysul.
Troughton, W. (1994), 'The trading history of the barque *Hope* (Aberystwyth) lost in the North
    Atlantic in 1892', *Ceredigion* XII (3), pp.85-101.
Williams, M.I. (1973), 'The Port of Aberdyfi in the eighteenth century', *National Library of Wales Journal*
    XVIII (1) pp.95-134.
Williams, W. E. (1987), 'The wreck of the barque *Spanker*', *Maritime Wales* 11, pp.163-169.

North Wales

Anon. (1980), 'The voyage of the brig *Albion* with emigrants from Caernarfon to North America'
    Maritime Wales 5, pp.31-42.
Bartley, D.A. (1992), 'Clwyd, Foryd or Port River of Rhuddlan', *Maritime Wales* 15, pp.51-73.
Cowell, J. (1990), *Liverpool to North Wales Pleasure Steamers: a Pictorial History 1821-1962*, S.B.
    Publications, Loggerheads, Salop.
Davies, I.E. (1989), 'The port of Conway', *Trans. Aberconwy History Society*, 1989, pp.4-8.
Davies, P.N. (1978) 'The discovery and excavation of the Royal Yacht, *Mary*', *Maritime Wales* 3, pp.25-32.
Davies, W. (1988), *The Sea and the Sand: the Story of HMS* Tara *and the Western Desert Force*, Gwynnedd
    Archives Service.
Eames, A. (1973), *Ships and Seamen of Anglesey 1558-1918*, Anglesey Antiquarian Society, Anglesey.
Eames, A. (1987), *Ventures in Sail. Aspects of the Maritime History of Gwynnedd 1840-1914*, Gwynnedd
    Archives Service, Merseyside Maritime Museum, National Maritime Museum, London.
Eames, A. (2001), 'Sea power and Sir Caernarfon, 1642-1660', *Maritime Wales* 22, pp.36-54.
Elis-Williams, M. (1984), *Packet to Ireland: Porthdinllain's Challenge to Holyhead*, Gwynnedd Archives
    Service.
Elis-Williams, M. (1985), 'Samuel Roberts, preacher and shipbuilder 1819-1875', *Maritime Wales* 9,
    pp.44-71.
Elis-Williams, M. (1988), *Bangor, Port of Beaumaris. The nineteenth Century Shipbuilders and Shipowners of
    Bangor*, Gwynnedd Archives Service.
Eustace E.F.J. (1985), 'Captain Hugh Hughes (1832-1872) of Caernarfon and two of his ships, *Flying
    Cloud* and *Isabella*', *Maritime Wales* 9, pp.72-79.
Evans, J.R. (1989). 'The Trefriw steamers 1847-1940', *Trans Aberconwy History Society* 1989, pp.13-16.
Evans, R. (2002). 'Parcel of poor fishermen: a rural, coastal community's maritime experiences, 1750-
    1800', *Maritime Wales* 23, pp.71-90.
Fenton, R.S. (1989), *Cambrian Coasters: Steam and Motor Coaster Owners of North and West Wales*, World
    Ship Society, Kendal.
Griffiths, I.W. (1989), 'John Griffiths, Morfa Nefyn, Caernarfonshire, and the schooner *Eleanor and Jane*',
    Maritime Wales 12, pp.66-72.
Hope, B.D. (1994), *A Curious Place: The Industrial History of Amlwch (1550 - 1950)*, Bridge Books,
    Wrexham.
Hughes, E. and Eames, A. (1975), *Porthmadog Ships*, Gwynedd Archives Service.
Jones, R. (2004), *Sailing the Strait. Aspects of Port Dinorwic and the Menai Strait*, Bridge Books, Wrexham.
Joyce, A.H. (1989), 'Captain's accounts for the schooner *John*, 1856-1857', *Maritime Wales* 12, pp.81-84.
Lecane, P. (2005), *Torpedoed! The RMS* Leinster *Disaster*, Periscope Publishing, Penzance.
Linnard, W. (1981), 'Boatbuilding and ship-repairing on the Conwy, 1686', *Maritime Wales* 6, pp.6-9.
Lloyd, L. (1981 a), 'The wreck of the barque *Premier* of Beaumaris on the coast of Newfoundland in
    1872', *Maritime Wales* 6, pp.125-129.
Lloyd, L. (1981 b), 'De Winton of Caernarfon: some extracts from the local press', *Maritime Wales* 6,
    pp.135-137.
Lloyd, L. (1983), 'The nightmare voyage of the emigrant ship *Oregon* in 1849', *Maritime Wales* 7, pp.118-
    120.

Lloyd, L. (1986), 'Merioneth associations of the brig *Atalanta* of Caernarfon 1864-1891', *Maritime Wales* 10, pp.76-88.

Lloyd, L. (1989), *The Port of Caernarfon 1793-1900*.

McKee, A. (1988 2nd edition), *The Golden Wreck: the Tragedy of the 'Royal Charter'*, New English Library, Sevenoaks.

McManus, B. (1999), 'The loss of the cadet school training ship HMS *Conway*' *Maritime Wales* 20, pp.84-95.

Owen, J.R. (2001), 'The letters of James Sparrow, surveyor of customs at Holyhead, to Sir Richard Bulkeley Williams Bulkeley, Bart, MP, February-March 1832', *Maritime Wales* 22, pp.14-31.

Owen, J.R. (2004), 'A nabob at Holyhead: Richard Griffith, Post Office packet agent 1815-1820', *Maritime Wales* 25, pp.27-55.

Roberts, D. (1999), *HMS* Thetis - *Secrets and Scandal, Aftermath of a Disaster*, Avid Publications, Merseyside.

Roberts, E.W. (1984), 'Establishing the *Clio*', *Maritime Wales* 8, pp.5-28.

Roberts, O.T.P. (1983), 'The sloop *Darling* of Beaumaris 1781-1893', *Maritime Wales* 7, pp.5-20.

Roberts, O.T.P. (1998), 'That the *Mary* yacht is certainly shipwrecked' *Maritime Wales* 19, pp.50-55.

Roberts, O.T.P. (2001), 'SS *Enterprize* – "y Stemar Bach"' *Maritime Wales* 22, pp.84-95.

Roberts, R.F. (1991), 'Ships built on the River Clwyd', *Maritime Wales* 14, pp.16-21.

Stammers, M.K. (1989), 'The maritime interests of the Wynns of Glynllifon, *c*.1761-1930', *Maritime Wales* 12, pp.34-37.

Stammers, M.K. (1987), 'The wreck of the *Franchise*', *Maritime Wales* 11, pp.97-100.

Thomas, D. (1932), 'Anglesey shipbuilding down to 1840', *Trans Anglesey Antiquarian Society 1932*, pp.107-118.

Thornley, F.C. (1962, 2nd edition), *Steamers of North Wales*, T. Stephenson & Sons, Prescot.

Turner, R. (1987). 'The schooner *Unicorn* of Caernarfon and the Davies family', *Maritime Wales* 11, pp.153-156.

Turner, R. (1990), 'Captain David Davies, Tal y Don, Nefyn and his family', *Maritime Wales* 13, pp.111-114.

Usher, G.A. (1955), 'An Anglesey disaster', *Trans Anglesey Antiquarian Society 1955*, pp.2-11.

Warren, C, Benson, J. (1997), Thetis *'The Admiralty regrets...', The Disaster in Liverpool Bay*, Avid Publications, Merseyside.

Wignall, S. (1978), 'The quest for Great Britain's first submersible the *Resurgam*', *Maritime Wales* 3, pp.67-74.

Williams, R.R. (1959), 'Anglesey and the loss of the *Royal Charter' Trans Anglesey Antiquarian Society 1959*.

The Dee Estuary

Armstrong, J., Fowler, D. (1996), 'The coastal trade of Connah's Quay in the early twentieth century', *Flintshire Historical Society Journal* 34, pp.113-133.

Boyd, J.I.C. (1991), *The Wrexham, Mold and Connah's Quay Railway*, Oakwood Press.

Coppack, T. (1973), *A Lifetime with Ships: The Autobiography of a Coasting Shipowner*, Stephenson & Sons, Prescot.

Cowell, J. (1990), *Liverpool to North Wales Pleasure Steamers: A Pictorial History 1821-1962*, S.B. Publications, Loggerheads.

Craig, R.S. (1963), 'Some aspects of the trade and shipping of the Dee in the eighteenth century', *Trans Historical Society of Lancashire and Cheshire* 115, pp.99-128.

Dixon, J., Pickard, G. (2002), *J. Crichton & Co. Shipbuilders: Saltney and Connah's Quay. A Pictorial Record*, Published by the Authors.

Gruffydd, K.L. (1984), 'Ships and sailors of the Dee', *Maritime Wales* 8, pp.29-49.

Gruffydd, K.L. (1985), 'Maritime Dee during the later Middle Ages', *Maritime Wales* 9, pp.7-31.

Gruffydd, K.L. (1988), 'History of the export of coal from Flintshire pre-Industrial Revolution', *Flintshire Historical Society Journal* 34, pp.53-88.

Hawkes, G.I. (1985), 'The Point of Ayr lighthouse', *Maritime Wales* 9, pp.32-43.

Hawkes, G.I. (1987), 'Shipping on the Dee: the rise and decline of the creeks of the port of Chester in the nineteenth century', *Maritime Wales* 11, pp.112-33.

Large, F. (1998), *Faster Than the Wind: a History of and Guide to the Liverpool to Holyhead Telegraph*, Avid Publications, Merseyside.

Morris-Jones, H. (1998), 'Shipbuilding on the Welsh side of the River Dee after its canalization in 1737'. *The Magazine of the Buckley Society*, 22, pp.4-11.

Pratt, D. (1981), 'Sidelights on the Dee navigation 1892-1912', *Maritime Wales* 6, 59-65.

Stammers, M.K. (1959), 'Coasting with the *Indorita*', *Maritime Wales* 26, 116-119.

General Index

Index of Vessels